Also by Paul Michael Garrett

Remaking social work with children and families: a critical discussion on the 'modernisation' of social care (Routledge, 2003)

Social work and Irish people in Britain: historical and contemporary responses to Irish children and families (The Policy Press, 2004)

'Transforming' children's services? Social work, neoliberalism and the 'modern' world (Open University/McGraw Hill, 2009)

For VB

Contents

Acknowledgements

Some of the ideas featured in this book have been presented and debated in various European locations. I am grateful, therefore, to Siniša Zrinščak and Marina Ajdukovic for inviting me to the University of Zagreb, in January 2011, to present my paper 'Theory and social work with children and families'. Griet Roets, Rudi Roose and Lieve Bradt kindly invited me to present 'Theory won't get you through the door: thinking about theory and social work', at the University of Ghent, in December 2011. Finally, some of the themes featured in the book were discussed with PhD students after I gave the paper 'A note on the "transformation" of social work' at the Universität Duisburg-Essen, in March 2012. Fabian Kessl was responsible for extending the invitation for me to travel to Germany and for facilitating a stimulating discussion. I am grateful to all these colleagues for their interest and generous hospitality.

I also want to thank the anonymous peer reviewers for their frequently helpful remarks in prompting me to revise some of the arguments featured in what follows. This includes those reviewers who commented on the proposal and draft of the book and those aiding my thinking through some of the issues raised in international peer-reviewed journals. Stephen Webb and Stan Houston regularly reproduce important work seeking to apply social theory within the domain of social work and, in some respects, this book extends a conversation with both of them.

Declan Coogan and colleagues in the School of Political Science and Sociology at the National University of Ireland in Galway facilitated my taking sabbatical leave in 2010–11. Having this additional time for research made it much easier for me to complete this project on time. The comments of John Cunningham also assisted me in writing this book. Students involved in the MA in Social Work and my undergraduate modules – 'Transforming children's services' and 'Welfare words' – have also contributed immensely to this book because of their enthusiastic attempts to make the connection in times of neoliberalisation between social work and social theory.

This is the second of my books to have been published by The Policy Press and, as before, Karen Bowler and her colleagues were efficient and always very helpful. I, however, am entirely responsible for the contents of this book, particularly its failings. These would have been much more extensive if Valeria Ballarotti had not been so keenly attentive.

Galway, Easter 2012

CHAPTER ONE

Introduction

Introduction

The National University of Ireland, in Galway, set up the first social work programme in the west of Ireland in 2004. One member of the first cohort of an enthusiastic and engaging group of students had a firm opinion on the role of theory in social work. After having undertaken a range of social work-related activities prior to her becoming a postgraduate student, she pronounced with some confidence: "theory won't get you through the door". Angela's succinct declaration, which resulted in lively exchanges during a module on social theory and social work, echoes an opinion widely held in and beyond the profession. On one level, her view may appear convincing and connect to our intuitive understanding, our 'common sense' (and, perhaps, personal experience) of social work.[1] Arguably, on difficult home visits, where social workers have to ask troubling questions or convey upsetting news, theoretical knowledge may not seem to be of much help. Although it may have sparked animated discussions at university, when the *real* work of social work has to be undertaken, theory becomes redundant if not something of a hindrance.

Some of the content of the module I was teaching Angela and her class may have seemed somewhat challenging. It may be understandable how student participants doubted the usefulness of wading through Bourdieu's dense and complex prose. He never had to plot his way across the varied topography of social work practice; he never had to complete a late Friday night visit to an 'unknown' family subjected to a child abuse investigation; he never experienced the feeling of trepidation, the dry mouth and the queasy tummy while climbing out of his car trying to find a flat number on an ill-lit estate (see also Ferguson, 2010a). In spite of such understandable objections, this book makes the case for the relevance of social theory, including Bourdieu's contribution. It will argue that theoretical engagement may help social workers to navigate those 'indeterminate zones of practice', those 'situations of complexity and uncertainty', which are also inescapably attached to questions of politics and power (Schon, 1992, pp 51, 53).

Rather than disparaging Angela's views, *Social work and social theory* can be read as an elongated response to them. More specifically, the book aspires to:

- place social theory at the core of social work pedagogy, emphasising that a 'sociological imagination' (Wright Mills, 2000) should lie at the heart of creative social work practice;

- create a departure from the dominant theoretical frameworks (promoted by Giddens, Beck and, to a lesser extent, Bauman) that have monopolised the social work academic literature in recent years;
- encourage readers to investigate critical, often difficult, literature lying beyond a closely regulated social work curriculum;
- be a useful teaching aid, prompting reflection and debate on a number of controversial themes and 'bigger picture' issues central to social work practice;
- be a challenging, but engaging, resource for social workers who seek to explore new, radical forms of theory and practice; and
- build a bridge between critical social theory and social work, thus producing a text that may also be of interest to students and academics involved in the kindred disciplines of sociology and social policy.

A suitable job for 'retired City bankers' and 'ex-insurance brokers'?

Bob Mullaly (1997, p 99) argues that many:

> social workers either turn cold or rebel at the mere mention of theory. Theory is viewed as esoteric, abstract, and something people discuss in universities. Practice on the other hand, is seen as common sense, concrete, and occurring in the real world. Social work is viewed by many as essentially a pragmatic profession that carries out practical tasks. Theory has little direct relevance and actually obscures the true (i.e. practical) nature of social work. Spontaneity and personal qualities of the social worker are more important than theory.

Allegedly, this is because '*doing* social work is more important than thinking about it' (Gray and Webb, 2009, p 6, emphasis in original). Indeed, some social workers may even tend 'to elevate theoretical ignorance to a level of professional virtue' (Mullaly, 1997, pp 99–100). The notion that social work is ill-served by theoreticians reflects a dominant understanding periodically reinforced by official statements stressing the 'practical' nature of the profession. A representative of the UK government has gone so far as to state that social work could be undertaken on an entirely voluntary basis by 'retired City bankers or ex-insurance brokers' (*The Guardian*, 2010a; see also Department of Education, 2010, p 2).[2] Although, in the period leading up to the 2010 election, the Conservative Party (2007) attempted to win favour with the profession, the assumption underlying the minister's declaration is that social work – perceived here as a form of loosely organised 'common sense' – could be done on the cheap, by well-intentioned (and evidently financially comfortable) laypeople. During a period of so-called 'austerity' when the government is intent on cutting public services, this faintly veiled agenda is particularly insidious (Elliott, 2010). Furthermore, the reference to the retired wealthy implies not only a blatant class bias, but also an understanding that life experience is the paramount factor for those discharging the social work role. Here, experience 'means something specific – primary experience, unmediated by theory, reflection, speculation, argument, etc. It is thought superior to other kinds of argumentation because it is rooted in reality: experience is "real" – speculation and theory are "airy-fairy"' (Hall et al, 1978, p 152).

Within this paradigm, theory and theorising have no relevance at all. Nonetheless, 'all practice is theory based' (Mullaly, 1997, p 99), it is merely that the theory is often implicit or unspoken. As Gray and Webb (2009, p 5) assert:

> [every] social work practice is the bearer and articulation of more or less theory-laden beliefs and concepts. Even those who try to refute the value of theory by claiming that social work is just 'good common sense' are, in fact, articulating a distilled version of philosophical theories about common sense.

The 'fallacy' of 'theoryless practice'

All social work practice is 'based on theorizing' and it remains a 'fallacy' to refer to 'theoryless practice' (Thompson, 2010, p 5):

> Even where the theoretical understandings cannot be directly articulated by a practitioner, they will still be there. That is practitioners will be making assumptions about a range of factors (the nature and causes of human behavior; how society works; the nature and causes of social problems; how best to communicate; how to recognize emotional reactions and so on) and basing these assumptions on concepts, wherever they are derived from. Some sort of conceptual framework (and therefore theory) is therefore inevitable. (Thompson, 2010, p 7)

According to Thompson, theory and practice are 'two sides of the same coin. To undertake social work activities is not to choose between theory and practice, but rather to fuse the two – to engage in actions (practice) that are shaped by knowledge and understanding (theory)' (Thompson, 2010, p xvi).

Dangers exist in simply relying on 'practice wisdom' given that for 'many years the accepted wisdom took little or no account of the significance of discrimination in people's lives, due to the individualistic focus of social work at that time' (Thompson, 2010, p 5). Furthermore, as Schon (1992, p 61) observes, 'systems of intuitive knowing are dynamically conservative, actively defended, actively resistant to change'. Indeed, it is possible to stretch such points a little further and to argue that 'practice wisdom' or unquestioned 'common sense' dominant in particular fields of social work, or within particular establishments, actually facilitated the 'corruption of care' and the installation and acceptance of abusive practices (Wardhaugh and Wilding, 1993).

In very broad terms, within social work in the UK, it is possible to outline four conflicting theoretical perspectives on how society is organised or should be organised and on the nature of personal and social change. These perspectives, sometimes implicit rather than openly stated, are far from static and evolve over time. Although derived from the UK, these frameworks can be applied to other national and cultural contexts, yet it is clear that their marginality or predominance may vary accordingly: for example, within the Republic of Ireland, it is difficult to identify – historically – any major current within the profession adhering to a 'socialist-collectivist perspective'. Unlike the UK, however, there have been consistent attempts to hold on to the vestiges of the 'therapeutic perspective' (and especially the importance of counselling) as this came under threat from an ascendant 'managerialist-technocratic perspective'.

A therapeutic perspective

It was 'psychoanalysis which gave social work ... [the] scientific patina and vocabulary so critical to its claim for professional recognition' (Jones, C., 2011, p 33). Some in social work have attempted to reinstall this perspective at the centre of theory and practice and there have been calls for a renewed 'emotionally intelligent relationship-based social work and psychodynamic understandings of practice' (Ferguson, 2010b, p 136). For Ferguson (2010b, p 130), 'car therapy work' would seem to fulfil a fulcrum role within this paradigm and counselling is viewed as a vital way of engaging with 'clients'. An emphasis on 'good authority' (Ferguson, 2011, p 97) and the sensory and tactile aspects of practice is also characteristic of this approach, whose disavowal of collective solutions to social problems is coupled with a nostalgic longing for the social work of the 1950s and early 1960s, a period when capitalism seemed more benign and 'problem families' were easily identified, managed and contained (see, eg, Spinley, 1953).

For a time, beginning in the late 1970s, psychoanalysis was displaced by an alternative approach that, emphasising self-fulfilment, focused on enabling people to gain power over their feelings and way of life. The tendency here was to overemphasise how individuals, free of the social and economic circumstances in which they are embedded, have the capacity to overcome personal suffering, for example, the work of Carl Rogers (1980). Cruder approaches are wilfully inattentive to the economic and social context in which the 'client' is situated.

In the 1990s, the UK saw the rise of a different therapeutic perspective associated with 'New Labour's therapeutic turn' (Langan, 2011, pp 154–7; see also Giddens, 1998) and the proliferation of 'positive psychology'. Noting the 'pervasive impact in contemporary social (and educational) policy' of this 'new wave of therapeutic entrepreneurs', Mary Langan (2011, p 163) refers to a veritable 'process of colonisation of social work training by the nostrums of mentoring, coaching and leadership derived from US corporations' (see also Furedi, 2004).

A socialist-collectivist perspective

Through a socialist-collectivist lens, seeking personal and social fulfilment is impossible given the constraints that capitalism imposes. In opposition to 'the psychodynamic model or framework that dominated social work theory and practice' until the mid-1970s, this perspective stresses the importance of collectivist solutions to personal problems (Bailey, 2011, p x). In the UK, 'radical social work' was promulgated by *Case Con*, the 'revolutionary magazine for social workers' during the period 1970–77, and Bailey and Brake's (1975) volume (Weinstein, 2011, p 11; see also Corrigan, 1982; Joyce et al, 1988). These critical interventions were always a minority current within the field and were ridiculed by right-wing critics as mere 'extramural speculation', even 'revolution on the rates' (Brewer and Lait, 1980, pp 106–10). However, social work courses influential in shaping radical social work developed at Warwick, Bradford and North London. More recently, a revival of radical social work has been articulated by Jones (1983, 2001) and Lavalette (2011a). Organisationally, the perspective is reflected in the politics of the Social Work Action Network (SWAN), which developed out of a 'Social Work Manifesto' initially circulated in 2004.

An individualist-reformist perspective

This perspective does not seek major social change but gradual improvement in conditions. Historically, it is connected with Fabianism and, in the 1970s and 1980s, with the constellation of approaches connected to 'anti-oppressive practice', which owe something to developments within social work in the US.

Perhaps the demand that social workers develop skills in 'intimate child protection practice' can be inserted within this 'individualist-reformist' framework (Ferguson, 2011). This orientation, also influenced, as we have observed, by therapeutic approaches, calls for a new emphasis on 'relationship-based' social work, which is particularly relevant when practitioners have to move among – what are dubbed – 'marginalized families' living in often 'poor and disgusting conditions' (Ferguson, 2011, p 97).

A managerialist-technocratic perspective

The managerialist-technocratic perspective perceives social work as a 'business' that, in its dominant lexicon, aims to provide an 'excellent' and 'quality' range of services to a diverse range of 'customers'. It can be associated with 'charging' for services and with the blurring of the distinctions between social workers and those who are ancillary and less trained. John Harris (2003) has provided a criticism of this approach in *The social work business*. There also tends to be an emphasis on electronic technologies and a hankering for forms of intervention that are said to – unambiguously – 'work'.

All four of these perspectives, far from being internally unified and homogeneous, appear to form alternatives that compete within the field of social work to gain supremacy and to exclude the competitors. Although there may be affinities and points of overlap, resulting in hybrid theoretical formations, they are, on the whole, identifiably different. They can also be associated with a range of theoretical models of social work intervention. For example, those supporting a socialist-collectivist perspective may be more likely to support forms of invention such as community development or groupwork. However, there is no 'neat fit' enabling us to 'read off' a particular form of intervention derived from a theoretical perspective on social work:

> Community-based strategies and group working clearly allow practitioners to 'collectivise' social problems and look at their structural and oppressive features – the public causes – at the heart of problems. But radical practitioners can also be involved in quality, supportive casework that involves advocating on behalf of, and alongside, service users. There are some methods that radical social workers would find hard, if not impossible to implement (for example, the use of cognitive behavioural therapy), but surely the key element is the *orientation* of the practitioner as they undertake good quality work: whom they involve in work processes and how they communicate and keep service users informed. (Lavalette, 2011b, pp 5–6, emphasis in original)

Weinstein (2011, p 22) has attempted to correct a common misunderstanding of the radical social work movement of the 1970s by pointing out that Bailey and Brake (1975), in their influential *Radical social work*, were not seeking to 'eliminate casework, but to eliminate casework that supports ruling class hegemony'.

Each of the four theoretical approaches has, in some ways, been challenged by feminist, anti-racist and postmodernist perspectives. Nonetheless, they appear resilient and are also apt to be expansionist: for example, attempts have been made to implant a 'managerialist-technocratic perspective' among the emerging social work professions in the former Eastern Bloc. This has resulted in professional and cultural tensions, particularly in areas of Eastern Europe, such as Croatia, which have a rich indigenous social work history.

Social theory defined, social theory resisted

Generally, theory represents an attempt 'to explain a phenomenon ... by providing a structured set of concepts that help us to understand the subject matter concerned' (Thompson, 2010, p 4). This broad definition can encompass theoretical models of social work intervention, such as 'crisis intervention', 'task-centred intervention' and so on (see Coulshed, 1988): that is to say, theoretical models of *how to do* social work. Yet, it can also include theoretical perspectives *on* social work: that is to say, ways of *thinking* about the nature of social work and its involvement in the 'bigger picture'. Indeed, bringing to the fore more encompassing reflections on how society is socially and economically organised, this latter dimension takes us onto the terrain of social theory.

Ransome (2010, p 1) informs his readers that 'social theory is the name given to theories about the human world. Social theory is the body of knowledge about the nature of social action and the various contexts in which it takes place'. Callinicos (1999a, p 9) believes that social theory is 'indispensable to engaging with the present'. Social theory:

> seeks to understand society as a whole; distinguishes between and makes generalizations about different kinds of society; is concerned in particular to analyze modernity, the social life, the forms of social life which have come to prevail first in the West and increasingly in the rest of the world over the past couple of centuries. (Callinicos, 1999a, p 2)

As Ransome maintains, classical modernist social theory was developed by a triumvirate of leading thinkers: Marx (1818–83), Weber (1864–1920) and Durkheim (1858–1917). The latter two figures will hardly feature in what follows, although the theorists featured in the second part of the book are implicitly in dialogue with them. Marx, however, is not only the focus of Chapter Four, but he will circulate – like a spectre – throughout *Social work and social theory*. Broadly speaking, however, the book will concentrate on critical social theory as developed in Europe by contemporary modernist thinkers.

The last decade has seen the publication of a range of books seeking, with differing degrees of success, to illuminate the usefulness of sociology and social theory for social work.[3] Beyond these important academic contributions, it could be argued that, since the very definition of social work provided by the International Federation of Social Workers (IFSW) locates the profession within the 'bigger picture', the coupling of social work and social theory should not be controversial. The IFSW maintains:

> The social work profession promotes social change, problem solving in human relationships and the empowerment and liberation of people to enhance well being. Utilizing theories of human behaviour and social systems, social work intervenes at the points where people interact with their environments. Principles of human rights and social justice are fundamental. (IFSW, 2000; see also Hare, 2004)

Clearly, this expansive definition of the profession and its key roles and activities (embracing 'social change', 'liberation', 'human rights', 'social justice') strongly suggests that social workers should be acquainted with social theory. Nonetheless, the struggle to incorporate an awareness of the possibilities provided by social theory has frequently met with resistance from those seeking to define and delimit what might be regarded as 'social work'.

Where are the 'case studies'? What about the 'applications'? Where is Foucault?

Social work and social theory is mostly derived from two modules I teach to postgraduate social work students. Drawing on a range of theorists and competing perspectives, it will encourage a new generation of social work students to recognise and examine the importance of critical social theory for understanding the structural forces shaping their lives and the lives of those with whom they work and provide services.

The book will address often quite complex ideas in an accessible way. However, I have been reluctant to introduce 'case studies' or similar boxed incursions, which risk 'breaking up' the text and disrupting its coherence and flow. Instead, to encourage debate on some of the key themes, I have opted to feature a series of 'Reflection and Talk Boxes' at the end of each chapter. The aim of this device (which can be skipped if it is not to the taste of particular readers) is to stimulate critical conversations and debates in class/seminar and fieldwork/workplace settings on key facets of the preceding chapter. In this context, the book's subtitle, 'making connections', is also in need of some clarification. While *Social work and social theory* seeks to prompt readers to think more theoretically and more critically, it does not propose that theory can, and indeed should, be mechanistically 'applied' to practice. Still, surprisingly popular ideas, such as those of Davies (1981), that social workers are 'maintenance mechanics' are – as well as being deeply ideological – likely to reinforce the notion that theory can be applied to practice in a fairly straightforward and unproblematic fashion (see also Reflection and Talk Box 1). Partly rooted in a positivistic understanding of intellectual inquiry, this way of perceiving theory also tends to be reflected in how social work curricula tend to map learning for future practitioners.

Schon addressed this perspective in a seminal paper in which he challenged the notion of 'professional practice as an exercise of *technical rationality* ... an application of research-based knowledge to the solution of problems of institutional choice' (Schon, 1992, p 52, emphasis added). The whole idea of *applying* theory to practice is deeply problematic because it pivots on the 'mistaken assumption that there are simple, direct one-to-one links that can be made between theory and practice' (Thompson, 2010, p xvii). Thompson has elaborated:

> practitioners do not simply use a theoretical knowledge base in a direct way ... but, rather, go through a more complex process of 'theorizing' practice – that is using a set of concepts to act as a framework for making sense of the situations we encounter in practice and how these relate to the wider context of social work and indeed of society itself. (Thompson, 2010, p xii; see also Robinson, 2003)

Social work 'involves dealing with complexity. Its challenges are far too demanding and multi-layered to be amenable to simple, formulaic approaches' (Thompson,

2010, p xv). The same writer's own emphasis, therefore, is on '*integrating* theory and practice' (Thompson, 2010, p 15, emphasis added). That is to say, 'theory should inform practice, but practice should also inform theory.... What we have is a dialectical relationship' (Thompson, 2010, pp 15–16). Indeed, this is a perception that will be shared by this book.

Social work and social theory cannot, of course, be an exhaustive survey; the book is inevitably informed by the author's political and personal inclinations and is liable to oversights and omissions. I am also mindful of the fact that some readers might find my references to social work in the UK and Ireland as somewhat limiting. The shells featured in the photograph that forms the book's cover image are from a particular place – a beach in Connemara in the west of Ireland; they are, like my own perceptions and the analysis in the book, derived from a particular time and place. Readers elsewhere may need to 'make connections' for themselves and taper some of the themes and issues featured in the 'Reflection and Talk Boxes' to fit local, particular circumstances.

Reflecting on the comments generated by readers of the book's initial proposal, there will be no space for Freire (1972) and the teachings of Gandhi. Neither, although he is likely to occasionally appear, is there a chapter devoted entirely to Foucault. I hope that the absence of such a chapter will not prompt any fretful Foucauldian purchasers to return the book and demand a refund. One hopes that they will be too 'self-responsibilised' to get overly annoyed about the omission. Despite Foucault's failure to adequately acknowledge and conceptualise resistance to power (Said, 2002), his usefulness in aiding thinking about social work is undeniable and it would be difficult to justify his exclusion from any taught social work programme. Reading *Discipline and punish* (Foucault, 1977) was an immensely enlightening experience that would shape my later understanding as a practitioner of the intent and meaning of the various assessment schedules introduced into social work with children and families in the UK from the early 1990s (see, eg, Garrett, 2003). Regrettably, however, to produce a text of the requisite length, the 'cut' had to be made somewhere. Although Foucault did not make it to this book's final edit, the copious literature already available on social work and Foucault will more than compensate for this omission.[4]

It is also conceded that the book could have been assembled in a variety of different ways. Throughout, as opposed to being divided into two parts, it may have dwelt, on a chapter by chapter basis, on a particular theorist. An alternative way of organising the material would have been to concentrate on the various 'society' paradigms that have emerged in recent years. A chapter might, thus, have elaborated on social work in a 'surveillance society' (Lyon, 2001a, 2001b, 2003, 2006) or social work in a 'risk society' (Webb, 2006; see also Llewellyn et al, 2008, pp 19–23).[5] Alternatively, chapters may have focused on the various 'isms' social theorists have produced and debated: for example, 'cosmopolitanism' (Fine, 2007). After consideration, these ways of putting the book together were rejected and, instead, it will be constructed as mapped below. First, however, one 'ism' deserves particular attention – feminism.

The 'death' of feminism and the 'post-feminist' era?

In the spring of 2011, the Universities Minister for the Conservative–Liberal Democrat administration in the UK blamed educated working women for the lack of jobs available for working-class men (*The Guardian*, 2011a). For the Minister, David Willetts, feminism was probably the 'single biggest factor' for the lack of social mobility. Leaving aside this 'Neanderthal take' on the country's unemployment crisis, as a Trades Union Congress (TUC) spokesperson aptly dubbed it, at least two other criticisms have been directed at feminism in the recent past. In the mid-1990s, Teresa Ebert (1996, p ix) argued that the 'dominant' feminist paradigm – which she referred to as 'ludic feminism' – had by then 'largely abandoned the problems of labour and exploitation and ignored their relationship to gender, sexuality, difference, desire, and subjectivity'. At a 'time when two-thirds of all labour in the world is done by women' (Ebert, 1996, p ix), Ebert maintained that leading feminist theorists, often situated in the more prestigious universities, had 'abandoned' bread-and-butter issues impacting on women's daily lives. Whereas these comments are, to some extent, accurate, the assertion that we are now in a 'post-feminist' era is far less tenable given the increasing 'feminisation of the proletariat' (Harvey, 2010, p 15; see also Bunting, 2011). Women now form 'the backbone of the global workforce' (Harvey, 2010, p 59) and are presently hit harder by public sector cuts in the UK labour market than men. Luann Good Goodrich (2010, p 109) refers to the stark

> gendered and racialized inequalities in the global economy and local labor markets, along with the commodification and devaluing of social roles, reproduction labor, and citizenship for women in general and poor, lone women in particular. Globalizing processes have produced a gendered and racialized global labor force that is deeply divided.... Specifically, more women are participating in global labor forces than ever before, yet associated social and economic gains are ambiguous at best, as a disproportionately high number of employed women are working jobs that are insecure, low-wage, without benefits, and part-time.

Yet, as a former president of the International Association of Schools of Social Work (IASSW) has remarked:

> The media in Western countries has confidently asserted that feminism is passé by claiming that we have entered the post-feminist era. To women like me, this is a strange paradox. For as women experience the feminisation of poverty, increased levels of sexual violence, the loss of welfare state benefits which women have accessed in the recent past, the threatened loss of livelihood and statehood, I marvel at the idea

that feminist claims have been realised and need consume the energies
of women and girls no longer. (Dominelli, 2002, p 1)[6]

Given the plurality of perspectives housed beneath the label 'feminism', it is more
accurate to refer to feminism*s*. Very broadly, these include: liberal feminists who
believe that gender equality is achievable within the parameters of capitalism and
social democracy; radical feminists who lay emphasis on the biological differences
and men's dominance over women throughout history and across cultures and
opt therefore for separatist strategies; and, finally, socialist or Marxist feminists
who maintain that there can be no socialism without women's liberation and no
women's liberation without socialism.

Feminist social work:

> arose out of feminist social action being carried out by women working
> with women in their communities. Their aim has been to improve
> women's well-being by linking their personal predicaments and
> often private sorrows with their social position and status in society.
> (Dominelli, 2002, p 6)

Importantly, feminist social work was rooted in the everyday concerns of women
using and women providing social work services (see also Thomas and Davies,
2005). Cree (2010) has maintained that the assessment of the impact of feminism
on mainstream social work ranges from potentially optimistic to the deeply
pessimistic. A number of achievements are, however, identifiable. For example, by
'placing gender on the social work map, feminist social workers have challenged
the gender neutrality regarding this social division usually upheld in traditional
professional social work theories and practice' (Dominelli, 2002, p 8). Feminist
social workers have 'problematised practitioner responses to women's needs'
(Dominelli, 2002, p 9): for example, 'mother blaming', the focus on 'dangerous'
mothers and the related failure to engage with fathers (for an early example,
see, eg, Milner, 1993). Feminist social workers and academics have also made an
important contribution to research and endeavoured to reform language practices
within social work.

No particular section of this book is specifically devoted to feminism, nor is
there a chapter entirely given over to a female theorist. However, the significance
of feminism is acknowledged and the book is informed by feminist analysis. As
Thompson (1997, p 43) observed, social work operates 'at the boundaries of
"normality" and "deviance" and so it is important that we recognise that our
conceptions of normality are "gendered"'. Furthermore, social work is work
undertaken mostly by women, oftentimes with and alongside women. In the
Republic of Ireland, for example, the most recent overview of the profession
indicated that 83.2% of the social work workforce are women (NSWQB, 2006).
Within a number of other jurisdictions, gender profiles of social workers reveal
similar findings.

Specifically in terms of the theoretical perspectives examined in this book, one cannot comprehend the deficiencies of the 'post-traditional order' theorisation explored in the next chapter without being mindful of its gender lacunae. Our understanding of 'primitive' patterns of capital accumulation, referred to in Chapter Four, is enhanced by Silva Federici's Marxist-feminist optic. Likewise, any interpretation of precarious employment patterns, discussed in Chapter Five, which fails to incorporate a feminist awareness will be unsatisfactory (Good Goodrich, 2010). Similarly, it is difficult to grasp the meaning of the work of Nancy Fraser, referred to in Chapter Nine, without being mindful of how gender differentiates and stratifies.

Chapter map

Social work and social theory is comprised of two parts and divided into 10 chapters. Part One, 'Debating modernity', will concentrate on debates about the shape of modernity. Such debates are significant for social work in at least two ways. First, social work is a product of modernity; and, second, over the past few years, the trajectory of modernity has been a focus of attention within the profession's academic literature. Chapter Two will focus on a range of theoretical interpretations and will begin, perhaps paradoxically, by referring to postmodernism and the notion that modernity is a concluded project. Although, the moment of postmodernism has now passed and we are, in some senses, *post-postmodernism* (Matthewman and Hoey, 2006), it remains important to have regard to this theorisation because of its prominence within social work literature, particularly in the late 1980s and 1990s.

For Gilroy (2000, p 60), modernity's 'new political codes must be acknowledged to have been compromised by the raciological drives that partly formed them and wove a deadly, exclusionary force into their glittering universal promises'. Partly prompted by this analysis, the chapter will go on to examine postcolonial theory. The final section of the chapter will dwell on the contributions of Anthony Giddens (1938–) and Ulrich Beck (1944–), for whom modernity is 'reflexive, rethinking its own achievements and failures' (Wagner, 2008, p 2; see also Giddens, 1994a; Beck, 1998). Here, it will be maintained that to understand Giddens' and Beck's theorisation, it is not only important to question the veracity of the world it *depicts*, but also to decipher the surplus meanings it *betrays* about the lives of the theorists themselves.

Chapter Three will introduce readers to the conceptualisations of 'Solid Modernity' and 'Liquid Modernity' associated with the work of the Polish sociologist Zygmunt Bauman (1925–). His recent writings have been said to 'travel light, burdened by neither research nor by theoretical analysis, but borne up by an unusual life wisdom, trained observer's eye, and fluent pen' (Therborn, 2007, p 106). However, a concise and critical articulation of his key ideas is important because, in recent years, his increasingly popular contributions have begun to percolate into the social work literature. Nevertheless, it will be maintained that a range of criticisms exist that can be directed at Bauman's theorisation.

Marxism 'represents both a form of revolutionary politics and one of the richest and most complex theoretical and philosophical movements in human history' (Young, 2001, p 6). Despite the current marginalisation of Marxism in social work, Chapter Four will maintain that Marx's *Capital* (Marx, 1990) continues to provide a devastating critique of capitalism and remains a vital resource for social workers seeking to understand and develop strategies of resistance to neoliberalisation. That is to say, Marx provides a number of 'reminders' or 'coordinates' that might help us to make sense of transformations taking place within the 'world of work' today. The chapter will be mostly concerned with *Capital* (Marx, 1990) and will reflect on Marx's analysis of time, toil (or labour) and technology in the context of social work's 'modernisation'. More fundamentally, Marx's critique seems all the more timely given the very scale of the current crisis, which, as Callinicos observes, 'invites, as it did in the case of its predecessor in the 1930s, reflection on the extent to which its causes are systemic, lying in the very nature of the capitalist mode of production' (Callinicos, 2010, p 7).

Building on the previous chapter, Chapter Five will focus on one of the book's prime concerns, neoliberalism. Six interconnected components of neoliberalism will be highlighted and explored in some detail: the relationship between neoliberalism and the 'embedded liberalism' it seeks to supplant or displace; the role of the state within neoliberalism; the gap dividing actually existing neoliberalism and its theory and rhetoric; the concept of 'accumulation by dispossession' and neoliberalism's redistribution in favour of the rich; the centrality of insecurity, precariousness or precarity; the renewed and retrogressive faith in incarceration and, more broadly, what has been termed the 'new punitiveness'; and pragmatism and how neoliberalism is apt to adapt to different national settings. The collapse of Lehman Brothers on 15 September 2008 'precipitated the biggest global financial crash since the great depression of the 1930s' (Callinicos, 2010, pp 1–2). The chapter will conclude, therefore, by commenting on the impact of the crisis on the neoliberal project.

According to the *Chambers English Dictionary*, 'to intervene' means 'to come or be between … to happen so as to interrupt: to interpose'. Taking forward the debate on modernity, the second part of the book will focus on the critical (and often political) 'interventions' of particular theorists. Seeking to interrupt or disturb mainstream perceptions of the everyday, each of them aspires to create new ways of looking at the world and envisages more equitable economic and social relationships. Moreover, their contributions could potentially aid practitioners in thinking about their day-to-day professional activities and the world in which they live.

Chapter Six will explore the work of Antonio Gramsci (1891–1937), which has, until recently, mostly been ignored within social work's academic literature. Perhaps not surprisingly in the context of the present economic crisis, his ideas are beginning to find a place in the profession's journals (MacKinnon, 2009; Singh and Cowden, 2009). After briefly outlining his biography, the chapter focuses on some of his key conceptualisations: Americanism, Fordism and Taylorism; Hegemony; Common Sense; and Intellectuals and Critical Reflection. Despite the obstacles confronting those reading his work, Gramsci's theoretical formulations continue to be of potential use and might aid our understanding of social work in contemporary times. Furthermore, *thinking* with Gramsci – and bringing him into dialogue with other theorists – might enable social workers to help construct counter-hegemonic strategies and a renewed sense of radical activism.

In recent years, some attempts have been made to ascertain if Pierre Bourdieu's (1930–2002) thought has relevance for social workers. Chapter Seven will begin by identifying some of the major challenges posed by the mammoth contribution of the French sociologist. Apart from Bourdieu's dense prose style and the misleading labels frequently attached to him (eg 'Marxist' or 'postmodernist'), a further area of difficulty relates to the actual theoretical content of his contribution. Three main flaws in Bourdieu's output relate to: his problematic engagement with multiculturalism, 'race' and ethnicity; his emphasis on the dulled passivity of social actors, particularly the working class; and his views on the nature of the state. Despite the potential drawbacks, however, Chapter Seven will make the case for *thinking with* Bourdieu because his conceptual categories of habitus, field and capital – along with the related ideas associated with doxa and symbolic violence – add considerably to social work's social theory foundations. His more overtly 'political' involvement also contains a number of key 'messages' for social work.

Attentive to the resilience of Marxist theorisation, *Social work and social theory*'s intellectual affinity with Gramsci and Bourdieu provides the book with its theoretical compass. The next two chapters, however, examine the work of Jürgen Habermas (1929–) and the theory of recognition, both of which have received some coverage in the social work literature, primarily thanks to Stan Houston's lucid explanations in the *British Journal of Social Work*. Alert to the promotion of Habermas's work in the area of child protection and related forms of endeavour (Hayes and Houston, 2007), Chapter Eight will engage with the potential difficulties in the work of the German thinker. For example, due to his unsatisfactory attentiveness to power differentials, his emphasis on the possibilities for unconstrained dialogue is less than convincing. In this context, bringing Habermas into dialogue with Gramsci, Bourdieu and the Russian literary theorist Mikhail Bakhtin (1895–1975) helps illuminate key factors Habermas neglects.

A number of writers located within the field of social work have suggested that the ethics and 'politics of recognition' provide a body of theorisation that can assist social workers in their day-to-day encounters with the users of social services. Chapter Nine will extend the existing theoretical parameters by drawing attention to some of the contemporary critiques directed at recognition theorists. The discussion will start with the German theorist Axel Honneth (1949–), whose work is now frequently promoted within social work. While Honneth's tendency to 'psychologisation' undermines his contribution, it will be suggested that a more compelling theoretical articulation of recognition is provided by the American feminist Nancy Fraser (1947–) whose work seems more congruent with more progressive social work discourses on the multifaceted nature of oppression and subjugation. More generally, however, recognition theory tends to focus too exclusively on micro-encounters and interactions and pays insufficient attention to the role of the neoliberal state.

Chapter Ten will draw attention to a number of additional writers whose work should, perhaps, be wider known within the social work literature in the future: the co-authored work of Luc Boltanski (1940–) and Ève Chiapello (1965–), Antonio Negri (1933–) and the autonomist Marxists, and Alain Badiou (1937–). All of them, although conceptually different, potentially signal new directions for social work's engagement with social theory. Critical readings of them can also help to displace the Giddens–Beck–Bauman orthodoxy that has dominated the profession's social theory repertoire in recent years.

Finally, the 'political' dimension to critical social theory continues to trouble many within the social work academy uncomfortable with any destabilisation of mainstream, officially endorsed understandings. One reviewer of my proposal for *Social work and social theory* stated that there was a need for me to 'make the content more objective. For example, the sentence [featured in my proposal] … "capitalism is an exploitative economic system which damages bodies and minds" could be highly contested'. 'I suggest', continued the same reviewer, 'a more *balanced* approach' (emphasis added). However, what follows seeks to be a scholarly, but still radical and disruptive read, situated among those books, actions, thoughts and dispositions that are irrevocably anti-capitalist. Inescapably, the book will also be influenced by the long economic crisis evolving in Europe and elsewhere. Perhaps readers seeking a more 'balanced' approach should look away now.

◀◀ Reflection and Talk Box 1: The 'maintenance mechanic' ▶▶

(Extracted from Martin Davies, *The essential social worker* [1981, pp 137–42])

Social workers are the maintenance mechanics oiling the inter-personal wheels of the community.... Motor mechanics hope to produce improvements in the running performance of vehicles after a routine service: they aim to get the car back on the road after a break-down. For most people, most of the time, the human way of life ensures self-maintenance; but for a minority, either because of defects at birth, deprivation during childhood, the onset of sickness or old age, the experience of an accident, the shock of bereavement or job-loss, or the ill-effects of political, economic or social planning or discrimination, self-sufficiency runs out and the need for a maintenance mechanic becomes apparent. This need pinpoints the heart of the social worker's role.

The social worker is contributing to the maintenance of society by exercising some control over deviant members and allocating scarce resources according to policies laid down by the state, but implemented on an individual basis. He is maintaining members in society by exercising control, by allocating resources, and by the provision of a wide range of supportive strategies designed to maximize self-respect and develop the abilities of individuals to survive and thrive under their own steam.... For example, work with a problem family can involve pressure to get a man to work.... He [the social worker] has to reconcile marginal individuals to their social position while simultaneously helping to improve them.

The maintenance strategy is two-pronged.... On the one hand, social workers are employed by the state to curb some of the excesses of deviant behavior. But social workers are also concerned with ameliorating the living conditions of those who are finding it difficult to cope without help. Their agencies' objectives lead them to make attempts to improve the quality of life of conflicting married couples, out-of-work teenagers, handicapped housewives, terminally-sick hospital patients.

The very idea of maintenance implies – indeed demands – a broad acceptance of the existing political and economic regime.... [It is] a reality-based view of contemporary existence for worker and client.

- What theoretical perspectives on society underpin the idea, articulated over 30 years ago, that the social worker is a 'maintenance mechanic'?

- Can you identify any problems, or gaps, in this theoretical perspective?

- Does the role of 'maintenance mechanic' adequately describe how you perceive your own role as a social work practitioner?

Notes

[1] Gramsci had a specific understanding of 'common sense' and this will be examined in Chapter Six.

[2] It is recognised that the UK is a differentiated social and political entity given the devolved administrations in Scotland, Wales and Northern Ireland.

[3] See, for example, Ferguson (2004), Webb (2006), Price and Simpson (2007), Llewellyn et al (2008), McLaughlin (2008), Cunningham and Cunningham (2008), Smith (2008), and Thompson (2010).

[4] Specifically in terms of social work and Foucault, Chambon et al (1999) provide a helpful volume with a valuable glossary: see also the chapter by Irving in Gray and Webb (2009) and Garrity (2010). Skehill (1999, 2004) has deployed a Foucauldian approach and used the associated literature on governmentality to analyse the history of social work in Ireland. As well as *Discipline and punish* (Foucault, 1977), readers new to Foucault are encouraged to look at the following: Foucault (1980, 1988a, 1988b, 1988c, 1988d). The theorisation of Nik Rose (2000) should also be examined (see also Miller and Rose, 2008). McKinley and Starkey (1998) have produced a collection examining Foucault in the context of management and organisational studies. Useful commentaries on Foucault include: Danaher et al (2000) and Moss (1988). Miller (1993), among others, has provided an accessible biography. Bourdieu's (2008, pp 138–41) homage to Foucault is interesting and Cronin (1996) has provided a comparison between the two French scholars. Readers might also wish to consult issue 55 of the journal *New Formations*, from Spring 2005, which is entirely devoted to a reappraisal of Foucault.

[5] Lyon (2001a, p 2) defines 'surveillance' as 'any collection and processing of personal data, whether identifiable or not, for the purposes of influencing or managing those whose data has been garnered'. He maintains that it is 'hard to find a place, or an activity, that is shielded or secure from some purposeful tracking, tagging, listening, watching, recording or verification device' (Lyon, 2001a, p 1). For Rose (2000, p 325) surveillance 'is "designed in" to the flows of everyday existence'. In short, we now live in, what Gary T. Marx has referred to as, a 'surveillance society' (in Lyon, 2001b, p 32; see also ICO, 2006, 2010). For a discussion on how these development relates to social work, see Garrett (2009, ch 5).

[6] Dominelli (2002, p 7) has defined 'feminist social work' as:

> a form of social work practice that takes women's experience of the world as the starting point of its analysis and by focusing on the links between a woman's position in society and her individual predicament, responds to her specific needs, creates egalitarian relations in 'client'–worker interactions and addresses structural inequalities.

Part One

Debating modernity

CHAPTER TWO

'How to be modern': theorising modernity

Introduction

Today, most theoretical perspectives derived from sociology and social theory tend to argue that modernity – itself a contested term – has *not* yet been exhausted. 'What is the nature of the modernity which we inhabit?' is a key question preoccupying many theorists, which gives rise to a plethora of alternative and competing views on what it is to be 'modern' and on how moderns *think, feel* and *act*. Deliberating on these matters is inescapably *political*: sociologists and social theorists should not be perceived as providing 'scientific' or 'objective' accounts of how we are evolving because they owe allegiances to particular political projects, which are intent of remaking the world in particular ways . Perhaps one of the best examples of this is Giddens, who, throughout the Blair years, appeared to provide a sociological 'road map' for the politics of New Labour. With his revealingly titled *Beyond left and right* (Giddens, 1994b), he furnished a 'book full of sneers at social democracy and the welfare state' and was to 'become the 'theoretician of the [former] British Prime Minister [Blair] and his New Labour regime, giving an intellectual gloss to a party that had lost – or rather severed – any connection to "first wave" social democracy' (Therborn, 2007, p 100).

It was postmodernists who 'stimulated an awareness of and a debate about modernity' and this chapter will begin by briefly looking at their contribution (Therborn, 2011, p 55). After briefly examining the derivation and definition of 'modernity', the focus will be on postcolonial theory. Important here is the failure of many theorists to locate modernity in the context of European expansion and the domination of subjugated populations. As Gilroy (2000, p 71) points out in his exploration of colonial modernity, it is 'not merely that European imperial powers wrongly deprived colonial subjects of their humanity, but that Europe has perpetrated the still greater crime of despoiling humanity of its elemental unity as a species'. Attention will then turn to the work of Giddens and Beck, whose work, at the turn of the century, began to dominate and delimit social work's engagement with social theory.[1]

Whatever happened to postmodernism?

Postmodernism is founded on an understanding that the period of 'modernity' has now ended: postmodernism, in short, represents a rupture or break with modernity. Terry Eagleton (2003, p 13) elaborates that 'postmodern' refers to the:

> movement of thought which rejects totalities, universal values, grand historical narratives, solid foundations to human existence and the possibility of objective knowledge. Postmodernism is skeptical of truth, unity and progress, opposes what it sees as elitism in culture, tends towards cultural relativism, and celebrates pluralism, discontinuity and heterogeneity.

Postmodernism is, of course, a complex and diverse body of theorisation but, in general terms, and as Eagleton's definition hints, postmodern perspectives have emphasised the significance of a whole series of contemporary transformations. These include: the increasing pace of change; the emergence of new complexities and forms of fragmentation; the growing significance of 'diversity', 'difference' and the pervasive awareness of relativities; the opening up of individual 'choice' and 'freedom'; and the increasing awareness of the socially constructed nature of existence. Jean-François Lyotard, in his enormously influential *The postmodern condition* (1984), defined the postmodern as 'incredulity towards metanarratives'; that is to say, a lack of belief in explanatory and all-encompassing accounts of society and/or historical transformation that purport to provide reliable accounts of the trajectory and character of social change.

Within a postmodernist framework, truth 'takes the guise of "truth" centred neither on God's word (as in the premodern) nor in human reason (as in the modern), [it] is decentred and localised so that many "truths" are possible, dependent on different times and places' (Parton and Marshall, 1998, p 243). Moreover, relativities, uncertainties and contingencies are no longer seen as marginal and problems to be overcome as yet beyond the reach of reason, but are central, pervasive and part of the core of individual lives.

Parton and Marshall (1998, p 245) suggest that, at best, the implications for politics, policy and practice of such perspectives are ambiguous; at worst, they may undermine many of the 'central values and principles of social work itself'. Nevertheless, dominant academic discourses circulating in the UK, America and Australasia during the 1990s were clear that the world (or at least its affluent western regions) had entered an unambiguously postmodern phase (Howe, 1994; Parton, 1994). In some senses, this development could be perceived as the social work academy belatedly seeking to 'jump onto' an already departed postmodernist train (Smith and White, 1997). That is to say, some social work academics' enthusiasm for postmodernism could, perhaps, be interpreted as indicative of a desire to merely ape colleagues working in sociology and literature departments who, for a number of years, had been peppering their papers with the 'postmodern' adjective. However, this new interest from social work academics coincided with these other disciplines beginning a shift to new theoretical terrains.

Furthermore, the social work academy's relatively short engagement with postmodern theorisation, failed to have an impact on social workers' own perceptions of their day-to-day activities. This may, in part, have been related to the often rather alienating and obscure vocabulary which some associated with postmodernism were apt to deploy. Writing in an Australian context, Camilleri (1999, pp 26–7) felt that:

> [for many] social workers, the adjective 'postmodern', which is now increasingly used in social work texts, appears to throw them into the middle of a conversation. There is a sense of everyone knowing what is going on except them. It is a conversation constructed in a language that is at best obtuse and at worst incomprehensible. It appears designed to produce confusion.

Nonetheless, he and his Australian academic colleagues (Pease and Fook, 1999) remained intent on seeking to reveal how postmodernist theorisation illuminated how society was changing and how social work practice could be progressively transformed in line with these changes. Indeed, in the 1990s, a number of social work academics were won over by facets of the postmodernist perspective. David Howe (1994), for example, argued that the emergence of social work from the mid-19th century could be seen to reflect more pervasive tendencies within modernity. In this context, for him, the three cornerstones of social work – care, control and cure – represented specific manifestations of modernity's three great projects. This vision, we might add, was typified by Abram Games' (1914–96) wonderful 1938 poster for Berthold Lubetkin's (1901–90) Finsbury Health Centre, where the building's gleaming, white facade is juxtaposed to the dark world of disease, neglect and ruin. Alongside, is the text: 'Modern medicine means the maintenance of good health and the prevention and early detection of disease. This is achieved by a periodic medical examination at Centres such as the Finsbury Health Centre, where modern methods are used'.

The high point of this modernist project in England was the attempt to rationalise and reorganise social work practices, skills and approaches. This, for Howe, was reflected in the Seebohm (1968) Report. In contrast, the evolution of social work in the 1990s was symptomatic of a postmodern condition, whereby a detectable 'blurring' of boundaries was taking place between professionals. In the area of interventions into the lives of children and families, this postmodern approach resulted in the creation of multidisciplinary Youth Offending Teams (YOTs) after the introduction of the Crime and Disorder Act 1998. Similarly, Howe identified other changes such as a 'switch from causation to counting, from explanation to audit' as representative of a postmodern shift (Howe, 1994, p 86).

Importantly also, there were divergences within postmodernist theorisation. Pauline Marie Rosenau (1991), for example, refers to a dichotomy between 'sceptical' and 'affirmative' postmodernists: the former is 'the postmodernism of despair', which, inspired by philosophers of Continental Europe, emphasises the impossibility of truth. The latter is a more optimistic form of postmodernism open to positive political projects and action. Bob Pease and Jan Fook (1999, p 12) draw a somewhat similar distinction and side:

> with those expressions of postmodern thinking that do not totally abandon the values of the Enlightenment project of human emancipation. Only 'strong' or 'extreme' forms of postmodernist theory reject normative criticism and the usefulness of any forms of commonality underlying diversity. We believe that a 'weak' form of postmodernism informed by critical theory can contribute effectively to the construction of emancipatory politics concerned with political action and social justice.

However, the aspiration to utilise what are deemed 'weak' forms of postmodernist theory does not eliminate some of the core problems associated with it (see Thompson, 2010, p 33).

It is, of course, easy to lampoon the worst excesses of postmodernism. In the broadly defined domain of 'cultural studies', for example, such excesses are not difficult to locate, as Eagleton (2003, pp 2–3) rightly complains:

> the politics of masturbation exert far more fascination than the politics of the Middle East. Socialism has lost out to sado-masochism. Among students of culture, the body is an immensely fashionable topic, but it is usually the erotic body, not the famished one. There is also a keen interest in coupling bodies, but not in labouring ones. Quietly spoken middle-class students huddle diligently in libraries, at work on sensational subjects like vampirism and … porno movies.

Before turning our attention to the resilience of modernity, one particular perspective on postmodernism merits brief attention: that of Fredric Jameson. Significantly, Jameson anchored postmodernism within capitalism, equating it with 'the saturation of every pore of the world in the serum of capital' (Anderson, 1998, p 55). This move – which restored capitalism to the core of the analysis – went entirely against the grain of most intellectual articulations of postmodernism (Jameson, 1991). Although some find his ornate prose style challenging, Jameson's Marxist interventions are greatly enriched by his capacity to incorporate a diverse range of artistic production: from architecture, to literature, to the movies of Alfred Hitchcock. For him:

> as realism was an embodiment, in literary form, of nineteenth-century capitalism, and modernism was the expression of … post-industrial capitalism of the early twentieth century, so … postmodernism is …

the expression on an aesthetic and textual level of the dynamic of 'late capitalism'. (Roberts, 2000, p 112)

In short, just as capitalism has an economic logic, 'it also has a cultural logic, and the cultural logic of late capitalism' is postmodernism (Roberts, 2000, p 112). According to Jameson, there are a number of characteristics integral to postmodernism and one of these is related to 'the emergence of a new kind of flatness or depthlessness, a new kind of superficiality' (Jameson, in Hardt and Weeks, 2000, p 196). Beginning in the late 1980s, this was mirrored, one might add, in the development a range of 'tools' for social work practice, such as the emblematic assessment schedules relating to the 'looking after children' (LAC) materials (Garrett, 2003). In recent years, Jameson appears to have concluded that it is theoretically preferable to have regard to what he now terms a 'singular modernity' (Therborn, 2007).

Defining modernity

Within sociology, the German Georg Simmel (1858–1918) was the first to use the term (Frisby, 2002). In recent times, it has been Giddens, along with Habermas and Marshall Berman, who have promoted its use. Contemporary social theory and sociology, though, do not hold the monopoly over the term. The word 'modernity' was first explored by 'poets, not political scientists; Charles Baudelaire elaborated the term in his essay "The Painter of Modern Life [1859–60]"' (Boym, 2001, p 19). The etymology takes us even further back in time because while Baudelaire:

> identified modern sensibility and coined the noun modernity, the adjective *modern* had its own history. Derived from *modo* it comes from the Christian Middle Ages; initially it meant 'present' and 'contemporary' and there was nothing radical about it.… In the eighteenth century 'to modernize' often referred to home improvement. (Boym, 2001, p 22, emphasis in original; see also Therborn, 2011, p 54)

Moreover, argues Boym (2001, p 22), it is 'crucial to distinguish modernity as a critical project from modernization as a social practice and state policy'.

Modernity was associated with the 'open horizon of the future, with unending progress towards a better human condition' (Wagner, 2008, p 1; see also Scott, 2006, ch 7). In this context, the historian Eric Hobsbawm has written about the impact of the 18th-century (and in particular the French) Enlightenment, with its associated stress on systematic rationalism and the notion that Reason was to provide the basis of all action. The various currents of the Enlightenment promulgated the 'belief in the capacity of man [sic] to improve his conditions'. Furthermore, the 'rationalism of the Enlightenment implied a fundamentally critical approach to society' (Hobsbawm, 2011, p 20).

More expansively, Lyon (1994, pp 19–20) has ventured that modernity:

refers to the social order that emerged following the Enlightenment. Though its roots may be traced back, the modern world is marked by unprecedented dynamism, its dismissal or marginalizing of tradition, and its global consequences. Modernity's forward-looking thrust relates strongly to belief in progress and the power of human reason to produce freedom.... Modernity is all about the massive changes that took place at many levels from mid-sixteenth century onwards, changes signalled by the shifts that uprooted agricultural workers and transformed them into mobile urbanites. Modernity questions all conventional ways of doing things, substituting authorities of its own, based on science, economic growth, democracy or law. And it unsettles the self; if identity is given in traditional society, in modernity it is constructed. Modernity started out to conquer the world in the name of Reason; certainty and social order would be founded on new bases.

Whilst Woodwiss considers capitalism to be the driving force of modernity, Lyon associates it with five key elements: differentiation; rationalisation (reflected in the bureaucracy and a bureaucratic sensibility); urbanism; discipline; and secularism. He also maintains that modernity can be connected to certain perturbing developments or ambivalences, such as those related to: alienation and exploitation; anomie and loss of direction; what Weber termed the 'iron cage' of bureaucracy; the evolution of a society of 'strangers'; and more patterns of 'control' (Lyon, 1994, pp 29–34).

Frankfurt School theorists have also dwelt on these themes and written about modernity in terms of 'administered society' (Marcuse, 1991) and the 'standardised life' (Adorno, 2000). Similar perceptions on the drawbacks of 'modernity' are examined in the work of Jürgen Habermas in Chapter Eight: more specifically, his conceptualisation that the 'system' is colonising the 'lifeworld'. Zygmunt Bauman (1989), whose work is explored in the Chapter Three, has emphasised how the search for 'order' has failed and even made life worse. However, more recently, he has argued that there are reasons to consider 'fluidity' or 'liquidity' as fitting metaphors when we wish to grasp the nature of the present.

Modernity as 'Eurocentric', modernity as genocide: the postcolonial critique

A common failure of theories of modernity is that they have tended to be 'Western' perspectives, which have not incorporated a satisfactory understanding of the evolution of other societies located elsewhere in the world. A number of writers, often, but not always, associated with 'postcolonial theory', have explored this lacuna. The key figure identified in this field of political and cultural critique is the late Edward W. Said (1935–2003).[2] He demonstrated that the 'habitual practices, and full range of effects of colonialism on the colonized territories and their peoples, could be analysed conceptually and discursively' (Young, 2001, p 18). Apart from Said (2003 [1978]), postcolonial theory is predominantly based on the work of Frantz Fanon (1925–61).

Two key facets of postcolonial and related theory warrant brief attention. First, the assertion that the 'equating of modernity with Europe reinforces a fundamental assumption of much intellectual thought today: that particular structures, emerging first from the West, would become universal' (Bhambra, 2007, p 1). Within this dominant conceptualization, the West is perceived as 'the "maker" of *universal history*' (Bhambra, 2007, p 2, emphasis in original); hence the 'implicit "Eurocentrism" contained within classical theories of modernity' (Bhambra, 2007, p 5). In his fascinating history of Iran, Mirsepassi (2000, p 6) has stated that the:

> project of modernization becomes one of 'development', or 'catching up' with, and homogenizing into, the economically, politically and culturally modern West. A major support to these projects is a group of theories presenting modernization as a rational and universal social project, superior to any other societal model in history.

Although, in more recent times, a good deal of theorising has endeavoured to embrace notions of 'multiple modernities', 'successive modernities' or 'alternative modernities' (Therborn, 2011, p 54), it cannot be disputed that Eurocentrism is still very much present in social theory.

By the time of the commencement of the First World War, 'imperial powers occupied, or by various means controlled, nine-tenths of the surface of the globe; Britain governed one-fifth of the area of the world and a quarter of its population' (Young, 2001, p 2). Nevertheless, a second and more pointed critique of much mainstream theorisation is that there has been a failure to appreciate that colonialism by 19th- and 20th-century European states meant that in many areas of the world, modernity was *imposed* from outside: 'modernity arrived … out of the barrels of guns' (Therborn, 2011, p 59). More emphatically, the project of modernity was impaired, in human terms, from its inception because of its racialised, even genocidal, character.

Gilroy (2000), for example, has drawn attention to the fact that seminal Enlightenment figures often held views of black people and colonised peoples that contaminated their thinking. Kant (1774–1804), for example, confidently observed that the 'Negroes of Africa have no feeling that rises above the trifling' (quoted in Gilroy, 2000, p 58). Furthermore, 'blacks are … so talkative that they must be driven apart from each other with thrashings' (quoted in Gilroy, 2000, p 60). These musings reveal that 'Kant's democratic hopes and dreams simply could not encompass the black community' (Gilroy, 2000, p 60). More broadly, these 'philosophical' interventions by Kant illuminate modernity's 'color-coded promises' (Gilroy, 2000, p 87).

Colonialism, and the domination or eradication of subjugated populations, can also been linked to later developments within the European heartland. For example, Aimé Cesare (1913–2008) was among the first to point out that fascism was 'a form of colonialism brought home to Europe' (Young, 2001, p 2). As will be noted in Chapter Three, Bauman's conceptualisation of 'solid modernity' and the Holocaust tends to omit the colonial dimension. Nevertheless, it was 'colonial societies and conflicts that provided the context in which concentration camps emerged as a novel form of political administration, population management, warfare, and coerced labor' (Gilroy, 2000, p 60). Despite conservative historiography's attempts to restore a more benign, even triumphalist, depiction of the British Empire, colonial nostalgia cannot disguise the fact that two:

> systems of morality coexist within modernity, one for 'us' and the other
> for 'them'. All of the 'liberal', 'enlightened', and 'progressive' triumphs
> in Western modernity have had their independent counterpart in
> utterly illiberal, violently totalizing, and destructive assaults on other
> peoples. (Mirsepassi, 2000, p 35)

The postcolonial critique has, therefore, provided a welcome corrective to a social theory that repeatedly failed to situate modernity within the project of Western expansion and colonialism. However, although distinctive, this critique is not the 'first to question the ethics of colonialism: indeed, anti-colonialism is as old as colonialism itself' (Young, 2001, p 6). Historically, Marxism has played a major role in anti-colonial resistance. Early Marxist theorisation, following Marx himself, assumed that capitalist penetration would lead to positive economic and social evolution and development. On account of this, there is a 'powerful tendency in postcolonial studies to dismiss Marx as a Eurocentric or even Orientalist thinker' (Lindner, 2010, p 27). Objecting to the hastiness of this critique, Linder's close reading has revealed that Marx 'gradually comes to reject Eurocentric assumptions' (Lindner, 2010, p 27). Subsequently, Rosa Luxemburg (1871–1919) was, perhaps, the earliest European Marxist thinker and activist who was to recognise the devastating impact of imperialism upon the Third World (Hudis and Anderson, 2004).[3]

Some of this may appear far too abstract and unlikely to be of much interest to social workers and associated workers. However, we can make the connections, and such theorisation can be viewed as relevant, in a contemporary sense, in a number of ways. First, renewed sensitivity to questions of neo-colonial exploitation is likely to have informed the development, from the 1980s onwards, of 'anti-racist' forms of social work theorisation and practice. Arguably, there may be a unifying thread connecting the critique of the universalising discourses of modernity and the critique of local authorities' provision of one-size-fits-all 'services', which simply disregarded the particular needs of specific minority ethnic groups (Garrett, 2004). This could be in relation to the provision of meals or, more substantially, in terms of adoption and fostering policy impacting on black and other minority ethnic children. In the early 1980s, for example, the Association of Black Social Workers and Allied Professionals in the UK challenged the hegemony of child placement policies and practices located within an assimilationist perspective, but also, more historically, the legacy of colonialism. Here, practitioners highlighted the potentially damaging consequences for black children of being placed with white adoptive and foster carers, but also, more broadly, drew attention to the impact of racism (Small, 1982).

Second, postcolonial approaches have remained alert to the impact on 'those oppressed through class or minoritarian status within the heartlands of contemporary capitalism' (Young, 2001, p 9). Young's argument is that the indigenous impoverished poor, often 'white', were themselves the target of colonising strategies. This is most apparent in terms of some of the language used to describe the living conditions of the urban poor towards the end of the 19th century. As McClintock (1995, p 120) notes, not only was colonial discourse 'systematically deployed to map urban space into a geography of power and containment', but the 'analogy between the slum and colony was tirelessly evoked'. She refers, in particular, to the mid–1880s and the literature on the 'discovery' of London's East End and the 'depiction of the slums as foreign lands' (McClintock, 1995, p 121). In more recent times, some of the policing strategies and surveillance tactics deployed in colonial zones, such as Kenya and Northern Ireland, have also found their way to the British 'mainland' (Kitson, 1991 [1971]). During the period of the former New Labour administrations, political rhetoric and social policy would refer to 'problem families' as being, seemingly, from another age: living anachronisms, 'anti-modern', seemingly 'out of time' families that were unable or unwilling to display a commitment to be self-activating, responsibilised neoliberal citizens (see also Haylett, 2001). What is more, as mentioned earlier, Ferguson's (2011, p 97) recent reference to 'marginalized families' living in often 'poor and disgusting conditions' can be interpreted, in part, as echoing this perspective. Indeed, over the past 25 years, a whole range of social work assessment schedules have been implicitly intent on colonising the lives of service users and moulding them into narrowly defined, normative families with 'acceptable' middle-class social aspirations and 'appropriate' ways of rearing children (Parker et al, 1991; Department of Health, Department for Education and Employment, and Home Office, 2000).

Third, as different countries are apt to construct and follow alternative routes to modernity, academic literature on social work should try to encompass diverse perceptions of the profession's core function. Bar-on (1999, p 9), for example, in his discussion on the development of social work in Africa, points out that social work training in Botswana originally took place in an agricultural college where students were taught 'cooking, knitting, vegetable gardening and the like'. In short, the activity constructed and identified as 'social work' was entirely different to that regarded as 'social work' in, for example, the UK. Nevertheless, there is still an inclination to impose dominant tropes of UK (perhaps, even more precisely, English) sociology onto countries with very different histories to the metropolitan centre. In Ireland, for example, this prompted an interesting exchange involving Powell (1998) and Skehill (1999) in which the latter criticised the former for transposing the theorisation of Giddens and Beck to an Irish context without sufficient regard to its cultural specificity.

A new sociological template for social work? Giddens and Beck

The now largely defunct postmodernist perspective tended to exaggerate the rupture that allegedly occurred with 'modernity', whereas most contemporary theorisations share the perspective that we still inhabit a period of modernity. In this context, the work of Giddens – rightly regarded as the intellectual architect of the 'Third Way' – has been immensely influential, despite his current marginalisation in the aftermath of Labour's defeat at the 2010 general election.

Giddens uses the phrases 'Post-Traditional Society' (Giddens, 1994a), 'High Modernity' or even 'Late Modernity' to distinguish the contemporary period. Moreover, he accepts that it is 'quite accurate' to characterise this period – as does the German social theorist Ulrich Beck (1998) – as a 'risk society' (Giddens, 1991, p 28; see also Giddens, 1998; Webb, 2006): Beck (1994) also refers to the phrase 'reflexive modernisation' to describe the current period. He has also – and to add to the terminological confusion – introduced the phrase 'second modernity' to complement his 'reflexive modernisation' formulation (Beck, 2000a).

A number of attempts have been made to import this sociology (and political outlook) into social work and related fields (Jordan, 2000, 2001). In an important article in the *British Journal of Social Work*, Harry Ferguson – drawing on Giddens and Beck – endeavoured to provide a new sociological template for social work in the 21st century (Ferguson, 2001). He maintained that 'life politics' should form the 'fundamental concerns of social work' in a 'post-traditional context' (Ferguson, 2001, p 41). Ferguson then went on to provide a lucid summary of the theoretical interventions of Giddens and Beck, particularly their understanding that Western societies have undergone a transformation that has had a profound impact on individual lives and on intimate relationships. Thus, it was argued that during a period of 'simple modernity', stretching 'roughly from the 1920s through to the 1970s, social life and intimate relations were relatively fixed' (Ferguson, 2001, p 42). For much of the 20th century, 'men and women essentially knew their place and the state intervened to ensure that those on the margins did not forget it' (Ferguson, 2001, p 42). Intra-familial dynamics were based on 'hierarchical authority relations' and there was, for example, no concept of children possessing separate rights, different from those of adults. Gender roles were clearly demarcated and social work played a major role in reinforcing and regulating dominant constructs of motherhood. Associated with these societal and familial patterns was the 'structured concealment' of issues such as sexual abuse (Ferguson, 2001, p 43).

In this 'post-traditional order', key components of 'simple modernity' begin to unravel, profoundly affecting issues of identity and relationships (see also Beck and Beck-Gernsheim, 1999). In the 'order of simple modernity, identity was structured through external controls imposed by the church, family experts and tradition itself (the binding nature of "how things have always been done")' (Ferguson, 2001, p 45). In a 'post-traditional order', however, 'the self' has become a 'reflexive' or 'biographical project' (Giddens, 1991, p 32; 1994b, p 82). Here, individuals have the opportunity to construct an identity and the task becomes that of working on one's own 'elective' biography (Ferguson, 2001, p 45). While traditional authority continues to have an impact, in 'reflexive modernity', it is from 'experts, global media and so on' that people 'draw information reflexively' in making their lives (Ferguson, 2001, p 45; see also Giddens, 1994b, pp 6–7, 86). We are now, in fact, 'a world of clever people' where, it is claimed, 'most people most of the time know most of what the government knows' (Giddens, 1994b, p 94).

'Individualisation' and what would appear to be an epoch of new freedom nonetheless has considerable disadvantages and psychologically destabilising factors (Beck, 1994, 2000a). 'The world we live in today ... is one of dislocation and uncertainty, a "runaway world"' (Giddens, 1994b, p 3). To live in this world 'has the feeling of riding a juggernaut' (Giddens, 1991, p 28). Consequently, 'individuals feel bereft and alone in the world in which she or he lacks the psychological supports and sense of security provided by the more traditional settings' (Giddens, 1991, pp 33–4). Many of the 'landmarks which previously provided orientation, meaning and personal anchorage place in a larger universe have vanished' (Beck and Beck-Gernsheim, 1999, p 44). 'Risk' has a growing impact on a range of personal and professional sites, increasingly encroaching on popular discourses (Beck, 1998, 2000b). This attentiveness to risk derives less from the 'proliferation of new dangers per se than from the "setting free" of individuals from normative institutional constraints' (Ferguson, 2001, p 46; see also Webb, 2006).

Owing to the dissolving of the constraints associated with 'simple modernity', there are now more and more areas of personal life requiring 'choice and responsibility' (Ferguson, 2001, p 46). In an 'individualised society each of us must learn ... to conceive of him/herself as the pivot round which life revolves, a planning office for his/her own abilities, preferences, relationships and so on' (Beck and Beck-Gernsheim, 1999, p 40). However, and importantly, social work has failed to take account of this seismic shift from the period of 'simple modernity' to a 'post-traditional order'. Related to this, it is maintained, is the profession's continuing allegiance to 'emancipatory politics', which has constituted the 'orientation of most forms of radical social work discourse' since Bailey and Brake's (1975) important collection (Ferguson, 2001, p 47). Crucially, because critical social work is 'tied to emancipatory politics', it is 'unable to deal *theoretically*, *politically* or *practically* with defining features of how people have to live in a post-traditional order' (Ferguson, 2001, p 47, emphases added). Indeed, Ferguson's central and most serious charge is that 'critical social work', still viewing the world through the lens of 'simple modernity', has exhausted its radical potential, and is no longer theoretically equipped to comprehend the 'post-traditional order'. Even more damaging, the practitioners committed to anachronistic 'emancipatory politics' are unable to adequately respond to the needs of users of services.

On a theoretical level, 'radical left critiques of social work' are still too influenced by 'Marx, Foucault and post-structuralism' and so fail 'to account for the reflexive ways in which the users of services and social workers "make" their own biographies' (Ferguson, 2001, p 48). According to Ferguson, there is a need to 'reconceptualize the fundamental concerns of social work' as 'life politics' (Ferguson, 2001, p 41). At the heart of this politics is 'a new relationship between the personal and the political, expertise and lay people, in which practices such as social work increasingly take the form of a methodology of life planning for late-modern citizens' (Ferguson, 2001, p 42). Ferguson (2001, pp 52, 50) asserts that a 'post traditional social work' education and practice must begin to acquaint itself with the 'new agenda of life politics'; an agenda that should, he has maintained, include '*compulsory* parenting classes' (*Society Guardian*, 2006, p 3, emphasis added).

Is this a 'post-traditional order'?

This assertion that we are now living in a 'post-traditional order' needs to be scrutinised in some detail because it provides a conceptual foundation for the suggestion that social work should now seek to reorient itself in the direction of the agenda of 'life politics'.

It could be argued that the 'radical rupture' notion is misleading because of the manifest resilience of key economic and social dynamics associated with the period of 'simple modernity'. Contesting Giddens' tendency to overemphasise globalisation, Hutton (in Hutton and Giddens, 2000), has questioned the existence of dynamics adequately reflecting something 'qualitatively different', marking clear 'discontinuity' with the past. He observes how 'key historical forms', such as the British monarchy, remain in place in the early 21st century. Hutton's observation is all the more topical in the wake of the royal wedding in spring 2011 and the Oscar-winning film *The King's Speech*. Indeed, this apparent – and maybe even surprising – new popularity of the British royal family is corroborated by a *Guardian*/ICM poll, where 63% of respondents maintained that Britain would be 'worse off' without the royal family (*The Guardian*, 2011b). More importantly, the inequality and immense imbalances in power associated with 'simple modernity' remain. The major change in the recent epoch, the 'true quantum leap', was the collapse of the Soviet Union, which can be associated with a reshaped capitalism that is 'much harder, more mobile, more ruthless' (Hutton, in Hutton and Giddens, 2000, p 9). Capitalism, however, as the dominant mode of economic life, provides continuity and spans the entire period from 'simple modernity', deep into a 'post-traditional order'.

A focal problem with the work of Giddens (and Beck) is that it fails to examine the continuing significance of these key 'historical forms', lacking patience with some of the analytical tools previously used to interpret them (Beck, 1994, p 12). Significantly, Beck dismisses social forms and institutions such as class, family or neighbourhood as 'zombie categories', which have been 'clinically dead for a long time, but are unable to die' (Beck, 1994, p 40; see also Beck, 2000a). Thus, for him, we are now in the presence of 'class parties without classes, armies without enemies, or a governmental apparatus which in many cases claims to start and keep things going which are happening anyway' (Beck, 1994, p 40).

This somewhat cavalier attitude to social reality does not seem to provide a sufficiently sturdy intellectual foundation for the idea that we have entered a 'post-traditional order' and that those working in social services should reorient their approach. Similarly, Giddens fails to acknowledge the continuing significance of forms of control that he simplistically discounts as anachronistic remains of an earlier epoch. His glib pronouncements on women's reproductive rights are a case in point: with the 'advent of more or less fail safe methods of contraception, reflexive control over sexual practices and the introduction of reproductive technologies of various kinds, reproduction is now a field where *a plurality of choices prevails*' (Giddens, 1991, p 219, emphasis added). However, in Ireland and other areas in Europe, women continue to be denied the right to choose abortion and access the alleged 'field where a plurality of choices prevails'.

More fundamentally, there appears to be an unwillingness to appreciate the real and contemporary significance of regulation patterns stemming from 'simple modernity'. Associated ideas centred on the so-called 'do-it-yourself biography' appear jarringly inappropriate in this context (Ferguson, 2001, p 46). Such questions are not merely abstract, academic musings in that they have a direct impact on those in contact with social services. In seeking to transport the ideas of Giddens and Beck into social work, Ferguson risks downplaying the continuing significance of religion in what is termed the 'post-traditional order'. His analysis may well obscure the profound influence that religious faith – be it Christianity, Islam or any other form of spiritual practice – can hold over individual action and choices. Indeed, it has been argued that in the first quarter of the 21st century, we have now entered a 'post-secular age' (Habermas et al, 2010).

It is crucial that social workers remain sensitive to this dimension in their engagement with the users of services. In this context, Ferguson (2003, p 701) claims, somewhat blandly, that 'now people have a choice about whether to be "religious" ... and actively choose and construct for themselves what the influence will be on their lives'. Religion, it seems, is to be taken off the supermarket shelf or left there for the next potential consumer to reflexively peruse: choosing a religion becomes like choosing a new lampshade in Ikea. This might be how some people relate to religion, but perhaps Marx's understanding is far more enlightening. For him, the social conditions that produced a religious sensibility were important: religion was the 'sigh of the oppressed ... the feeling of a heartless world and the soul of soulless circumstances' (quoted in McLellan, 2000, p 72). In this way, religion fulfils deep existential yearnings and has profound explanatory power for social actors. As Eagleton (2003, p 100) has maintained:

> To speak of a post-religious age is to speak a good deal too hastily. The age may look that way in Leeds or Frankfurt, but hardly in Dacca or Dallas. It may seem irreligious to intellectuals, but not to

peasant farmers or office cleaners. In most stretches of the globe, including the United States, culture never ousted religion in the first place. Even in some regions where it did, religion is creeping back with a vengeance. On the planet in general, it is still by far the most resourceful symbolic form.

This is illuminated, of course, by geopolitical developments over the past half-century. Indeed, the Iranian revolution of 1979 was the first 'major revolution since Cromwell's time that was not inspired by a secular ideology but appealed to the masses in the language of religion, in this case the idiom of Shi'ite Islam' (Hobsbawm, 2011, p 412; see also Sayyid, 2003). More narrowly – in terms of social work – the significance of religion is revealed by some of the circumstances surrounding the death of Victoria Climbié.

Adjo Victoria Climbié, known to child welfare professionals in England as Anna Kouao, died in London in February 2000 after suffering neglect and violence from her aunt, Marie Therese Kouao, and her aunt's partner, Carl Manning. In January 2001, they were convicted of the murder of the nine-year-old and were sentenced to life imprisonment. Significantly, religion seems to have played a major role in the child's appalling predicament. The preposterous connection drawn by two London-based pastors between the child's incontinence and her being 'possessed by an evil spirit' appears, in fact, to have been a main motive for the aunt's abuse of the child (Secretary of State for Health and Secretary of State for the Home Department, 2003, pp 32, 35). It is therefore vital for social workers to recognise that Evangelical Churches – such as the Universal Church of the Kingdom of God and the *Mission Ensemble pour Christe*, where Victoria was taken by her aunt – continue to provide some people with the answers they seek, promising them 'deliverance from "witchcraft, bad luck or evil"' (Secretary of State for Health and Secretary of State for the Home Department, 2003, p 36). In the light of such realities, locating users of services in the type of world envisaged by the 'life politics' theorists risks producing shallow and uninformed assessments. In short, there is a need to try to situate people within their own particular 'habitus' – as will be argued in Chapter Seven. This entails recognising a person's cultural rootedness and assessing how tradition might continue to shape their behaviour. Here, there is a complex, dialectical interplay of factors related to contemporary global capitalism, the resilience of traditions and people being embedded in/dislocated from communities.

Theorising families

The assertion that the family domain has undergone major changes is central to the analysis promoted by Giddens (1998) and Beck (see Beck and Beck Gernsheim, 1999, p 46). This aspect of the 'life politics' argument is particularly important because dynamics *inside* families relate to the daily activities of social workers. Again echoing Giddens, Ferguson (2001, p 44) contends that there has been a 'structural transformation in the social organisation of intimacy', which has resulted in significant changes in terms of how couples relate to each other. In a 'post-traditional order', there is a move towards negotiated relationships, where the individuals involved are less likely to be encased in the gender roles associated with 'simple modernity'. It is, however, acknowledged that 'hegemonic masculinity' can still limit choices, nor 'can marriage be said to be a "meeting of equals" in many ethnic and cultural groupings in Britain or amongst the travelling community in Ireland, for instance' (Ferguson, 2001, p 44). Leaving aside the crudely reductive view that familial patterns of 'simple modernity' may only linger in minority communities, another range of problems stems from this particular facet of Ferguson's analysis.

It could be argued that there was a good deal more fluidity in gender roles in intimate relationships during the period of 'simple modernity' than the 'life politics' analysis allows for. This was particularly the case in those countries where capitalist and patriarchal hegemony was (temporarily) usurped. However, even within societies defined by the primacy of market relations, feminism had an impact on the 'private sphere' and intimate relations (Goldman, 1969, pp 227–41). Despite Giddens' (1998, pp 89–99) identification of the 'democratic family' and the emergence of a so-called 'democracy of emotions' (Giddens, 1994b, p 16), there appears to be a paucity of detailed empirical evidence deployed to support his analysis. On the contrary, some of the available empirical work exploring the texture of contemporary relationships between couples has actually revealed the continuing significance of traditional gender roles. This is particularly the case in terms of love, intimacy and the gender division of 'emotion work' in heterosexual relationships (see Duncombe and Marsden, 1993).

Specifically in relation to social work, we are also advised that during the period of 'simple modernity', social work 'both reinforced and was largely influenced by an ideology of maternalism which saw intervention in family life largely reduced to the regulation of motherhood' (Ferguson, 2001, p 43). Clearly, the tenacity and commitment of feminist social workers and their impact on social work theory and practice cannot be undervalued. However, research still points to social work's enduring reinforcement of maternalism, even in the so-called 'post-traditional order', where intervention continues to focus, 'by and large, on the woman' when child protection issues are a focal concern (Holt, 2003, p 59; see also Milner, 1993; Krane and Davies, 2000; Turney, 2000). The notion of extensive social change in relation to motherhood is countered by Joanne Baker's (2009, p 286) empirical research, which examined the de-traditionalisation and self-determination of young mothers. She points to the dangers of 'conflating de-traditionalization with emancipation from constraint' and maintains that her interviewees' 'experiences of motherhood are still strongly influenced by the ideology that positions it as an essentially sacred … endeavour that devolves naturally to and is carried out instinctively by women' (Baker, 2009, p 287).

The kids are alright? Children in the 'post-traditional order'

Related to the notion that the personal relationships of men and women have been entirely reshaped, there is an assertion that the position of children has now fundamentally changed (Ferguson, 2001, pp 42–3). During the period of 'simple modernity', from the 1920s to the 1970s, relationships 'between adults and children were based on hierarchical authority relations with little or no concept of children having rights to negotiate or to be heard in ways that were separate from their parents and carers' (Ferguson, 2001, pp 42–3). Although Giddens (1991, p 97) makes a persuasive case that 'parent–child relations are increasingly subject to negotiation on both sides', this development does not eliminate an encompassing context in which children are structurally positioned in similar ways to the bygone days of 'simple modernity' (see Prout, 2000). This is apparent in a number of different areas, both inside and beyond the family. In the UK, for example, even older children are 'locked out' of the democratic process because they are still denied the franchise. Recent years have also seen the 'demonisation' of certain groups of children seen as 'troublesome' or ambiguously disruptive. This has resulted in an increase in the numbers of children incarcerated (Goldson, 2009). There has also been a range of television 'reality shows' – such as 'Supernanny', 'The House of Tiny Tearaways' and 'The World's Strictest Parents' – which promote 'positive' methods of parenting, but which appear intent on managing, regulating and containing children.

Perhaps the events surrounding the death of Victoria Climbié again highlight some of the problems with the claims of the 'post-traditional order' theorists. For example, unlike a number of instances described in other child death inquiries, Victoria was *not* hidden from the gaze of social workers and other welfare professionals. What is striking, in fact, was her sheer visibility. Indeed, the child was an in-patient in two hospitals and was also a 'cause of concern' for four different local authority social services departments in North London. Cast in the 'traditional' role of the child *seen* and not *heard*, she was rarely addressed in her first language by those professionals charged with safeguarding her. Since Victoria was merely a child, the police treated concerns about her welfare less seriously. As the Laming Report suggests, 'a comparison with adult victims is instructive' here: allegations of serious crimes against an adult would have been 'investigated by a detective, but a crime committed against a child would be dealt with by an officer with no detective training at all'. As the Report concluded, 'it is wrong that the victims of crime are disadvantaged in terms of the training and expertise of the investigating officer, simply because they are children' (Secretary of State for Health and Secretary of State for the Home Department, 2003, p 311).

None of these comments in Laming's report would seem to support the idea that children are recognised as people in their own right who are heard and responded to in the same way as adults. Indeed, the failure to adequately recognise and engage with children was apparent in social workers' involvement with Baby Peter Connolly, who died in August 2007 (Garrett, 2009). Beyond the UK, the way in which children – particularly the children of the poor – are treated in Ireland would seem to further undermine the analysis. A key issue has been the deaths of children and young people in care and the failure of the Health Service Executive (HSE) to produce robust and reliable data. Mirroring the findings of the Ryan Report, which examined the abuse of children in institutions in the past, little value seems to be attached to these children (Commission to Inquire into Child Abuse, 2009; see also Garrett, forthcoming). In March 2010, it was reported that the HSE had not published a single report into the death of a child in state care since it was formed in 2005 (Garrett, 2012).

As young consumers in the sphere of market relations, some children may, of course, now have more power and choice, yet it would be wrong to interpret this development as reflecting far-reaching shifts that would bolster the 'post-traditional order' perspective (see Klein, 2001, ch 3). Both in terms of the family and wider encompassing patterns, there appears to be sufficient evidence to undermine the idea that we have moved from an era of 'simple modernity' into a 'post-traditional order'.

The 'do-it-yourself' or 'elective biography'

An additional problem is that proponents of the 'post-traditional order' and 'life politics' perspectives place far too great an emphasis on human agency, failing to recognise the structural constraints affecting an individual's capacity for action (Jeffery, 2011). This is not to argue that social structure deterministically dictates individual action, but rather to endorse the view that it is necessary to develop a more balanced:

> conception of social structure where agents are not conceived as acted upon mechanistically, as cultural dopes, as mere bearers of structural properties, while at the same time *not giving in to a social world of pure contingency where everything is possible, where the destiny of individuals is conceived as purely in their own hands.* (Lopez and Potter, 2001, p 88, emphasis added)

The 'life politics' perspective (embedded in a particular theoretical perception on modernity) can, however, be interpreted as doing just this: promoting a body of ideas which strongly suggests that the 'destiny of individuals' is 'in their own hands'. This amplification of voluntarism and the minimising of constraint are reflected in the context of contemporary social policymaking (Hoggett, 2001; Prideaux, 2005). Perhaps, in many respects, on the account of this renewed emphasis placed on agency, volition, personal choice and 'self-actualisation', we are witnessing the dull echo of ideas and myths central to the ideology of corporate capital. These myths are embedded in discourses centred on consumption and consumer choice and are found in Nike's 'Just Do It' and Microsoft's 'Where do you want to go today?' slogans. Given this encompassing ideological context, it does not surprise when it is maintained that social work needs to 'develop an orientation which fully understands', among other things, the '*choices* open to *consumers* of services' (Ferguson, 2001, p 53, emphases added).

While 'simple modernity' was a period of 'limited – and limiting – choice for people' our current times are characterised by the 'do-it-yourself' or 'elective biography' (Ferguson, 2001, p 42). However, contrary to Giddens' claims that 'where a person lives, after young adulthood at least, is *a matter of choice* organised primarily in terms of the person's life planning' (Giddens, 1991, p 147, emphasis added), child welfare professionals developing 'aftercare' plans for 'looked-after' children will readily appreciate the wide range of structural constraints limiting the choices actually available. The lack of subtle interrogation of agency, choice and aspiration at the core of 'life politics' perspectives is also detectable in Beck's contributions (see Beck, 2000a). He, and his partner, claim that individuals are 'becoming the legislators of their own way of life, the judges of their own transgressions, the priests who absolve their own sins and the therapists who loosen the bonds of their own past' (Beck and Beck-Gernsheim, 1999, p 5). No evidence is furnished for the idea that individuals are becoming atomised in this way and are cut adrift not only from economic constrictions, but also from historical and contemporary bonds, mores and expectations. More fundamentally, there is the suspicion that what Giddens and Beck present as indicators of *universal* processes are in fact the *specific* experiences of their elite group of metropolitan, mobile, Euro- or American-centric, affluent, professorial males.

Men on the move: the 'autotelic self'

Giddens' (2007) later work reveals a striking lack of reflexivity, consistently failing to acknowledge how the author's own habitus and specific milieu may have impinged on his worldview and policy proposals. He simply makes no reference to the fact that his life may be somewhat different from that of people getting by in the deindustrialised heartlands of Britain (Charlesworth, 2000a) or of other European countries (Bourdieu et al, 2002). Even though a universalising 'we' is apt to be deployed by the champions of 'life politics', it is legitimate to assume that what might be true for them, might not be true for everyone (see, eg, Ferguson, 2001, 2003). This unsettling use of 'we' is never adequately interrogated or deconstructed. Whose world is being described? What is the relationship of this 'we' to its 'others'? Who are the 'others'? Indeed, there is a need to be cautious when referring to 'we' in the 'diaspora space' that is the UK in the first quarter of the 21st century – a space inhabited by people from a range of diverse cultural backgrounds and 'homelands'. This would seem to be particularly the case in relation to Giddens' comments on work and the related issue of poverty. Indeed, his own structural location may somewhat impair his recognition of the constraints that limit many people's ability to 'foster the autotelic self' (Giddens, 1994b, p 192).

Giddens fails to embark on what Beck (1994, p 5) himself calls an act of 'self-confrontation', which becomes apparent when exploring the concept of the 'autotelic self' in greater detail. In his characteristic prose, Giddens (1994b, p 192) advises us that the 'autotelic self' refers to a person 'able to translate potential threats into rewarding challenges, someone who is able to turn entropy into a consistent flow of experience'. The 'autotelic self' does not, he goes on, 'seek to neutralise risk or suppose that "someone will take care of the problem"; risk is confronted as the active challenge which generates self-actualisation' (Giddens, 1994b, p 192). However, as Deacon and Mann (1999, pp 421–2) point out, Giddens' argument that the 'autotelic self' is one that does not expect others to take care of the problem 'can all too easily be translated into compelling individuals to be responsible, irrespective of their ability to address the problem'. The notion is, moreover, central to the ideology of neoliberalism.

Hoggett (2001, p 43) has provided a sustained critique of ideas centred on the 'autotelic self', noting that Giddens' conceptualisations are 'riddled with borrowings from popular "how to do it" culture, particularly from the United States, which are essentially self-management guides about everything from physical fitness to negotiation'. Hoggett (2001, p 44) has also gone on to persuasively relate this criticism to the 'tremendous stress upon making people fit for labour' in contemporary social policy. Moreover, the same author has wisely suggested that the concept of the 'autotelic self' – and related ideas concerned with gaining 'mastery' (Ferguson, 2001, p 41) – can be viewed as 'gendered, expressing an essentially masculine experience of autonomy' (Hoggett, 2001, pp 45–6). Indeed, a number of feminist writers have criticised Giddens and other theorists, such as Beck, because they appear to 'run the risk of re-instating the disembodied and disembedded subject of masculinist thought and lead to a tendency towards voluntarism' (Adkins, 2004a, p 198). Lois McNay (1999, pp 97–8) is also suspicious of this body of theory because 'a tendency to voluntarism can arise which manifests itself in an overemphasis on the emancipatory expressive possibilities thrown up in late capitalism'. Similarly, Beverley Skeggs (2004a, p 82) has referred to 'an agency-overloaded self'. Moreover, 'other forms of self-making are pathologized; people who do not display the requisite reflexivity are seen to be lacking, not fully formed selves, and this lack is moralized and individualized' (Skeggs, 2004a, pp 81–2).

Specifically in relation to working lives, Giddens unselfconsciously confides that despite the uncertainties of the 'post-traditional order', 'leading scholars', such as him, 'can get a job more or less as they wish' (quoted in Hutton and Giddens, 2000, p 37). In contrast, his contributions fail to take account of the fact that, for many people, jobs are precariously held and are a constant source of fear and stress during a period of neoliberalisation. However, *men* in his position are mobile, prized and structurally enabled to exercise *choice*. Many esteemed university professors, 'holders of an institutionalized form of cultural capital' (Bourdieu, 2001a, p 36), are able to enjoy lifestyles that are denied most people. This dimension is particularly significant during a period of neoliberalism when a 'few star professors' (Walters, 2003) or 'celebrity chairs' (Mooney, 2003) enjoy access to the media and to senior politicians. Giddens is, perhaps, something of a 'case study' in this regard. The following excerpt, devoid of the slightest hint of self-irony, illustrates the author's insular orientation:

> It is February 1998. I am on my way to Washington DC. On board also are Tony Blair, Cherie Booth.... We are off to the White House to meet Bill and Hillary Clinton, Al Gore and a group from the US cabinet. We are flying in Concorde. (Giddens, 2007, p xi)

At the White House, he then goes to dinner:

> Standing in line to shake hands with the President, I am next to Harrison Ford on the one side and Barbra Streisand on the other, who both chat to me amiably. Later we are entertained by Stevie Wonder and Elton John at twin pianos. (Giddens, 2007, p xi)

Given Giddens' circle of acquaintances, it is understandable how he may struggle to comprehend what 'work' means to those inhabiting different structural locations. He asserts, for example, that like 'so many areas of social life, work was until recently experienced by many as fate.... In current times, even among deprived groups work is rarely approached as fate' (Giddens, 1994b, p 91). Again, no empirical evidence is deployed to support this contention. Furthermore, the implication that work is no longer a 'given set of conditions, offering little autonomy for action' is also likely to be contested by alienated groups of workers, including many social workers (Jones, 2001; Harlow, 2004; James, 2004; Carey, 2007).

Underpinning the 'life politics' analysis is a failure to recognise the structural (and personal) significance of poverty. For Beck (2000b, p 43), poverty is 'to some extent' another 'zombie category'. Giddens complacently contends that poverty 'probably used to be more a condition than it is now' (quoted in Hutton and Giddens, 2000, p 27). Moreover, he is comfortable about importing the vocabulary of the Right into his 'third way politics' discourse on 'benefit dependency' (Giddens, 1998, p 115). Again, emphasising acts of personal volition, his programme of 'positive welfare' calls for 'active risk-taking' on the part of the poor. For benefit claimants, counselling might also be viewed as 'more helpful than direct economic support' (Giddens, 1998, pp 116–17). That is to say, the stress remains on lifestyle changes and lacks any indication that Giddens truly acknowledges that poverty also derives from structural factors connected, as will be argued in Chapter Five, to neoliberalisation.

Trashing 'emancipatory politics' in the 'post-traditional order'

Social work can, of course, be associated with regulatory and controlling practices and functions. However, the 'life politics' orientation aims to politically marginalise any potentially emancipatory possibilities associated with the profession and its more progressive values. 'Emancipatory politics', Ferguson (2001, p 47) tells us, seeks a transformation in 'unequal power relations to improve the life of the oppressed'. It is 'concerned to reduce or eliminate exploitation, inequality and oppression' and 'makes primary the imperatives of justice, equality and participation' (Giddens, 1991, pp 211–12).Yet this orientation forms part of the moribund, or old, 'politics of the left and right' (Ferguson, 2001, p 47). Ferguson (2001, p 48), again following Giddens' lead, does not entirely dismiss 'emancipatory politics', but rather deems 'life politics' to be a superior articulation of the 'new fields of selfhood and action in a post-traditional order'.

According to Ferguson (2001, p 42), 'emancipatory politics' is 'simplistic' and contains an 'over-structural focus'. Hence, a 'post-traditional social work' should help to develop the 'means to enhance the capacities of (vulnerable) clients to practice life-planning and gain mastery over their lives'. Widening the focus, politics is, it is asserted, moving 'beyond traditional left and right divisions' (Ferguson, 2001, p 42).

To summarise, within this theoretical paradigm, 'emancipatory politics' is associated with a range of noble endeavours, yet it is perceived as an anachronistic form of politics. Social workers' attachment to this 'old politics' would, therefore, undermine their role in the 'post-traditional order'. Indeed, 'life politics' theorisation pivots on the conviction that the emancipatory struggles embedded in the relations of production (class), reproduction (patriarchy) and neo-colonialism ('race' and ethnicity) have now become superfluous. Indeed, this understanding is perhaps *the* central idea located at the core of the 'life politics' perspective.The notion that emancipatory struggles are unnecessary is also integral to Beck's 'zombie categories' and to associated ideas, such as the idea that the 'dynamism of the labour market, backed up by the welfare state has dissolved the social classes within capitalism' (Beck, 2000a, p 43). Similarly, it is related to Giddens' view that 'no one any longer has any alternatives to capitalism' and that the 'demonizing of the large corporations, so popular among sections of the left at one time, does not make sense now' (Giddens, 1998, p 43; 1994b, p 89); a view that, of course, after the 'crash' of 2007/08, and revelations about the conduct of the investment banking sector, seems particularly misplaced (Callinicos, 2010). Nevertheless, confidently stating that 'no one any longer has any alternatives to capitalism', Giddens (1991, p 124) confided over 20 years ago that:

> Life politics *presumes* (a certain level of) emancipation … from the fixities of tradition and from conditions of hierarchical domination. It would be too crude to say that life politics focuses on what happens once individuals have achieved a certain level of autonomy of action, because other factors are involved, but this provides at least an *initial orientation*. (Emphases added)

Conclusion

It will be maintained throughout this book that this 'initial orientation' provides an unsatisfactory conceptual foundation for grasping what it is to be 'modern' and – more specifically – for theoretically understanding some of the dynamics connected to social work. 'Life politics' – a politics of choice, lifestyle and self-actualisation – also fails to theoretically equip social workers to respond to the structurally generated hardships that many users of services have to confront. In short, what is presented as 'new thinking' lacks the conceptual and political insight and vocabulary to recognise the direction of social and economic transformations. 'Life politics' remains, in fact, part of the ideology of the comfortable when what is needed is a reaffirmation of the primacy of 'emancipatory politics' (Lavalette, 2011a).

In contrast, however, Zygmunt Bauman (2011a, p 12) has argued that a core element in what he terms the 'liquid modern human condition' is that the individual is 'now appointed to the position of chief manager of "life politics" and its sole executive'. Chapter Three will explore his theorisation in more detail and will dwell on his 'solid' and 'liquid' modernity conceptualisations.

◄◄ Reflection and Talk Box 2 ►►

- Does the term 'postmodernism' still have any relevance for social work?

- Can the theorisation associated with 'postcolonial' perspectives illuminate any aspects of social work in your national setting?

- Do we now live in a 'post-traditional' society? What are the flaws in the thinking of Giddens and Beck?

- Does the contemporary role of children in society provide evidence that we how inhabit a 'post-traditional order'? Illustrate your response with reference to your work as a practitioner or social work student?

- Does the 'post-traditional order' theorising place too much emphasis on people's ability to transcend their social, political and economic circumstances? Can you discuss this in the context of a particular client group?

- What is your understanding of 'life politics'? Can this idea provide a new theoretical foundation for social work?

Notes

[1] Parts of this chapter draw on, and radically rework, previously published articles in the *British Journal of Social Work*: 'The trouble with Harry: why the "new agenda of life politics" fails to convince', vol 33, no 3, pp 381–97; and 'More trouble with Harry: a rejoinder in the "life politics" debate', vol 34, no 4, pp 571–83. I am grateful to Oxford Journals for granting me permission to use some of this material.

[2] Towards the end of his life, Said distanced himself from this body of theory. See also the journal *New Formations*, vol 59, published in 2006, for a useful collection on the 'reframing' of postcolonial studies following the attack on Iraq.

[3] In *The accumulation of capital*, published in Germany in 1913, Luxemburg maintained:

> 'From the very beginning, the forms and laws of capitalist production aim to comprise the entire globe as a store of productive forces. Capital, impelled to appropriate productive forces for purposes of exploitation, ransacks the whole world, it procures its means of production from all corners of the earth, seizing them, if necessary by force, from all levels of civilisation and from all forms of society. (Quoted in Hudis and Anderson, 2004, pp 55–6)

Following the Bolshevik Revolution, for the 'first time, a government of a powerful state was explicitly opposed to western imperialism in principle and practice' (Young, 2001, p 10). In 1920, Lenin's Comintern 'offered the first systematic programme for global decolonisation in its "Theses on the National and Colonial Questions"' (Young, 2001, p 10).

CHAPTER THREE

'Solid' modernity and 'liquid' modernity

Introduction

In recent years, questions related to modernity have, on occasions, dwelt on the notion that we have shifted from a period of 'solid modernity' to one of 'liquid modernity'. The main sociologist associated with this theorisation is Zygmunt Bauman. Now in his 80s, Bauman remains an exceptionally prolific, influential and, more recently, controversial sociologist (Tester, 2004). He was born in Poland in 1925, but left in the late 1960s and arrived – after short stays in Israel, Canada and Australia – at the University of Leeds, where, since 1990, he has been an Emeritus Professor.

Attention has been drawn to his allegedly working for Poland's intelligence services from the end of the Second World War until 1953 (Edemariam, 2007; Ramesh, 2010). Irrespective of the precise accuracy of such reports, it is impossible to comprehend Bauman's role without locating it in the context of the civil war that erupted in Poland following liberation from Nazi rule (see Tester and Jacobsen, 2005). Furthermore, he has been lambasted for what has been regarded as an alleged lack of scholarly detail in his later work. Derbyshire (2004, p 49), for example, has criticised Bauman's 'theoretical impressionism', maintaining that his apparent reliance on 'nothing more substantial than articles in the *Guardian* and the *Observer* colour supplements' is 'objectionable'. Perhaps there is some truth in this critique, but Bauman's 'defence of a morally committed sociology' remains compelling, serious and should be taken into account, albeit critically, within any book seeking to address social theory and social work (Tester and Jacobsen, 2005, p 21).[1]

What follows does not seek to provide a comprehensive account of Bauman's sociology and its relationship to social work (see Bauman, 2000a). Neither does it aim to bring his work into sustained dialogue with other social theorists even though the synthesising of multiple theoretical 'voices' has heuristic advantages (see, eg, Houston et al, 2005). Rather, this chapter will provide a short critical introduction to key conceptual facets of Bauman's work as these relate to the first part of the book. Largely relying on his own words, the first two sections are devoted to an examination of some of his main themes and theoretical preoccupations. Initially, this will focus on 'solid modernity', the most fascinating aspect of Bauman's work, and his critique of those political projects driven by 'reason' and 'science' that, for him, have resulted in failure. Indeed, the Holocaust provides his most devastating illustration of this dynamic (Bauman, 1989). The second section will concentrate on Bauman's more recent theorisation on how modernity has transformed from 'solid' to 'liquid' form (Bauman, 2000b, 2002a, 2003, 2005, 2006, 2008, 2009, 2010, 2011a). Within the social work literature, Ferguson (2004, 2005, 2008) has drawn attention to Bauman's notion of 'liquid modernity' and argued that it has day-to-day resonance for social workers. This conceptualisation of contemporary life encompasses a range of interrelated concerns about the 'wasted lives' of those on the margins (Bauman, 2004, 2011b), the preoccupation with 'security' (Bauman, 2000c), globalisation (Bauman, 1998a), consumption and 'failed consumers' (Bauman, 1998b), and the demise of the nation state (Bauman, 1998a). The third section briefly discusses social work and social and penal policy in the Republic of Ireland in an attempt to assess Bauman's potential contribution to an understanding of contemporary social work.

'Solid' modernity: the search for 'order' and the Holocaust

Modernity and the Holocaust (Bauman, 1989) remains Bauman's most famous book and gained him most attention in academic circles in the West and beyond. Here, he argues that a typical way of regarding the Holocaust is to simply focus on 'the *Germanness* of the crime' and this risks becoming an 'exercise in exonerating everyone else, and particularly *everything* else' (Bauman, 1989, p xii, emphasis in original). One of the problems with this approach is that the:

> message which the Holocaust contains about the way we live today –
> about the quality of the institutions on which we rely for our safety,
> about the validity of the criteria with which we measure the propriety
> of our own conduct and of the patterns of interaction we accept and
> consider normal – is silenced, not listened to, and remains undelivered.
> (Bauman, 1989, p xii)

Consequently, he refers to a 'long-overdue task of formidable cultural and political importance; the task of bringing the sociological, psychological and political lessons of the Holocaust episode to bear on the self-awareness and practice of the institutions and the members of contemporary society' (Bauman, 1989, p xii). Thus, his central message is that there is an urgent need to assimilate the 'lessons of the Holocaust in the mainstream of our theory of modernity and of the civilising process and its effects' (Bauman, 1989, p xiv). Related to this analysis is the 'unspoken terror' that the Holocaust could 'be more than an aberration': that it could have been 'another face of the same modern society whose other, more familiar, face we so admire. And that the two faces are perfectly comfortably attached to the same body' (Bauman, 1989, p 7).

He concedes, however, that a number of obstacles embedded in mainstream perspectives – certainly at the time he was writing – prevented a more rigorous sociological approach to the Holocaust. One of these is that the Holocaust is perceived as 'something that happened to the Jews; as an event in *Jewish* history' (Bauman, 1989, p 1, emphasis in original). Alternatively, the Holocaust is referred to as a product of something 'primeval and culturally inextinguishable' or a '"natural" predisposition of the human species' (Bauman, 1989, p 2). Unconvinced by this analysis, Bauman maintains that the Holocaust was 'not an irrational outflow of the not-yet-fully eradicated residues of pre-modern barbarity. It was a legitimate resident in the house of modernity; indeed, one who would not be available in any other house' (Bauman, 1989, p 17). That is to say, if we are to try and comprehend the Holocaust, it needs to be viewed as an occurrence that cannot be entirely disassociated from the trajectory of modernity. Modernity's dominant rationality and the organisational forms – particularly bureaucracy – that this produced are also of significance in this context. Thus, he argues that the Holocaust should be looked at as a sociological 'laboratory' and proposes that we seek to comprehend it as 'a rare, yet significant and reliable, test of the hidden possibilities of modern society' (Bauman, 1989, p 12).

This conceptualisation relates to Bauman's analysis of bureaucracy as the organisational form that led to individuals becoming complicit in genocide while remaining 'sitting at their desks' (Bauman, 1989, p 24). This was partly because the causal 'connections between their actions and the mass murder were difficult to spot' (Bauman, 1989, p 24). Moreover, the hierarchical and functional division of labour impacts on how violent actions are carried out, in that the 'practical and mental distance from the final product means … that most functionaries of the bureaucratic hierarchy may give commands without full knowledge of their effects' (Bauman, 1989, p 99). The classifying practices deployed by bureaucracies also risk failing to 'perceive and remember' the human beings hidden behind technical terms and labels (Bauman, 1989, p 105).

An 'inescapable side-effect of order building' is that 'each order casts some parts of the extant population as "out of place", "unfit" or "undesirable"' (Bauman, 2004, p 5). Furthermore, a key and disturbing characteristic of the Holocaust is that most of the perpetrators of the genocide were ostensibly 'normal people', not 'monsters', but 'civilised', even 'cultured', individuals (Bauman, 1989, p 19). Indeed, 'civilized manners showed an astounding ability to cohabit, peacefully and harmoniously with mass murder' (Bauman, 1989, p 110). Three conditions erode the moral inhibitions that ordinarily deter people from committing acts of violence against vulnerable or potentially vulnerable populations: the violence is authorised; actions are routinised; and the victims of the violence are dehumanised.

Perhaps what perturbs him most is the 'distinct modern flavour' of this particular genocide project and its granular operative modalities (Bauman, 1989, p 88). Bauman (1989, p 90) also maintains that rage and 'fury are pitiably primitive and inefficient as tools of mass annihilation'. Contemporary 'mass murder is distinguished by a virtual absence of all spontaneity' and the 'prominence of rational, carefully calculated design' (Bauman, 1989, p 90; see also Marcuse, 2001). Violence – and its deployment – is vitally important to this formulation (see Young, 2007, ch 5). Often it is 'invisible' and '*enclosed … in segregated and isolated territories*, on the whole inaccessible to ordinary members of society; or evicted to the "twilight areas" … or exported to distant places' (Bauman, 1989, p 97, emphasis added).

Bauman emphasises the spatial dimension to the Holocaust, since responsibility 'arises out of proximity of the other' and becomes 'silenced once proximity is eroded' (Bauman, 1989, p 184). It was such 'a separation which made it possible for thousands to kill' (Bauman, 1989, p 184). Thus, Jews (and other problematic populations, such as leftists, Roma, gypsies and 'asocial families') had to be removed from the 'horizon of German daily life' (Bauman, 1989, p 189; see also Marcuse, 2001). Bauman maintains that the committing of 'immoral acts … becomes easier with every inch of social distance' (Bauman, 1989, p 192). More fundamentally, 'morality seems to conform to the law of optical perspective. It looms large and thick close to the eye. With the growth of distance, responsibility for the other shrivels' (Bauman, 1989, p 193). In this sense, it seems that 'we feel mostly through the eyes' and, consequently, morality would appear to have a 'vanishing point' (Bauman, 1989, pp 155, p 193).

Bauman's analysis implies, therefore, that the Holocaust should not be interpreted as a facet of humankind's inexplicable tendency to evil actions. Rather, it represented a historical occurrence in which the search for an 'order', rooted in the bureaucratic sensibility of 'solid modernity' and instrumental ways of thinking and acting, was *pushed to the limits*. Indeed, he maintains that the Holocaust 'inverted all established explanations of evil deeds', for it 'suddenly transpired that the most horrifying evil in human memory did not result from the dissipation of order, but from faultless and unchallengeable rule of order' (Bauman, 1989, p 151). In one of the most compelling sections of his book, he illuminates how 'science' and academia played key roles in furnishing an intellectual and 'objective' foundation for the Nazi's annihilation project. For example, the 'department in the SS headquarters in charge of the destruction of European Jews was officially and blandly designated as the section of Administration and Economy' (Bauman, 1989, p 14). Nonetheless, even today:

> widespread opinion solely underestimates the degree to which initiatives (indeed, some of the most gruesome among them) were generated by the scientific community itself … and the extent to which racial policy itself was initiated and managed by the recognized scientists with academically impeccable credentials. (Bauman, 1989, p 110)

Thus, 'expertise' provided a 'modern form of authority', which dissolved 'personal responsibility' into the 'abstract authority of technical know-how' (Bauman, 1989, p 196; see also Pine, 1997). More generally, the 'organization of the Holocaust could be made into a textbook of scientific management' (Bauman, 1989, p 150; see also Badiou, 2007).

'Liquid' modernity: 'safe ports are few and far between'

As Bauman became more prolific, his conceptualisation of modernity radically altered. Today, there 'are reasons to consider "fluidity" or "liquidity" as fitting metaphors with which to grasp the nature of the present, in many ways *novel*, phase in the history of modernity' (Bauman, 2000b, p 2, emphasis in original). This understanding has given rise to a range of books such as *Liquid love* (Bauman, 2003), *Liquid life* (Bauman, 2005) and *Liquid fear* (Bauman, 2006). Indeed, what could be regarded as the 'Bauman brand' is now one associated with a 'liquid' world that is entirely unlike that experienced during the period of 'solid modernity'. In this sense, Bauman's theoretical perspective appears to rest fairly comfortably alongside the postmodernist theorisation referred to in Chapter Two (see also Bauman, 1993, 1995, 1997; Tester, 2004, pp 13–14; Tester and Jacobsen, 2005). However, his comments on this association remain somewhat ambiguous:

> I was uneasy with the common uses of the 'postmodern' idea. I tried hard ... to keep a distance from the pronouncements of the 'end of modernity' and tried even harder to manifest exception to the celebratory mood of the preachers and enthusiasts of the 'postmodern bliss' ... I defined postmodernity as 'modernity minus its illusions' – modernity coming to terms with its own un-fulfil-ment and un-fulfillability. I use the term 'postmodernity' primarily to connote the 'second disenchantment'. (Bauman, in Beilharz, 2001, p 339)

One of the most striking facets of his recent work is its pervasive pessimism, reflected in the identification of the 'jading of the modern state' (Bauman, 2000b, p 133; see also Bauman, 2000c). This is partly connected to the manifest failure of political projects to produce meaningful social change to enhance the quality of human lives. Each 'form of social design has been proved to produce as much misery as happiness if not more' (Bauman, 2000b, p 134).

In this baleful context, the whole idea of what amounts to 'progress' has become devolved and people have become de-collectivised and socially atomised. If the 'flipside of the "solid modern" domination-through-order-building was the totalitarian tendency, the flipside of the "liquid-modern" domination-through-uncertainty is the state of ambient insecurity, anxiety and fear' (Bauman, in Bauman and Haugaard, 2008, p 112). There is a 'profusion' or 'excess' of options, yet a palpable 'scarcity of reliable signposts and authoritative guides' (Bauman, in Bauman and Haugaard, 2008, p 115). In short, the 'liquid-modern' world is a global milieu characterised by existential bleakness: a world where 'safe ports are few and far between, and most of the time trust floats unanchored vainly seeking storm-protected havens' (Bauman, 2000b, p 136). Elsewhere, a rather typical Bauman metaphor likens our experience to that of 'airline passengers who discover, high in the sky, that the pilot's cabin is empty' (Bauman, 2000b, p 133). As patterns of work have altered, capital has 'become exterritorial, light, unencumbered and disembedded to an unprecedented extent, and … is in most cases quite sufficient to blackmail territory-bound political agencies into submission' (Bauman, 2000b, pp 149–50).

In his recurrent preoccupation with popular culture, Bauman perceives television programmes such as *Big Brother* and *Weakest Link* as 'public rehearsals of the disposability of humans' (Bauman, 2002a, p 63). He avows that this human disposability mirrors the uncertainty most people frequently associate with employment. However, for those condemned to 'wasted lives' (Bauman, 2004) – on the margins of society – the situation is even more precarious. Here, Bauman has in mind groups such as refugees who have to contend with multiple burdens and differing, but interrelated, forms of oppression. In addition 'to the usually brandished charges of sponging on the nation's welfare and stealing jobs, refugees can now stand accused of playing a "fifth column" role on behalf of the global terrorist network' (Bauman, 2002b, p 84). That is to say, refugees – and frequently other categories of migrants – fulfil the role of scapegoats for those fearful of their own fragile predicament.

Assessing this theorisation for social work

Bauman's preoccupations clearly relate to a number of social work concerns. First, therefore, how can his theorising of 'solid' modernity, with its dangers of instrumental thinking and the passion for 'order', be assessed in terms of aiding our understanding of social work? This seems to be a relevant question because, despite there being some interest in Bauman's utility for social work in recent years, this aspect of his theorisation is usually neglected.

'Solid' modernity': the search for 'order', the Holocaust, and the corruption of care

Social work is, of course, a highly differentiated field, but, as mentioned in Chapter Two, Howe (1994) has argued that the emergence of the activity from the mid-19th century onwards is a manifestation of modernity's three great projects: care, control and cure. In this context, his analysis of modernity is potentially of great relevance. However, his theoretical interpretation of the Holocaust remains problematic.

Many social workers refused to align themselves with Nazism and, more generally, Bauman pays insufficient attention to the resistance that fascism prompted *within* Germany. More generally, one of the main criticisms of his perspective on the Holocaust is that he fails to satisfactorily conceptualise Nazism and to situate it within an economic context – a crisis of capitalism (see Trotsky, 1972). The assertion that bureaucracy 'has a logic and a momentum of its own' remains open to challenge because of the various competing versions of modernity available at the time of the rise of Nazism (Bauman, 1989, p 104). For example, international socialists in Germany and elsewhere in Europe during this period were committed to furthering modernity and Enlightenment values, yet their political project ran entirely counter to that of the fascists. Bauman fails to recognise that the Nazis had a *particular* and *specific* modernist project. Furthermore, fascism – associated with a cult of violence and absolute allegiance to the leader – can, in fact, also be perceived as a 'counter-modern movement' (Hallsworth, 2005). Additionally, recent research suggests that the Auschwitz-based image of the Holocaust as 'faceless, conveyor-belt, industrial murder is distorted', given that most Jewish victims died in archaic and primitive ways by, for example, being shot at close range on the edge of pits and trenches (Steele, 2009, p 33).

Second, the substantial gaps in his analysis result in too narrow a conceptual focus. Bauman's analysis of 'solid modernity', and his paradigmatic Holocaust example, glosses over the way in which social class functioned. Indeed, his substantial body of work since the early 1990s has neglected class analysis. He has also failed to incorporate gender and, more broadly, the social regulation of (and within) families (see, eg, Pine, 1997). Certainly, omitting discussion on masculinity undermines his analysis, for, as Kathleen Taylor (2009, p 2) has argued, 'men are far more likely to wreak violent death than women'. His perspective is also – as some of the theorists of postcolonialism discussed in Chapter Two might assert – Eurocentric. He concedes, though, that what partly prompted Western powers to challenge Hitler's regime was that it was beginning to adopt barbaric tactics against white Europeans previously reserved for subjugated peoples living in the colonies (Bauman, 2002a, p 109; see also Badiou, 2007). His failure to theorise events such as the atomic bombing of Hiroshima also means that his analysis is somewhat skewed and fails to ask more politically disruptive questions.

However, turning specifically to the resonance of Bauman's ideas for social work, they may serve as a corrective to a somewhat complacent, even sentimental, understanding that the profession has always been a benign activity, constantly aligned with the forces of social justice. What of social work during the period of National Socialism? This chapter cannot address this matter in any detail because most of the archival sources are, of course, only accessible to German-speakers (see Lorenz, 1993). We do know that social workers were not entirely compliant with Nazism: Alice Salomon (1872–1948), a former president of the International Association of Schools of Social Work (IASSW) who was an opponent of the regime, was expelled from Germany. Nevertheless, social work was, of course, a diverse field of activity with many different strands, preoccupations and internal tensions (Crew, 1998). What troubles Kunstreich (2003) is just how easily some components of social work – its institutional ways of *seeing* and *acting* – appeared to be annexed to the political and social project of National Socialism (see also Pine, 1995, 1997). In a manner consistent with the analysis of Bauman, he maintains that the 'participation of social workers and the social welfare establishment ... was fostered by already familiar social technology procedures that were all too easily harnessed ... to the exclusionary and murderous purposes of the Nazi regime' (Kunstreich, 2003, p 24). Kunstreich (2003, p 25) refers, for example, to the process of *selektion* and the 'singling out those who did not fit in with the normative concept of the "ideal German"' (Kunstreich, 2003, p 26). Also important was the interest in social hygiene, which was 'construed as a purification process through which those deemed to be deviant, inferior, or degenerate' had to be eliminated. This gave rise to a range of 'reform' practices that attempted to contain those perceived as contaminating society (Kunstreich, 2003, p 26; see also Pine, 1995). Furthermore, this policy fixation – impacting on social work activity – was reflected in discourses and practices of eugenics and sterilisation, which stretched beyond Germany (see, eg, Broberg and Roll-Hansen, 1996). In many countries, practices of sterilisation carried on, and even increased, *after* the Second World War (Hietala, 1996; Mottier and Gerodetti, 2007; Swansen, 2007). Indeed, 'eugenic thinking never really went away' (Burdett, 2007, p 8; see also Blair, 2006). As if to substantiate this notion, a senior academic in the UK has called for the sterilisation of parents who abuse children (Pemberton, 2010). A Conservative Party member of the House of Lords has also expressed his concerns that planned welfare changes risk encouraging 'breeding' among the poor (*The Guardian*, 2010b).

A related aspect of Bauman's work on scientific rationality and 'solid modernity' that remains relevant for contemporary social work is his concern for those inhabiting those 'twilight areas' that are 'off-limits for a large majority (and the majority which counts) of society's members' (Bauman, 1989, p 97). This sequestration of certain groups of people and their relocation within specific areas and institutions perturbs him because this process potentially facilitates the use of violence. Today, the evolution of policy impinging on social work is rarely situated within a 'scientific' discourse; rather, it is placed within a discursive framework in which 'social inclusion' – more recently, in the UK, the 'Big Society' (Cameron, 2010) – and an overarching moral or ethical register are deployed. Nonetheless, the conduct of 'care' practices in the 'twilight areas' should also cause concern in that they may still reflect some of the trends that have troubled Bauman.

Given the instances of institutional abuse that have tainted the reputation of social work and associated spheres of 'expertise', Wardhaugh and Wilding (1993) have used Bauman's observations to better comprehend how contemporary 'care' practices can become corrupted (see also Levy and Kahan, 1991; Waterhouse, 2000; Butler and Drakeford, 2003). Scrutinising reports on institutional abuse, they investigated the possible reasons why some 'care' organisations and staff deviated from an ethic of care and respect for persons. Influenced by *Modernity and the Holocaust* (Bauman, 1989), they argue that the corruption of care depends on the neutralisation of normal moral concerns. For people to be abused in institutional settings, they normally have to be regarded as 'beyond the bounds of moral behaviour which [normally] governs relations' between people; that is to say, the victims come to be seen as 'less than fully human' (Wardhaugh and Wilding, 1993, p 6). Frequently, admission procedures to institutions, for example, involve the erasure of a person's sense of identity, which is compounded by a pervasive 'culture of obeying orders without question' and a lack of effective external monitoring of institutional practices (Commission to Inquire into Child

Abuse, 2009, vol 2, p 80). Groups regarded as 'morally dirty' can be perceived as particularly vulnerable when segregated and isolated. Indeed, this dimension has been highlighted by the Commission to Inquire into Child Abuse (2009), which examined Industrial Schools that were used to contain neglected, abandoned and ambiguously 'troublesome' children in the Republic of Ireland (see also Arnold, 2009). Within such institutions, as Bauman detects, 'expertise' served to bolster the notion that those detained should be *appropriately* regarded as pariahs in need of tough treatment. That is to say, 'experts' performed important 'definitional labour' in relation to those confined (Goffman, 1971 [1959]): a doctor responsible for medical inspections in the Industrial Schools, for instance, described the detained children as 'terrorists' (Commission to Inquire into Child Abuse, 2009, vol 4, p 29).

Bauman's perspective can, therefore, serve as a theoretical lens through which to view the management of 'problem populations' both historically (in terms of the treatment afforded to workhouse paupers and the children of the poor) and in a more contemporary sense (in places of confinement or quasi-confinement). With regard to the latter dimension, the findings of a report commenting on the bulging prison system in the Republic of Ireland are relevant. Prison chaplains have observed a 'growing disregard for the dignity of the human person and a worrying erosion of compassion'. Conditions are reported to be 'an insult to the dignity of any human being and an affront to the basic tenets of decency' (Irish Prison Chaplains, 2010, p 10). 'Warehoused' in stultifying environments with insufficient rehabilitative possibilities, the predicament of today's prisoners is, in fact, disquietingly similar to that of detainees in Industrial Schools in the past:

> We feel that the situation within the prison system is now so bad that we have no option but to challenge the prevailing culture, a culture of conformity which resists any criticism or challenge, is apparently unable to hear any alternative views and is unwilling to listen to the opinions or suggestions of those who do not conform to the dominant way of thinking that exists within the management structure. (Irish Prison Chaplains, 2010, pp 10–11)

In the much-criticised St. Patrick's Institution, the way that prisoners (aged 16 to 21) are 'managed' raises particular concerns. This is the state's largest facility for young offenders and national and international bodies have repeatedly condemned deplorable conditions over the past 25 years. This is not only because the detention of young people under 18 is in direct contravention of the United Nations Convention on the Rights of the Child, which forbids the imprisonment or detention of children with adults, it is also because the Ombudsman for Children is explicitly prohibited from investigating complaints or allegations by the young people located there. Like the inmates of Industrial Schools in the past, 'young people detained in St. Patrick's Institution are not allowed to wear their own clothes (unlike every other prisoner in every other prison)' (Irish Prison Chaplains, 2010, p 19).

Examples such as this are not, of course, limited to the Republic of Ireland. Within most 'civilised' countries, there is a panoply of ostensible 'care' locations in which people are vulnerable to being treated as mere 'material' (Badiou, 2007, p 8). This was illustrated by UK research revealing that an estimated 150,000 dementia patients (many located in 'care' homes and hospitals) are being inappropriately prescribed antipsychotic drugs. According to a research charity, this contributes to 1,800 deaths each year (Alzheimer's Research Trust, 2009). In such contexts, the danger is that issues for the carers/guards risk becoming mere questions of organisation or technique, which reduce 'residents' to specimens of a category. The neutralisation of moral concerns may be expressed in cultural stereotyping and exploitative practices, with the most vulnerable individuals and groups being those lacking resources of material and symbolic capital (Bourdieu and Wacquant, 2004).

In his discussion on child incarceration and 'repositories for managing the unwanted' (Goldson, 2009, p 88), Goldson concludes that the 'low level of social value accorded to such children ... renders them particularly prone, by omission or commission, to systematic maltreatment within socio-political contexts where those responsible operate with impunity' (Goldson, 2009, p 89). Here, four 'intersecting and mutually reinforcing processes' play a key role: 'othering', 'veiling', 'euphemism' and 'circumspection' (Goldson, 2009, pp 96–100). More broadly, 'international evidence reveals that children in custodial institutions are particularly prone to violence and harm' (Goldson, 2009, p 93). This insight became highly relevant in the summer of 2010 when the British government eventually agreed to publish a 'secret manual' that revealed techniques used to *deliberately* inflict pain on children as young as 12 in private prisons (see Children's Rights Alliance for England, 2010). More generally, in institutional settings where resources are limited and the stress is placed on survival and 'getting by', emphasis on control and 'order' maintenance can result (Mental Health Commission, 2011a). Indeed, a constellation of factors could contribute to the evolution of what Stanley Cohen (2001, p 11) has referred to as the development of 'micro-cultures of denial within particular institutions'. The power of these cultures is such that they risk overriding or nullifying the professional codes of ethics to which relevant staff rhetorically adhere.

These contributions examining aspects of confinement, when wedded to those of Bauman, are significant because they can – so to speak – switch on 'warning lights' within social work and social care. What is more, new marginalised zones – or 'twilight areas' – are being created in contemporary penal and social policy (Garrett, 2007a). Clearly, the parallels drawn here do not imply a direct correlation between policies pursued in 1930s Germany and present-day developments within social policy in Western Europe. They merely identify a shared and ambiguous *tendency* to locate particular populations (those regarded as 'troublesome' and 'out of place') within enclosures that may not even, in the ordinary sense of the word, be 'prisons', but which remain zones of varying degrees of violence, confinement, enclosure, monitoring and supervision (see Butler, 2004). Additionally, such developments can be analytically linked to a series of policies and practices relating to 'detention' and 'detainees' that have become more central in the context of 'national security' in the UK and elsewhere.

'Liquid modernity' = 'liquid social work'?

Ferguson (2004, 2005, 2008), Bauman's chief proponent in the field of academic social work, has concentrated on 'liquid modernity'. In his 'reflections' on the Victoria Climbié case and his attempt to dismantle 'critical social work theorising', Ferguson asserts that child protection, 'like social work and welfare practices more generally', mirror 'the contingent, "liquid" nature of modern life itself' (Ferguson, 2005, pp 794, 788). More emphatically, child protection should be viewed 'as a mobile form of "*liquid welfare*"' (Ferguson, 2005, p 788, emphasis added). However, this importation of Bauman's more recent ideas into the theorisation of social work seems a little overconfident and too definitive. Certainly, Bauman's social theory – and the contributions of Ferguson derived from it – shed some light on the transformation from the 'Seebohm factories' (Simpkin, 1983), ushered in during the late 1960s and early 1970s, and the new 'workscapes' envisaged for social workers today in the UK and elsewhere (see, eg, Conservative Party, 2007). Nonetheless, to perceive such 'reforms' as entirely attributable to 'liquid modernity' is misleading since it obscures the impact of neoliberalisation. Moreover, there are a number of additional problems with the 'liquid modernity' formulation that undermine its theoretical usefulness for social work and related spheres of activity.

First, despite Ferguson's (2004, p 198) acknowledgement that child protection has always been a 'mixture of solid and melting forms', he – influenced by Bauman – tends to overemphasise the radical difference in working lives during the so-called 'liquid' and 'solid' periods. This is unconvincing because many workers – especially those regarded as 'surplus' to capitalist processes of production and distribution – experienced work that was fragile, temporary and insecure even *during* the period of so-called 'solid modernity'. These were characteristics of employment for many 'unskilled' workers, women workers, black and other minority ethnic workers often on the periphery of labour markets. In short, capitalism – for many – was *never* particularly 'solid', in that work and life were continually saturated with 'ambient insecurity, anxiety and fear' (Bauman, in Bauman and Haugaard, 2008, p 112). It may be that Bauman, and those seeking to apply his work, are too prone to dwell on the experiences of a 'labour aristocracy' during the period identified as 'solid modernity': relatively high-waged groups concentrated in manufacturing sectors in the metropolitan centres. Neoliberalisation and attempts to eradicate 'embedded liberalism' (Harvey, 2005; see also Chapter Five) have clearly had an impact on the lives of such workers, but it would be erroneous to universalise their experiences. A second problem with the 'liquid modernity' perspective is that it risks mirroring the promotional rhetoric of neoliberalisation, which tends to extol the merits of 'speed', 'flexibility' and 'fluidity' (see also the discussion on Boltanski and Chiapello in Chapter Ten). A third criticism relates to mobility and the valorisation of the mobile in contemporary social theory (Ferguson,

2010a, 2010b; see also Cresswell, 2001; Skeggs, 2004b). Bauman himself is apt to acknowledge that people have differential and structurally mediated capacities to be mobile and that there is, in fact, 'blatant inequality of access to mobility' (Bauman, 2002a, p 83). Even more bluntly, travelling 'for profit is encouraged; travelling for survival is condemned' (Bauman, 2002a, p 84). However, many of those indebted to Bauman's more recent work appear less cautious in their foregrounding of mobility and this is detectable in the theorising of the car and how it shapes work (Dant, 2004; Laurier, 2004). Ferguson (2004, 2008, 2010a) and Smith (2003) have also emphasised the significance of the car, and – as we have seen – 'car therapy work' (Ferguson, 2010b, p 130), without taking into account that car manufacture, marketing and usage are contextually embedded in the socio-economic fabric of capitalism. In addition, due to so-called 'austerity' measures, many public sector workers, such as social workers, are having their mobility *restricted* because of cuts to car mileage reimbursement rates for home visiting (Mickel, 2011).

A fourth, and final, criticism of the 'liquid modernity' construct is the centrality it assigns to computer-based technologies and other electronic communications. Here, there is a failure to recognise how individuals and groups are differentially positioned because of the uneven development that is integral to the patterning of capitalist production and consumption. Steyaert and Gould's (2009, p 743) contribution on the 'digital divide' reminds readers that on a global level, 'only 1.5 billion people have access to the internet': this 'is approximately 22 per cent of the world's population of 6.6 billion'.

Conclusion

Bauman's work can, perhaps somewhat schematically, be divided into three phrases. Phase one, roughly coterminous with his period in Poland, can be associated with Marxism and dialectical materialism; phase two, following his arrival in Leeds, initially related to his theorisation of 'solid modernity' and its harmful, even calamitous, consequences; phase three is reflected in his preoccupation with 'liquid modernity'. What holds his contributions together, however, is that all 'his books are drenched in solidarity with – and sympathy for – people caught and suspended in the webs of power, oppression, persecution, poverty and potential extermination' (Tester and Jacobsen, 2005, p 24). Moreover, his theorisation might prompt us to try and illuminate that 'deep and secret bond' between Nazism and the apparent 'innocence of democracy' (Badiou, 2007, pp 4–5). Indeed, underpinning this chapter is the understanding that his 'solid modernity' theorisation, although remaining deeply problematic, is more useful for social work than his ideas associated with 'liquid modernity', which have, in recent times, begun to achieve some prominence within the profession's academic literature. However, Bauman's theorisation is lacking because he fails to provide any exploration of the centrality of capitalism. The next chapter, therefore, will

—

focus on the understanding that capitalism provides the motor for modernity. In this context, Marx's (1990) *Capital* will provide a basis for examining this assertion.

⏮ **Reflection and Talk Box 3** ⏭

- Can we reasonably speak of 'liquid modernity' and 'liquid social work'?

- What messages does the work of Bauman convey for contemporary social work?

- Can we relate any of Bauman's insights to what Wardhaugh and Wilding call the 'corruption of care'? Can we connect their analysis to any instances of institutional abuse?

- Does Bauman's work prompt any thoughts on asylum seekers in contemporary society?

- Is Bauman's vision unduly bleak? For example, he quotes Woody Allen: 'More than at any other time in history, mankind faces a crossroads. One path leads to despair and utter hopelessness. The other leads to total extinction. Let us pray we have the wisdom to choose correctly' (quoted in Bauman, 2002a, p 86).

- What other key issues for social workers emerge from this chapter?

Note

[1] This chapter makes use of and reworks an article previously published as 'From "solid modernity" to "liquid modernity"? Zygmunt Bauman and social work', *British Journal of Social Work*, vol 42, no 4, pp 634–51.

CHAPTER FOUR

Modernity and capitalism

Introduction

For some writers, the term 'modernity' is of little use and functions to mask the centrality and significance of capitalism. Jameson, for example, proposed, as a 'therapeutic recommendation', substituting capitalism for modernity in all the contexts in which the latter appears (quoted in Callinicos, 2006, p 50). A similar position has been taken by Woodwiss (1997), who has also historically located the renewed interest in the concept:

> I wish to question the general sociological utility of the concept formerly known as capitalism – modernity.... In my view, the term 'modernity' as a specifically sociological sign has its origins in the representation of American society contained in the work of sociologists like Daniel Bell [author of the influential *End of ideology*, 1960] and David Riesman [author of *The lonely crowd*, 1950], and given a technologically determinist inner logic ... in the 1960s. This was a representation that identified the combination of liberal democracy, a capitalist economy, an 'open' class structure and an individualistic value system as the antithesis of totalitarianism whether fascist or communist. (Woodwiss, 1997, p 2)

Woodwiss (1997, p 4) recommends that 'we restore ... capitalism, to its rightful position of pre-eminence within sociological discourse'.

Despite remarkable transformations having taken place within modernity since the publication of Marx's *Das Kapital* (henceforth, simply *Capital*) in 1867, this chapter will stress the continuing relevance of the book for those working in social work and associated fields. In short, it provides a devastating critique of capitalism and remains a vital resource for those seeking to understand and develop strategies of resistance within capitalism during a period of crisis and so-called 'austerity'.

It could argued that the suggestion that *Capital* may be of relevance and potential importance for social workers in the early years of the 21st century is a rather unfashionable, obtuse, even contrary and provocative notion. As we approach the bicentennial of Marx's birth – in 2018 – the world in which his book appeared would seem to be radically different from the 'new world order' (Derrida, 1994). However, it was not a left-wing tabloid, but an October 2008 issue of the London *Financial Times*, which published the headline – 'Capitalism in convulsion'. Indeed, the convulsions and crises of that period, still with no decipherable outcome at the time of writing, illuminate the sheer instability of capitalism (Harvey, 2010). As the historian Eric Hobsbawm has observed, what 'never lost contemporary relevance is Marx's vision of capitalism as an historically temporary mode of human economy and his analysis of its ever-expanding and concentrating, crisis-generating and self-transforming *modus operandi* ' (Hobsbawm, 2011, p 11). Moreover, the 'globalised capitalist world that emerged in the 1990s was in crucial ways uncannily like the world anticipated by Marx' (Hobsbawm, 2011, p 5).

While mindful of Marx's model of the British political economy and his crucial distinction between 'necessary labour' and 'surplus value', this chapter will focus more on the *social* critique of capitalism that is embedded in *Capital*. Readers seeking a detailed exploration of Marx's political economy of capital and his theory of labour value may, therefore, wish to avail themselves of supplementary sources (eg Harvey, 2005, 2006a, 2006b, 2010). Marx's theorisation contains three interlocking parts, each of them in effect models of how crucial elements of the capitalist system operated.

> [One] model was concerned with the 'economy' itself, conceived of as the creation of the circulation of capital. A second model dealt with the social organization of that economy, and how it controlled the exploitation of one class by another. The third model set out the operation of the 'ideological apparatus' which is woven around the society and economy. (Worsley, 2002, p vii)

The first part of the chapter, and foundation for what follows, will very briefly examine the plethora of factors, or arguments, which suggest that *Capital*, and more broadly Marxism, may now appear to be largely irrelevant. Having noted some of these, it will then be maintained that *Capital* remains relevant for social workers and those working in associated fields because Marx helps to illuminate facets of what can be termed 'actually existing capitalism'. It will also be argued that *Capital* is still important because it reminds us that capitalism, despite its ability to bedazzle and seduce, *hurts*: that it is an exploitative economic system that damages bodies and minds and undermines – what if often referred to in more contemporary times as – health and 'well-being' (Bergdolt, 2008). In this context, it is significant that Marx is perturbed and outraged by how the lives of children were being destroyed by the dynamic, unregulated power of capital and this dimension will be discussed in the third section of the chapter.[1]

Social work and Marxism

Marxism had considerable influence on social work in the not-too-distant past. In *The road not taken*, Michael Reisch and Janice Andrews (2002), for example, perhaps surprised many by alerting their readers to the impact of Marxism within social work in the US throughout the 20th century.[2] In the UK, Marxism has had an impact on the theorisation and practice of some social workers stretching from the New Leftism of the late 1960s and into the period of the Conservative–Liberal Democrat government. Many social workers, members of the Labour Party and also smaller and explicitly Marxist parties have attempted to organise themselves industrially and endeavoured to develop a social work *praxis* underpinned by Marxism. The project to locate social work activity within the matrix of social and economic relations structured by capitalism was apparent across of a number of influential 'radical social work' textbooks published during the period of Labourism's demise and the installation of Thatcherism. Most notable here, as observed in Chapter One, were Bailey and Brake's (1975) *Radical social work* and a range of books commissioned and published by Macmillan (eg Corrigan and Leonard, 1978; Jones, 1983; Simpkin, 1983; for reflections on this period, see also Bailey, 2011; Weinstein, 2011). A small group of academics continue to apply Marxist conceptual categories, such as 'alienation', to contemporary social work (eg Jones, 2001; Ferguson and Lavalette, 2004, 2006; Lavalette, 2011a, 2011b). However, many consider Marxism as largely irrelevant to social workers, and others, in the first quarter of the 21st century. According to Marxism's detractors, reading volumes such as *Capital* is rather a 'waste of time' because Marxism is an anachronistic 'grand narrative' – a now jaded, formulaic, even 'oppressive' body of ideas and practices. Even more emphatically, Marx is often presented as the 'scapegoat for all the ills of the social world' (Bourdieu, in Bourdieu and Wacquant, 2004, p 126).

The assertion that Marxism is no longer of any theoretical or practical utility is lodged within a myriad of interconnected arguments. For the sake of brevity, three main criticisms will be highlighted. The first deems the 'collapse' of the USSR and the crumbling of the Berlin Wall to be irrefutable evidence for the intellectual exhaustion of Marxism. Such an argument is rhetorically bolstered by reference to how states once viewing themselves as 'socialist' have subsequently rushed to embrace capitalism, while even nominally 'socialist' states, such as China, appear committed to neoliberalisation (Harvey, 2005; Walker and Buck, 2007). This criticism merely assumes that the former Soviet Union and its satellites were unambiguously 'socialist'. However, it could be countered that these political, economic and military entities were in fact *degenerated* workers' states (Trotsky, 1971). Indeed, following Foucault (by no means a Marxist), the demise of the Soviet Union and the satellite regimes of the so-called 'Eastern Bloc' countries may result in the 'unburdening and liberation of Marx in relation to party dogma, which has constrained it, touted it and brandished it for so long' (Foucault, 1988d, p 45).

Furthermore, the introduction of unrestrained capitalism in former 'socialist' states, often by means of so-called 'economic shock therapy', led to the pillaging of public services and a tremendous concentration in wealth. In Russia, for example, this 'put seven oligarchs in control of nearly half the economy within a few years' (Harvey, 2010, p 29). The simultaneous and wholesale assault on public health provision caused death and hardship (Klein, 2007). The United Nations (UN) reported that, since the early 1990s, the Russian Federation has seen 'a marked increase in male mortality over and above the historical trend' and the number of additional deaths during 1992–2001 is estimated at an astonishing 2.5–3 million. The UN report further remarked that in the 'absence of war, famine, or health epidemics there is no historical precedent for the scale of loss' (United Nations Development Programme, 2005, p 23). A fledging social work profession has had to respond to this mass immiseration (Iarskaia-Smirnova and Romanoz, 2002). Living standards have improved, and now come close on average to the 'level of late 1970, though with much higher social and regional differentiation. However, even after the years of economic growth, many Russians are much poorer than in the late Soviet period' (Kagarlitsky, 2009, pp 45–6).

A second more theoretically driven assertion is that Marxism is no longer able to grasp the complexities of contemporary life and that the focus on the centrality of class, determined by the positioning of a group or an individual in relation to the dominant means of production and distribution, is reductive. It is maintained that subjectivity is a far more complex issue and questions relating to 'identity' are now much more significant than economic class. Other theorists couple this critique to a more fundamental charge that Marxism, itself a product of modernity, has proved unable to analyse and interpret the direction or trajectory that modernity has taken. A more insightful analysis of contemporary developments, they would argue, is supplied by different theoretical paradigms. As mentioned in the previous chapter, these include: 'postmodernist' theorising; ideas associated with the 'risk society' (Beck, 1998); the claim that we have now entered a period of 'liquid modernity' (Bauman, 2005); or that we have now entered a period that needs to be analytically attentive to the evolution of 'life politics' (Giddens, 1991).

Capital is a reflection *of*, as well as a reflection *on*, a particular era. Gaps and omissions also exist, of course, in a book first published in 1867. It is preoccupied with a period of rapid industrialisation and, understandably, Marx did not deal with (de)industrialisation, as experienced in the late 20th and early 21st centuries in a number of Western European countries (see Charlesworth, 2000a). He was also unable to fully appreciate the seductive lure of mass consumption and how capitalism – with its technologies and its inducements – *appears* to furnish pleasures as well as hardships and pain. This is connected to the evolution of the 'consumer society' (Jameson, 2000) and what motivates people to enter into and remain attached to the 'spirit of capitalism' (see Boltanski and Chiapello, 2005; Soper, 2007; see also Chapter Ten). Writers such as Bourdieu have also argued that there is a need to expand the notion of capital to include more than economic assets (see also Chapter Seven). Others have maintained that Marx was clearly unable to predict the speed of movements of capital, aided by computer technology, in the 21st century. These are valid points, proving that it would be erroneous to assume that we can *mechanically* apply Marx's work in manifestly different times and circumstances, and assume that *Capital* holds the key to, for example, every particular problem encountered by social workers and associated groups of workers. Yet, as Hobsbawm explains:

A number of central features of Marx's analysis remain valid and relevant. The first, obviously, is the analysis of the irresistible global dynamic of capitalist economic development and its capacity to destroy all that came before it, including even those parts of the heritage of the human past from which capitalism had itself benefited, such as family structures. The second is the analysis of the mechanism of capitalist growth by generating internal 'contradictions' – endless bouts of tensions and temporary resolutions, growth leading to crisis and change, all producing economic concentration in an increasingly globalised economy. (Hobsbawm, 2011, p 14)

Perhaps, like Gramsci (whose contribution will be explored in Chapter Six), there is a need to reject any perception of Marx as 'a "shepherd wielding a crook", or some Messiah who left us a string of parables laden with categorical imperatives and absolute, unchallengeable norms, lying outside the categories of time and space' (Morton, 2003, p 123). Rather, we have to 'do our own work', and ponder if, in our particular time, place and professional field, some of the ideas adumbrated by Marx in the late 19th century may still hold contemporary resonance and meaning within neoliberal modernity (Garrett, 2009).

A third criticism is entirely sceptical about the worth of Marxism, but also more generally critical of social theory and abstract reflection. This form of criticism, mentioned at the outset of this book, is rooted in an impatient, blinkered, anti-intellectualism that condemns anything beyond the 'practical' and is merely interested in the 'here and now'. This perspective – rhetorically non-ideological, in truth deeply ideological – is discursively embedded in the idea that social work must deploy approaches and forms of intervention that *unambiguously* 'work', and which are manifestly 'evidence-based'. *Social theory and social work*, in seeking to draw attention to *Capital*, is, however, committed to promoting critical and dialectical thinking *in* and *on* social work and – while not diminishing the importance of the 'practical' – to reaching beyond it if only to arrive at a more informed and rounded understanding.

To social workers committed to such an endeavour, Marxist analysis offers an indispensable counter-hegemonic perspective on our neoliberal times. Capitalism is deeply fissured through its own internal contradictions. There is, therefore, a pressing need for an analysis of these contradictions and this requires the deployment of theoretical tools such as those that Marx pioneered. The task is not to regurgitate Marx's texts, but to extend, revise and adapt them in ways that can address the complexities of our times. In re-examining *Capital*, therefore, the focus will be on how it might help us gain a better understanding of some of the key components associated with, what is often referred to as, the 'modernisation' or 'transformation' of social work today (see also Garrett, 2009).

Marx and 'actually existing capitalism': the *work* in social work

It is, perhaps, difficult for 21st-century readers of *Capital* to appreciate that Marx's searing critique applied to an earlier period of 'modernisation' in which large-scale factory manufacture was *new*. For example, in describing and castigating the conditions workers (many of them children) had to endure as match producers, Marx was investigating a *new* industry that did not begin until the 1830s. Interrogating the misleadingly hyperbolic 'spin' in support of 19th-century laissez faire economics (Perelman, 2000), his research project furnishes a number of 'coordinates' that can also be applied to contemporary transformations within the 'world of work'. More specifically, *Capital*'s articulation of the three interrelated questions of Time, Toil (or labour) and Technology provides telling insights into the changing nature of *work* within the field of social work.

Time

The late Daniel Bensaid (2002, p 74) suggested that volume one of *Capital* is 'the book of stolen time'. Marx did not produce a theory of time, but time and temporality played a central role in his 'conceptualization of change and historical development, on the one hand, and his economic theories of surplus value and commodification, on the other' (Adam, 2004, p 37). Certainly, Marx was preoccupied by capital's 'drive towards a boundless and ruthless extension of the working day' (Marx, 1990, p 411). Indeed, in pursuit of social discipline during the period of capitalism's imposition, 'an attack was launched against all forms of collective solidarity including sports, games, dances, ale-wakes, festivals, and other group-rituals that had been a source of bonding and solidarity among workers' (Federici, 2004, p 83). The owners of capital were intent on prompting a swift and radical cultural shift, inducing the emerging industrial working class to fundamentally *remake* their idea of what constituted a reasonable number of working hours per day. This pivoted on the need to lengthen 'the working day beyond the limits set by the sun, the seasonal cycles and the body itself, as constituted in pre-industrial society' (Federici, 2004, p 135).

For the greater part of the 18th century, it was custom and practice to work a mere four days each week (Marx, 1990, p 387). However, the imposition of a new time discipline transformed the whole mode of existence of the working class. Thus, the length of the working week was extended and fluctuated 'within boundaries that are both physical and social. Both these limits are of a very elastic nature, and allow a tremendous latitude' (Marx, 1990, p 341). A working day was carved out under the Factory Acts, but 'small thefts of capital from workers' meal-times and recreation times' continued and were described by factory inspectors as the 'petty pilfering of minutes' (Marx, 1990, p 352). Capital thus 'haggles over meal-times, where possible incorporating them into the production process, so that food is added to the worker as to a mere means of production, as coal is supplied to the boiler, and grease and oil to the machinery' (Marx, 1990, p 376).

The motivation for such actions was the employers' recognition that within a capitalist system, 'moments are elements of profit' (Marx, 1990, p 352); hence the 'drive towards the extension of the working day, and the werewolf-like hunger for surplus labour' (Marx, 1990, p 353). Marx went on to interpret the introduction of night-working and the shift system (occurring at the time in many cotton mills) as reflecting capital's incessant quest for 'surplus labour' and additional profit:

> The prolongation of the working day beyond the limits of the natural day, into the night, only acts as a palliative. It only slightly quenches the vampire thirst for the living blood of labour. *Capitalist production therefore drives, by its inherent nature, towards the appropriation of labour throughout the whole of the 24 hours in the day.* (Marx, 1990, p 367, emphasis added)

The worker was, therefore, a mere commodity within the evolving system of capitalist production and the exploitative relations that were at its core. Hence, for Marx (1990, p 375), it was 'self-evident that the worker is nothing other than labour-power for the duration of his whole life, and … all his disposable time is by nature and by right labour-time, to be devoted to the self-valorization of capital'.

Within Marx's complex gothic scenography, capital drains the life from those forced to sell their labour (see Carver, 1998, ch 1). For him, capital is 'dead labour which, vampire-like, lives only by sucking living labour, and lives the more, the more labour it sucks' (Marx, 1990, p 342). Capital:

> asks no questions about the length of life of labour power. What interests it is purely and simply the maximum of labour-power that can be set in motion in a working day. It attains this objective by shortening the life of labour power, in the same way as a greedy farmer snatches more produce from the soil by robbing it of its fertility. (Marx, 1990, p 376)

In short, 'the "free" worker is compelled by social conditions to sell the whole of his active life' (Marx, 1990, p 382). Importantly, this situation also gave rise to opposition because as soon as the working class, stunned and disoriented by the noise and turmoil in the factories, had partly recovered its senses from 'the shock and awe' the new system of production prompted, it began to resist (see Klein, 2007).[3] The factory legislation attempting to regulate the length of the working day was, therefore, the object of a 'long class struggle' (Marx, 1990, p 395).

In social work, time is usually viewed as conceptually unproblematic despite an implicit day-to-day thematic preoccupation with temporal matters (Munro, 2011). In practice with children and families, assessments are implicitly underpinned by ideas about time (eg ideas associated with the discourse of 'child development'). Similarly, practice is often rooted in notions concerning how it is damaging for children to drift (in time) in 'care'. Often lengthy office exchanges take place on when 'cases' should pass from 'intake' or 'short-term' to 'long-term' teams.

In other areas of practice, social workers intervene with people with a limited lifetime (the terminally ill) or work with people with a frayed or muddied sense of time (eg those with Alzheimer's disease). In certain spheres, social workers seek to assist victims of abuse needing time to recover. Furthermore, the profession is embedded in the understanding that key social work values (such as 'respect for persons') are, seemingly, 'timeless'.

In the context of Marx's observations, therefore, it is fruitful to examine how the labour in social work is dictated by considerations of time. This can be seen in terms of issues related to: the duration of work; the length of contracts; the mapping of the 'working day'; and how the boundaries between 'home' and 'work' are, for many, becoming more porous. In terms of the tempo of work, this can be seen in how quickly assessments need to be completed: for example, a number of centrally devised assessment schedules contain time limits for completion. More generally, some forms of communication – such as emails – compress or 'speed up' work.

Here, it might be countered that as the majority of social workers, certainly in the UK, are unlikely to be employed in the private sector, questions relating to time, profit and surplus value do not apply. It could be responded, however, that 'welfare' is increasingly becoming a site of capital accumulation and that social workers and related groups of workers are now more likely to find themselves located in the private or quasi-private sector (Scourfield, 2007; Carey, 2008): for example, within so-called 'social work practices' or working for one of the 'local authority trading companies' that Ernst & Young are aiding a number of councils to establish (Le Grand, 2007; see also Cardy, 2010; Dunning, 2011). Second, 'the time-is-money assumption permeates *every* aspect of daily life as naturalized and unquestioned fact' (Adam, 2004, p 125, emphasis added). Expressed another way, social work is a form of labour that, even if deployed in settings where there is no direct private sector employer, remains located within a matrix of economic and social relationships determined by capital. Moreover, public sector organisations are increasingly modelling themselves on private sector approaches to work and the measurement of 'performance' (Clarke et al, 2007).

Toil

Issues related to the 'performance' of workers, and the governance and organisation of workplaces at particular times in particular places, is central to *Capital*. In the period when Marx was writing, the factory – and the disciplinary regime associated with it – was, of course, of immense significance. It not only subjected the 'previously independent worker to the discipline and command of capital', it created 'in addition a hierarchical structure amongst the workers themselves' (Marx, 1990, p 481). As a result, factories were characterised by a 'barrack-like discipline' (Marx, 1990, p 549):

An industrial army of workers under the command of a capitalist requires, like a real army, officers (managers) and NCOs (foremen, overseers) who command during the labour process in the name of capital. The work of supervision becomes their established and exclusive function. (Marx, 1990, p 450)

The aim of this mode of organisation was to maximise the productivity of labour and, hence, profits. For those falling outside the sphere of production, a panoply of other disciplinary institutions, providing differing degrees of confinement, were evolving (such as Poor Law institutions) in order to regulate and manage the dissident and recalcitrant (Federici, 2004).

In terms of organisation within factories, a central feature was the division of labour implemented to increase profits. Marx outlined, for example, how the production of carriages was being split up so that individual workers carried out 'specialised' or 'exclusive' functions with the 'manufacture as a whole being performed by these particular workers in conjunction' (Marx, 1990, p 456). Thus, the 'individual workers are appropriated and annexed for life by a limited function: while the various operations of the hierarchy of labour-powers are parcelled out among the workers according to both their natural and their acquired capacities' (Marx, 1990, pp 469–70):

> After the various operations have been separated, made independent and isolated, the workers are divided, classified and grouped according to their predominant qualities…. The one-sidedness and even the deficiencies of the specialized individual worker become perfections when he is part of the collective worker…. [H]is connection with the whole mechanism compels him to work with the regularity of a machine. (Marx, 1990, p 469)

Indeed, the 'violence of the ruling class was not confined to the repression of transgressors. *It also aimed at a radical transformation of the person*' (Federici, 2004, p 136, emphasis added; see also Federici, 2011). This point is particularly important because it highlights how the human body was central to the installation of capitalism. Working within the feminist-Marxist tradition, Federici (2004, pp 137–8) has maintained that the 'body … came to the foreground of social policies because it appeared not only as a beast inert to the stimuli of work, but also as the container of labor-power, a means of production, the primary work-machine'. From the 17th century:

> anatomical analogies were drawn from the workshops of the manufacturers: the arms were viewed as levers, the heart as a pump, the lungs as bellows, the eyes as lenses, the fists as hammers. But these mechanical metaphors reflect not the influence of technology per se,

but the fact that the *machine was becoming the model for social behaviour.* (Federici, 2004, p 145, emphasis added)

Federici (2004, p 146) claims that we can, in fact:

> see the development of the 'human machine' as the main technological leap, the main step in the development of the productive forces that took place in the period of primitive accumulation. *We can see, in other words, that the human body and not the steam engine, and not even the clock, was the first machine developed by capitalism.* (Emphasis in original)

Federici's analysis is entirely in tune with Marx's condemnation of workplace organisation within capitalism:

> A worker who performs the same simple operation for the whole of his life converts his body into the automatic, one-sided implement of that operation.... The collective worker, who constitutes the living mechanism of manufacture, is made up solely of such one-sided specialist workers. (Marx, 1990, p 458)

This industrial configuration ensures the 'conversion of a partial task into a life-long destiny' (Marx, 1990, p 559). For Marx (1990, p 460), the 'constant labour of one uniform kind disturbs the intensity and flow of a man's vital forces, which find recreation and delight in the change of activity itself'. Elsewhere in *Capital*, he deplored 'riveting each worker to a single fraction of the work' (Marx, 1990, p 464) and 'the lifelong annexation of the worker to a partial operation' (Marx, 1990, p 477). Not 'only is the specialized work distributed among the different individuals, but the individual himself is divided up, and transformed into the automatic motor of a detailed operation' (Marx, 1990, p 481). This system 'mutilates the worker, turning him into a fragment of himself' (Marx, 1990, p 482). In a memorable paragraph, Marx declares:

> Unfitted by nature to make anything independently, the manufacturing worker develops his productive activity only as an *appendage of that workshop*. As the chosen people bore in their features the sign that they were the property of Jehovah, so the division of labour brands the manufacturing worker as the property of capital. (Marx, 1990, p 482, emphasis added)

Nonetheless, he attempted to view these developments dialectically, recognising that, on the one hand, this division of labour 'appears historically as an advance and a necessary aspect of the economic process of the formation of society, on the other hand, it appears as a more refined and civilized means of exploitation' (Marx, 1990, p 486). Marx was, however, clear that large-scale industry '*does away with all repose, all fixity and all security as far as the worker's life situation is concerned*' (Marx, 1990, pp 617–18, emphasis added). Such a description, observable at industrial capitalism's inception, appears to foreshadow some of the descriptions of working lives in the 21st century, although present-day theorisation is often rooted in the repudiation of Marxism and attached, as we have seen earlier, to notions such as 'liquid modernity' (Bauman, 2005; see also Chapter Three).

Fredric Jameson makes the important point that it is capitalism that continually and 'systematically dissolves the fabric of all cohesive social groups without exception, *including its own ruling class*' (quoted in Hardt and Weeks, 2000, p 136, emphasis added). Indeed, the fact that capitalism demolishes all repose, fixity and security reverberates into the early 21st century and describes, for many, their present-day working lives. Particularly during a period of neoliberalisation, temporary and precarious employment patterns are insidiously normalised: 'flexible working, another magic word of neo-liberalism, is imposed, meaning night work, weekend work, irregular working hours, things which have always been part of the employers' dreams' (Bourdieu, 2001b, p 34). Such practices also contribute to depression and other forms of mental distress (Bourdieu et al, 2002).

Clearly, Marx's interpretation might enrich contemporary understandings of how capital seeks to order, pattern and choreograph bodies in places of work. Despite a lack of sufficient appreciation of how gender structures the division of labour, *Capital* continues to furnish useful insights into how workers are often compelled to focus on one small aspect of production or 'service delivery' (Harlow, 2004; Baines, 2006). Although social work has always been a less spatially rooted and fixed activity than factory work (Ferguson, 2004), for over three decades, and within a number of national settings, a consistent current of critique has revealed how practice has become more standardised, routinised and fragmented.[4] Not all of these contributions have been explicitly Marxist and none have suggested equivalence between the late 19th-century production of carriages and child care assessments today. Nonetheless, through the promotional rhetoric of schemes such as the 'looking after children' (LAC) system formulated in the UK in the late 1980s, it is easy to recognise how it contributed to the fragmentation and cheapening of the work of social workers (Garrett, 2003). In Canada also, it has been argued that the increasing use of centrally devised assessment schedules and the 'standardisation' of 'service delivery' means 'that it is easier for those without social work credentials to assume the work, thus lowering the costs of labour' (Baines, 2004a, p 279).

These developments may be understood in terms of the labour management technique known, after its founder Frederick W. Taylor (1856–1915), as Taylorism (Braverman, 1974, 1998; see also Chapter Six). Boltanski and Chiapello (2005, p 439) have argued that forms of Taylorist work organisation can be compared to army-like discipline and modern warfare because within this regime of domination:

the difference between human beings vanishes: assembly-line workers lose all particularity, since workers at the same post are completely interchangeable. If a worker fails, he can immediately be replaced, just as in modern warfare – mass warfare – the infantryman who falls is immediately replaced in the post he occupied by some other.

Bourdieu (2003a, p 29) has referred to the more recent evolution of 'service-sector Taylorism'. For him, the 'prototype of the unskilled worker of the "new economy"' is the supermarket checkout worker, whom:

> bar-coding and computerization have converted into a genuine assembly-line worker, her cadence timed, clocked, and controlled across a schedule determined by variations in the flow of customers: she has neither the life nor the lifestyle of a factory worker, but she occupies an equivalent position in the new structure. (Bourdieu, 2003a, p 30)

Returning specifically to social work, it is apparent that information and communication technologies (ICTs) are facilitating not entirely dissimilar processes in the UK (White et al, 2009; Broadhurst et al, 2010), Australia (Tregeagle and Darcy, 2008) and Canada (Baines, 2004a, 2004b). How, therefore, can Marx help to illuminate some of these developments?

Technology

Concerned with the introduction of machinery within the *new* workplaces of the mid-19th century, Marx (1990, p 560) analyses how the 'constant advance of technology' was harnessed to the interests of capital. He was clear that the 'machine is a means for producing surplus-value' and that its deployment was serving to further oppress workers by stretching or elongating the working day (Marx, 1990, p 492). Thus, the 'most powerful instrument to reduce labour-time suffers a dialectical inversion and becomes the most unfailing means for turning the whole lifetime of the worker and his family into labour-time at capital's disposal' (Marx, 1990, p 532).

However, Marx understood that 'machinery' was not to blame for this development. As he lucidly remarked, it 'took both time and experience before the workers learnt to distinguish between machinery and its employment by capital, and therefore to transfer their attacks from the material instruments of production to the form of society which utilizes those instruments' (Marx, 1990, p 555). That is to say, it was not the machinery (or, for today's readers, the 'technology') that is the problem, but its 'imbrication within the relations that embrace it ... the concern for profit and domination that has canalized technological development' (Adorno, 2003, p 118).

Within social work and related fields, the deployment of ICTs is contributing to the slow evolution of a new 'techno-habitat' for social workers (Dyer-Witheford,

1999; see also Sapey, 1997; Harlow and Webb, 2003; Geoghegan and Lever, 2004). A number of writers have focused on how the 'call centre' is beginning to have a new prominence in the fields of health, social work and social care (Coleman and Harris, 2008; Hanna, 2010). More generally, it is important to relate issues bound up with the introduction of ICTs to the earlier reference to the Taylorisation of social work. These technologies – and what I have termed elsewhere social work's 'electronic or e-turn' (Garrett, 2009) – are potentially aiding employers' attempts to supervise and regulate places of work and to monitor and track the productivity of individual workers.

Surveying recent developments in Canada, Donna Baines (2004a, p 277) has observed:

> Taylorization has taken place, in part, through the integration of computer packages that increase the pace and volume of work, the gathering of statistics, the monitoring of worker productivity through E-supervision. Some models of E-supervision involve the use of computer-based packages that remind workers of pre-set time limits for certain parts of the job (for example the completion of intake and assessments), the order in which these tasks must be completed and when workers must seek supervisory approval before moving on. The computer package does not permit workers to complete tasks in other than the prescribed order. Failure to complete the tasks on time is reported electronically to the supervisor.

'The social factory': capitalism and the harm caused to health and well-being

Capital describes how the weight of the entire range of social institutions was brought to bear upon the working class in order to prepare them for their new role in economy and society: to turn them into reliable workers and citizens, and to keep them and their children that way. (Worsley, 2002, p 47). As Federici (2004, p 64) observes, at the:

> beginning of capitalist development, we have the impression of being in an immense concentration camp.... In Western Europe, we have the Enclosures, the Witch Hunt, the branding, whipping and incarceration of vagabonds and beggars in newly constructed work-houses and correction houses, models for the future prison system.

Marx, in fact, was particularly intent on illuminating the harm caused to children and other vulnerable people within the sphere of production. Indeed, his perspective lays a very strong emphasis on the welfare of children and he observed that many were treated 'just the same as parts of the machine' (Marx, 1990, p 469). Not only were children apt to be killed, injured or suffer from 'intellectual degeneration artificially produced by transforming immature human beings into mere machines for the production of surplus value' (Marx, 1990, p 523), but due to the employment of mothers, they were victims of 'an unnatural estrangement' from their primary nurturers (Marx, 1990, p 521).

Although gelling with notions related to the 'attachment' needs of children (Bowlby, 1990), opinion on the employment of mothers might strike readers as rather anachronistic in terms of gender politics. Admittedly, sex and gender are not important analytical categories in his theoretical works (Carver, 1998, p 26). Reference is made, however, to gender and power dynamics *inside* the family, in the context of social relations structured and ordered by capital. Thus, male factory operatives are cast in a less-than-heroic light: the 'capitalist buys children and young persons. Previously the worker sold his own labour-power, which he disposed of as a free agent, formally speaking. Now he sells his wife and child. He has become a slave-dealer' (Marx, 1990, p 519). Many male workers, in part accepting free-market ideology, were also indignant that factory legislation jeopardised their own exploitation of their wives and children (MacGregor, 1996).[5]

More broadly, capitalist forms of production damage bodies and minds, shorten workers' lives, and contribute to environmental and ecological devastation (Davis, 2006). In other words, Marx's critique highlights the fact that an economic system driven by the maximisation of capital overrides a traditional core value of social work – 'respect for persons'. In its 'blind and measureless drive, its insatiable appetite for surplus labour, capital … usurps the time for growth, development and healthy maintenance of the body' (Marx, 1990, p 375). It may be argued that Marx's comments are now entirely misplaced because the form of capitalism he describes has now ended, superseded by a more benign, even 'cool capitalism' (McGuigan, 2009). Undoubtedly, capitalist strategies in the early 21st century are markedly different from those of the 19th century, but in our contemporary world:

> the fate of whole strata of populations, and sometimes of whole countries, can be decided by the … speculative dance of Capital, which pursues its goal of profitability with a blessed indifference to the way its movement will affect social reality. That is the fundamental systematic violence of capitalism. (Žižek, 2000, p 15)

Furthermore, across the globe, capitalism continues to injure and mutilate the bodies of workers who continue to 'lose limbs, digits, fingernails, eyes: they develop repetitive strain injuries, respiratory diseases, diseases from exposure to asbestos, pesticides, and other hazardous substances … relations of industrial production are scratched into the body' (Orzeck, 2007, pp 503–4). Transformations in contemporary workscapes have also given rise to a plethora of post-industrial health hazards. The proliferation of work-related complaints such as 'exhaustion, burn-out, alcohol and drug-related problems, premature heart attacks and strokes, and a whole host of mental and emotional problems related to anxiety and depression' are likely to impact on social work and related forms of work (Gill and Pratt, 2008, p 18; see also May, 2005).

Marx's powerful exposé and critique of capitalism casts a revealing light on *present* practices. His concern about the health of workers can also be 'brought into conversation' with more contemporary discourses that circulate around, rather problematic (and often) shallow, notions of 'well-being' and 'happiness'.[6] Without seeking to diminish him to a mere liberal reformer, Marx's perspective is pertinent to issues presently located within a discourse focused on the 'work–life balance'. His insights can also be connected to contemporary struggles resisting attempts to increase the time that people spend working (either within the formal domain of the workplace or at home). Moreover, his work might encourage a critical questioning of employers promoting 'flexibility', activating '24/7' responses and referring to more 'choice' for 'customers'. Within the sphere of social work and social care, following the setting up of the Social Care Register in April 2003, it was:

> clear from the Codes of Practice that being a social care worker is not seen as a nine-to-five job, in which there is left a clear separation of work/home/private life. Indeed, the criteria gave both employers and the General Social Care Council (GSCC), via the registration process, unprecedented regulation over the workforce, whether in office, pub or at home. (McLaughlin, 2007, p 1274; see also McLaughlin, 2010)

Developments such as this reflect some aspects of the thinking of Henry Ford, the US car manufacturer, who – during the period of rapid mass industrialisation around the First World War – was keen to intervene in the private lives of his employees, exerting control over their free time.

As Gramsci predicted, those tendencies, which were only 'latent' then, may become 'at a certain point, state ideology' (quoted in Forgacs, 1988, p 191). Ford's intrusion into the private sphere of individuals is not dissimilar to the surveillance practices undertaken by the GSCC, allegedly to protect the vulnerable public in whose lives social workers intervene.[7] Furthermore, given the aspiration to erode the boundary between home and work, practitioners may, over time, find their workplace 'abolished altogether, or rather dissolved into life' (Bauman, 2002a, p 149).[8]

Offering a more persuasive account than Bauman's 'liquid modernity' formulation, the autonomist current within Marxism, which we will look at in more detail in Chapter Ten, maintains that the 'mass worker' of the Fordist era has been replaced by the 'socialised worker' in 'a new epoch in which the factory is increasingly disseminated out into *society as a whole*' (Gill and Pratt, 2008, p 6, emphasis in original). Autonomists refer to the 'social factory', as opposed to the liberal notion of 'work–life balance', in order to conceptualise how the 'whole life experience of the worker is harnessed to capital' (Gill and Pratt, 2008, p 17). This conceptualisation is 'largely understood in terms of time. Thus, it is 'not so much that work extends across different spaces (the home and, with mobile devices, almost everywhere)', but that the temporality of life becomes governed by work (Gill and Pratt, 2008, p 17). As a Toshiba advertisement campaign maintained in 2006, 'the working day is so yesterday' (quoted in Gregg, 2011, p 34). In this context, 'labour is deterritorialized, dispersed and decentralized' (Gill and Pratt, 2008, p 7), with the whole of society being placed at the disposal of profit.

Conclusion

Having 'recourse to history ... is meaningful to the extent that history serves to show that-which-is has not always been' (Foucault, 1988d, pp 36–7). Reading *Capital* today can also be recognised as part of the struggle to remember. Marx was not *against* change and would have viewed such a stance as futile and preposterous. For him, the 'present society' was 'no solid crystal, but an organism capable of change, and constantly engaged in the process of change' (Marx, 1990, p 93). He recognised that capitalism was, in some senses, an advance on previously and outmoded forms of economic organisation. In a similar vein, Jameson (2000, pp 225–6) urges us to:

> do the impossible, namely to try and think positively and negatively all at once; to achieve ... a type of thinking that would be capable of grasping the demonstrably baleful features of capitalism along with its extraordinary and liberating dynamism simultaneously.... We are somehow to lift our minds to a point at which it is possible to understand that capitalism is at one and the same time the best thing that has ever happened to the human race, and the worst ... catastrophe and progress all together.

In this sense, *Capital* remains, in a number of ways, a useful resource for a more politically alert, activist, anti-capitalist form of social work (see Lavalette, 2011a). However, the task is not to regurgitate Marx's texts, but to extend, revise and adapt them in ways that can address the complexities of our times. In other words, readers need to ascertain if and how his analytical categories and orientation to the world are meaningful for social workers and those working in related fields. Marx's book is rooted in the maxim *De Omnibus Dubitandum* ('We ought to question everything') and this served as his guiding principle. Reading *Capital* might also redirect social workers to become more 'reformist' or 'reform'-oriented. This understanding might appear somewhat odd given that Marx is typically viewed as the creator of an uncompromising blueprint for total revolution. However, *Capital* strongly suggests that Marx saw no contradiction in pursuing reform *and* revolution: the two were, for him, dialectically related and there are no indications that he perceived *meaningful* reform as diluting the possibility of revolution (Marx and Engels, 1978; see also Hobsbawm, 2011, p 61). This understanding is most clearly reflected in Marx's constantly seeking to instigate parliamentary reforms, more specifically, factory legislation, to improve the lot of factory operatives.

Indeed, the Factory Inspectors (in themselves perhaps something of an inspiration for social work) are depicted in a very favourable way and Marx relied on their detailed reports to provide illustrations of the death and hardship that capital was generating (see MacGregor, 1996). In acting in this way, perhaps Marx was also seeking to reveal how forces of counter-hegemony to capitalism might be mobilised within civil society (see Chapter Six). This tactic and the commitment to construct oppositional alliances might have great contemporary resonance for social workers committed to the 'liberation of people', enhancing 'well-being' and ensuring that principles of 'human rights and social justice are fundamental' (IFSW, 2000). In a temporal, economic and political context where the 'social state' is under threat, such ethical commitments are more than discursive ornamentation and need to be embodied in actual social work *praxis*.

Another important dimension to *Capital* is that while it passionately argues for the reform of capitalism, it reaches *beyond* mere reform. That is to say, like those today seeking to counter neoliberal globalisation, the book is rooted in the belief that 'another world is possible' (Klein, 2001) and that there are other ways of being 'modern' (Garrett, 2009). This understanding is vital because, as Marx argued, the 'advance of capitalist production develops a working class which by education, tradition and habit looks upon the requirements of that mode of production as *self-evident natural laws*' (Marx, 1990, p 899, emphasis added). Indeed, in our current period, neoliberalism 'comes to be seen as inevitability' (Bourdieu, 2001b, p 30).

As Chris Harman (2008) makes plain, 'neoliberalism' is a much-debated term. Some, such as Harman himself, are wary of the notion that we are experiencing a new variant of capitalism, which is reflected in new patterns of capital accumulation, heightened levels of exploitation, the erosion of welfare, new levels of insecurity and precarious types of work. His emphasis, and that of a number of other commentators on the left, remains on 'capitalism' and the stress is apt to be placed on the *continuities* between what some regard as 'neoliberalism' and more entrenched and historically prevalent modes of exploitation and resistance. An alternative perspective is detectable in Bourdieu (1998a). The next chapter, therefore, will focus on neoliberalism.

⏮**Reflection and Talk Box 4**⏭

- How might Marx's *Capital* translate into an effective resource for social workers in the first quarter of the 21st century?

- Marx wrote *Capital* in the 19th century: if Marx was writing in the first quarter of the 21st century, what new types of exploitation might interest him?

- How do social work practitioners, students and social work academics *experience* their work across the dimensions of Time, Toil (or labour) and Technology discussed earlier?

- In what ways does capitalism impact on the health and 'well-being' of you and those you provide services for?

- Can a capitalist society treat the welfare of children as 'paramount'?

- Are those working in social work and associated fields able to achieve a satisfactory work–life balance? Can your views be connected to the dynamics of capitalism?

Notes

[1.] The chapter will only focus on the first volume of *Capital*. Tucker (1972) provides a more extensive selection. A different version of this chapter was published as 'Marx and "modernization": reading *Capital* as social critique and inspiration for social work resistance to neoliberalization', *Journal of Social Work*, vol 9, no 2, pp 199–221. I am grateful to Sage Publications for allowing me to make use of my earlier work.

[2.] Marxism 'represents both a form of revolutionary politics and one of the richest and most complex theoretical and philosophical movements in human history' (Young, 2001, p 6). There are many currents within Marxism (for a helpfully accessible summary, see Joseph, 2006). In the 1980s, there emerged a diverse body of theorisation referred to as 'post-Marxism', which is with 'some notable exceptions, an intellectual and academic "practice", as opposed to a revolutionary one' (Tormey and Townshend, 2006, p 4).

[3.] Cruddas (2011) refers to the 'double movement' in capitalism. 'On the one hand, capitalism destroys traditions, families, communities, cultures and yet, on the other, this destruction created alliances, solidarity and resistance to everything becoming a commodity – our land, labour, relationships.'

[4.] Simpkin (1983) and Fabricant (1985) provide early examples. See also Harris (1998, 2003), Jones (2001), Carey (2003, 2008), Baines (2004a, 2004b, 2006, 2010), Ferguson and Lavallette (2004), Dustin (2007), Coleman and Harris (2008), and Munro (2011).

[5.] For a fuller discussion on the theme of Marx and gender, see Terrell Carver (1998, ch 10).

[6.] For texts containing critical engagement with such themes, see Kendall and Harker (2002), Mancini Billson and Fluehr-Lobban (2005), Sointu (2005, 2006), Ferguson (2007), Jordan (2007), and Rustin (2007).

[7.] The UK Coalition government announced in July 2010 that the GSCC was to be abolished and its powers transferred to the Health Professions Council.

[8.] Related to this point, an 'ethic of paid work' has to be balanced by an 'ethic of care' for, as Fiona Williams (2001, p 474) has maintained, there 'exists a fundamental tension between the practical acknowledgment of care and the political privileging of the work ethic' (see also Williams, 2005).

Modernity and the unfinished neoliberal project[1]

Introduction

During the final decade of the 20th century, opposition to 'neoliberalism' became the rallying cry for a wide and disparate conglomeration of 'anti-capitalist' groups. This opposition was, however, in contrast to the parties of the mainstream parliamentary left. As Hobsbawm (2011, p 396) observed shortly after the economic 'crash', no leader from any party of the 'European left in the past twenty-five years has declared capitalism to be unacceptable as a system'. Perhaps, rather surprisingly, the only public figure to do so 'unhesitatingly was Pope John Paul II' (Hobsbawn, 2011, p 396). This was particularly apparent in a encyclical on 'human work', which was published shortly after Ronald Reagan became US President and Margaret Thatcher and her first administration were installing neoliberalism in the UK (Pope John Paul II, 1981). Even read over 30 years later, the pamphlet remains remarkable in that it is a trenchant defence of workers' rights within functioning social democracy (see Table 5.1).[2]

Table 5.1: The Pope's defence of workers' rights in a period of neoliberalisation

Stressed the need for 'new movements of solidarity of the workers and with the workers' (p 30).
Concerned about the 'violation of the dignity of human work' and the 'scourge of human unemployment' (p 30).
Emphasised a principle 'that has always been taught by the Church: the principle of the priority of labour over capital' (p 30).
Gave 'prominence to the primacy of man [sic] in the production process, the primacy of man over things' (p 44).
Maintained that the 'right to private property is subordinated to the right of common use' (p 51).
Criticised 'rigid capitalism' (p 52).
Argued that workers 'should be assured of the right to strike, without being subjected to personal penal sanctions for taking part in a strike' (p 76).

Source: Pope John Paul II (1981).

The following decade, the Pope returned to the same theme in an interview published in Turin's *La Stampa* newspaper. Here, he criticised unbridled capitalism and said that, for all its faults, communism had some positive aspects and 'seeds of truth' that should be preserved. The pontiff also said that there were some countries in the world where capitalism was still 'almost as savage' as it was at the end of the 19th century. Moreover, the 'proponents of extreme capitalism, in any form, tend to overlook the good things achieved by Communism, the struggle against unemployment, the concern for the poor'. In the Eastern Bloc, the cost for this was 'paid for by the degradation of many other sectors of the lives of citizens'. Nevertheless, the more 'humane facets of capitalism had developed 'in large part thanks to socialist thought' and the struggle of the trade unions (*The Independent*, 1993).

Over recent years, it has been recognised in Europe and elsewhere that neoliberalism has had a major impact on the trajectory of social work (Ferguson, 2008; Garrett, 2009). The private sector, for example, has become increasingly important with regard to the 'delivery' of care for older people since the NHS and Community Care Act 1990, and this has been particularly the case in the adult and learning disability sectors, where large corporate providers now dominate the market (Harris, 2003). Residential care is now 'a commodity … there to be traded and exploited for its surplus value like any other commodity' and, as a consequence, 'the quest for profitability means that business values, reductions in costs and income generation have been prioritised over and above the quality of care' (Scourfield, 2007, pp 162, 170). Indeed, in 2011, the abuses committed against residents at the Castlebeck-owned Winterbourne View hospital and the financial affairs of the care home chain Southern Cross highlighted again some of the problems attached to privatisation (Coward, 2011; Scourfield, 2012).

The private sector's role in providing children's homes and related children's services is increasing as a number of local councils, such as Essex, seek to sell off residential services (Pemberton, 2011). There has also been a 'stampede of private equity firms into the foster-care sector' (Mathiason, 2007). Under the New Labour administration, the *Care matters* agenda which has mapped the future direction of services for children and young people in public care also emphasised the role of the private sector, not only in terms of the promotion of 'social work practices', but in a more pervasive sense (Secretary of State for Education and Skills, 2006; Le Grand, 2007). In seeking to provide a 'first class education' for 'looked after' children, for example, it maintained that for some children, private boarding schools 'provide an excellent means of stability and support' (Secretary of State for Education and Skills, 2006, pp 59–60). Related to this emphasis on the role of the private sector, the government was keen to highlight the role of HSBC (Hong Kong and Shanghai Banking Corporation) in funding private tutoring for children in care (Secretary of State for Education and Skills, 2006, p 65; Department for Education and Skills, 2007, p 76). More generally it has been asserted that 'major companies' do 'valuable work with vulnerable children and young people in the community as part of their corporate social responsibility programmes, increasing their access to structured leisure activities and the world of work' (Department for Education and Skills, 2007, p 102). However, this 'world of work' is never historicised, and rarely interrogated or examined.

This chapter will examine how neoliberalism – often discursively constructed as a politically, economically and socially neutral form of 'modernisation' – can be understood in terms of its key elements. The chapter will furnish readers with an accessible synthesis of some of neoliberalism's main components. It aims to provide an introductory resource for educators and students keen to bring into view the 'bigger picture', which, on occasion – partly on account of the imposition of tightly controlled and centrally devised curricula – risks being elided, subjugated or obscured during the period of professional formation in social work and associated fields.

Defining neoliberalism

Those seeking to grasp the meaning of neoliberalism should be attentive to at least six overlapping and interconnected dimensions: how we might define neoliberalism in relation to the 'embedded liberalism' it endeavoured to supplant; the role of the state; the concept of 'accumulation by dispossession' and its corollary redistribution in favour of the rich; the centrality of insecurity and precariousness; the renewed and retrogressive faith in incarceration and, more broadly, what has been termed the 'new punitiveness' (Pratt et al, 2005); and the incongruence between neoliberal rhetoric and practice. In conclusion, the chapter will focus on the crisis, which initially began to be detectable in 2006 and then erupted in 2008, and its implications – still far from clear – for the neoliberal project.

Erasing 'embedded liberalism'

For Pierre Bourdieu, neoliberalism is best perceived as a:

> conservative revolution' that 'ratifies and glorifies the reign of ... the financial markets, in other words the return of the kind of radical capitalism, with no other law than the return of maximum profit, an unfettered capitalism ... pushed to the limits. (Bourdieu, 2001b, p 35)

More theoretically, we can perhaps comprehend neoliberalism as seeking to succeed the type of 'embedded liberalism' that was dominant in most of the industrial West from the end of the Second World War to the 1970s (see Hall et al, 1978; Hall and Jacques, 1989). During this period, 'market processes and entrepreneurial and corporate activities were surrounded by a web of social and political constraints and a regulatory environment that sometimes restrained ... economic and industrial strategy' (Harvey, 2005, p 11). In contrast, the neoliberal project seeks to 'disembed capital from these constraints' (Harvey, 2005, p 11). Thus, to different degrees, depending on the specific cultural and national context, neoliberalisation 'seeks to strip away the protective coverings that embedded liberalism allowed and occasionally nurtured' (Harvey, 2005, p 168). Neoliberalism seeks to inject a fresh and reinvigorated emphasis on 'competition' at all levels of society, including those areas of life and social interaction previously perceived as *beyond* the reach of competition and commodification (Cooper, 2008). Indeed, the 'survival of the fittest and Social Darwinism have been given a new impetus by neoliberal globalization, after their post-Fascist quarantine' (Therborn, 2007, p 75).

Neoliberalisation is a process entailing:

> much 'creative destruction', not only of prior institutional frameworks and powers (even challenging traditional forms of state sovereignty) but also divisions of labour, social relations, welfare provisions, technological mixes, ways of life and thought, reproductive activities, attachments to the land and habits of the heart. (Harvey, 2005, p 3)

Thus, the aim has been to install a new 'common sense' and to ensure that people begin to *think* and *act* in a manner conducive to neoliberalism (Forgacs, 1988). Indeed, it has been argued that neoliberalism:

> has been ingested into the body politic so successfully that it has become the prevailing commonsense of everyday life.... Just as in the aftermath of the Second World War we all became 'social democratic subjects' in one way or another, we may have now become similarly constituted as 'neoliberal subjects', in ways that we do not fully recognise. (Thompson, 2008, p 68)

In this way, neoliberalisation can be perceived as bound up with an individual's sense of self, setting in motion and sustaining a multiplicity of 'identity projects' that are compatible with capitalism. Related to this, in terms of working practices, neoliberalism favours 'flexibility' and is hostile to all forms of social solidarity and identification that can potentially restrain capital accumulation (Brown, 2003).

Neoliberalism seeks to *remake* work and workscapes and to alter the aims, aspirations and affiliations of a range of professional groups and fields (Garrett, 2003, 2009). This, in turn, is likely to prompt resistance because those providing and those receiving social work services, for example, are unlikely to quietly accept some of the more troubling dimensions of neoliberal 'modernisation'. For example, people – be they the providers or users (and these categories are, moreover, fluid) – are apt to 'find ways of surviving, negotiating, accommodating, refusing and resisting' and do not merely 'act like automatons envisaged in the governmental plans and strategies of the powerful' (Clarke, 2005, p 159).

The global imposition of neoliberalism has 'been highly uneven, both socially and geographically, and its institutional forms and socio-political consequences have varied significantly' (Brenner and Theodore, 2002, p ix). Consequently, when seeking to examine developments in different national settings, it remains important to recognise that neoliberalism, rather like McDonalds, comes to speak the 'local language'. This 'implies thinking about neoliberalism in ways that foreground "unevenness", rather than a fluid spread across a flat landscape' (Clarke, 2004, p 94). In the case of the UK, during the Blair administrations (1997–2007), the 'Third Way' provided an intellectual foundation or narrative for New Labour's shift towards neoliberal policy 'innovations' and 'solutions' (see also Giddens, 1998, 2003). Indeed, it can be viewed as the dominant discourse through which restructuring proceeded and 'through which the meanings of welfare, work and Labour' were remade (Haylett, 2001, p 44). As observed earlier, Giddens was the key figure within the New Labour intelligentsia and, even if his ideas, preoccupations and prejudices did not always result in specific 'reforms' to welfare programmes and practices, they provided the atmosphere or 'mood music' for New Labour 'modernisation' (Giddens, 2001, 2007; see also Chapter Two). More fundamentally, the 'Third Way' was a neoliberal way and under 'Blair and Brown, the City of London was pumped up into the most deregulated trading centre in the world' (Watkins, 2010, p 13).

Throughout the period of New Labour, an embedded neoliberal rationality characterised the party's vision. This is not, of course, to argue that the former government's *entire* project of organisational, thematic and professional 'reform' focused on social work was unambiguously rooted in neoliberalism. Nonetheless, neoliberalism served, often implicitly, to provide the dominant, or hegemonic, core for the 'transformation' of children's services and associated sectors and spheres (see Garrett, 2009). Some academics and political commentators maintained that New Labour's neoliberalism was 'an uncomfortable and strained construction rather than an essential political character' (Clarke et al, 2007, p 146). However, following Blair's ascendancy, the party became increasingly comfortable with the neoliberal agenda. What Stuart Hall (2003, p 19) referred to as the 'subaltern programme, of a more social-democratic kind' became much more subdued, increasingly marginal and marginalised.

None of this is, of course, to suggest that the Conservative–Liberal Democrat Coalition, with its 'cocktail of born-again monetarism and regressive social policies', is preferable for social workers in Britain (Elliott, 2010, p 26). The emphasis that David Cameron has placed on the role of philanthropy and charity in providing what are now public services has made it plain that his party's vision of the 'future' is likely to be even more damaging than that imagined by the defeated Labour administration (see Finlayson, 2007; Toynbee, 2010a). Ideas rooted in the notion that Britain is a 'broken society' are central to the hegemonic endeavours of the present government (Cameron, 2010). For the Conservatives especially, the 'broken society' is 'the baleful outcome of social-democratic politics' and the 'source of the corrosion of social life can be found in the excesses of government' (Finlayson, 2010, pp 25–6). Unsurprisingly the 'effects of neoliberal competitiveness and inequality are... ignored' (Finlayson, 2010, p 26). For the ruling administration, the solution to the 'broken society' is to construct a 'Big Society' (Ellison, 2011). According to Cameron, this 'is about a real cultural shift – we know that the era of big government ... didn't work. We want to build a Big Society where local people feel empowered' (Cabinet Office, 2010, p 1). However, it remains clear that the government is intent on cutting jobs and services within the public sector and the political aspiration is to usher in 'eternal austerity' and a 'permanently shrunken state' (Toynbee, 2010b, p 27). This political project furnished the economic and social context for the riots during the summer of 2011 (Klein, 2011).

Reshaping the state

The core function of the neoliberal state is to furnish an 'apparatus whose fundamental mission [is to] facilitate conditions for profitable capital accumulation on the part of both domestic and foreign capital' (Harvey, 2005, p 7). The key point is that processes of neoliberalisation seek to *retool, reconfigure, radically change and remake the state, its role and core functions.* In this sense, therefore, Osborne and Gaebler's (1992) popular and influential work in the early 1990s and notions such as 'reinventing government' and creating government intent on 'steering not rowing' are entirely consistent with the process of neoliberal reconfiguration.

A misguided perspective maintains that neoliberalisation heralds a relentless and irrepressible 'rolling back' of the state with the 'market' and 'market mechanisms' being *entirely* left to 'take over' society. However, within the neoliberal paradigm, the state *continues* to play an active role in that it creates and preserves an 'institutional framework' for capital (Brenner and Theodore, 2002; Munck, 2005). Here, Harvey's (2010, p 48) 'state–finance nexus' conceptualisation, 'a confluence of state and financial power that confounds the analytic tendency to see state and capital as clearly separable from each other', is insightful. The 'state–finance nexus' functions as 'the "central nervous system" for capital accumulation' (Harvey, 2010, p 54). Moreover, each state possesses its own shifting and fluid nexus, which becomes the focus of struggle for defining some sort of 'rough consensus' as to how social life will be regulated and ordered (Harvey, 2010, p 63). Beyond the nation-state constellation, there is also a global 'architecture for an international version of the state–finance nexus' (Harvey, 2010, p 51); hence the operation of the World Bank, the IMF, G20 and so on.

Since a second phase of global neoliberalism began in the 1990s, there has been more of a commitment on the part of governments to *roll out* new policies rather than *roll back* the state (see also Munck, 2005); hence the emphasis on 'positive' or 'proactive' state interventions evident in policies pivoting on 'activating' the unemployed (or 'jobseekers') and in discourses and practices focused on 'social inclusion' and 'prevention' (Garrett, 2009). Specifically in relation to social work, recent years have also witnessed something of a 'boom', with the profession becoming a 'growth industry even in countries that ideologically would rather do without it' (Lorenz, 2005). Despite the 'anti-big government' rhetoric often associated with neoliberalism, there has been little diminution in the actual size of governments in the West. Indeed, 'big government' has not gone away even in a world supposedly governed by neoliberal rules. Capitalism can 'no more do without the state today that it could do in the Keynesian period' (Harman, 2008, p 97), as initially illustrated during the Northern Rock crisis in the UK in 2007 and in the subsequent response of the US administration to the collapse of the investment banks the following year (Jacques, 2008). The neoliberal state remains, therefore, a variegated and dispersed amalgam, which also includes spaces, of course, for potential opposition. As Bourdieu (2001b, p 34) reminds us, it is simply not convincing to baldly claim, as some more mechanistic interpreters of Marxism may do, that the state is merely:

> an instrument in the hands of the ruling class. The state is certainly not completely neutral, completely independent of the dominant forces in society, but the older it is and the greater the social advances it has incorporated the more autonomous it is. It is a battlefield.

It is also important to recognise that the 'state is not a "thing" reducible to fixed, static boundaries but an active and creative process of institution-building and intervention' (Coleman and Sim, 2005, p 104). The neoliberal state has, in fact, multiple identities and multiple boundaries. So, elaborating on Bourdieu's metaphor, the state may be less a 'battlefield' and more an expansive terrain on which occurs a series of *seemingly* discrete and unconnected skirmishes.

Restoring class power

Whatever *local* shape it may take in specific places and at specific times, neoliberalism remains a philosophy and series of practices that universally aspires to restore class power through vast transfers of income to the richest groups in society. Figures released by the US government on children (0–17 years) reveal that, in 2009, 21% (15.5 million) lived in poverty. This marked an increase up from 16% in 2000 and 2001. In 2009, 36% of black children, 33% of Hispanic children and 12% of white, non-Hispanic children lived in poverty. These are increases from 35%, 29% and 10%, respectively, in 2007. Significantly, the percentage of children who lived in families with very high incomes (600% or more of the poverty threshold) nearly doubled, from 7% in 1991 to 13% in 2009 (ChildStats.gov, 2011). Merrill Lynch has reported that the world's 'high net worth individuals' (HNWIs) 'expanded in population and wealth in 2010 surpassing 2007 pre-crisis levels in nearly every region'. Moreover, the 'global population of Ultra-HNWIs grew by 10.2% in 2010 and its wealth by 11.5%' (Merrill Lynch and Capgemini, 2011).

The main 'substantive achievement of neoliberalization … has been to redistribute, rather than to generate, wealth and income' (Harvey, 2005, p 159). This 'accumulation by dispossession', Harvey explains, is nothing but the 'continuation and proliferation of accumulation practices which Marx had treated as "primitive" or "original" during the rise of capitalism' (Harvey, 2005, p 159). Some of the characteristics of this dispossessing dynamic include the corporatisation, commodification and privatisation of hitherto public assets and the opening up of 'new fields for capital accumulation in domains hitherto regarded off-limits to the calculus of profitability' (Harvey, 2005, p 160). Moreover, the state:

> once neoliberalized, becomes a prime agent of retributive policies, *reversing* the flow from the upper classes that had occurred during the era of embedded liberalism. It does this in the first instance through the pursuit of privatization schemes and cutbacks in those state expenditures that support the social wage. (Harvey, 2005, p 163, emphasis added)

'Accumulation by dispossession' also includes reneging on key commitments negotiated with trade unions in relation to wages and the terms and conditions of employment, including pensions. Since the ending of corporate 'partnership' arrangements – involving the government, trade unions and the private sector – the Republic of Ireland has provided a good example of this form of attack. In the UK, so-called 'austerity' measures, and ideas associated with the 'Big Society', have provided a discursive foundation for strategies of 'dispossession'. The 'fundamental mission' is to 'create a "good business climate" and therefore to optimize conditions for capital accumulation no matter what the consequences for employment or social well-being' (Harvey, 2006b, p 25). Thus, the:

> neo-liberal state is particularly assiduous in seeking the privatization of assets as a means to open up fresh fields for capital accumulation. Sectors formerly run or regulated by the state (transportation, telecommunications, oil and other natural resources, utilities, social housing, education) are turned over to the private sphere or deregulated. (Harvey, 2006b, p 25; see also Cooper, 2008; Federici, 2011)

Rendering insecure and precarious

A fourth defining characteristic of neoliberalism can be associated with the aspiration to inject new forms of insecurity into people's working lives. This new insecurity, impinging on social workers and on the lives of many of those engaging with them, is frequently discussed in terms of 'precariousness'. As Luann Good Goodrich (2010, p 109) observes, in the past three

> decades workers across the globe have been confronted by a general deterioration and narrowing of their employment options. Research shows such trends are resulting in deepening poverty, widening income and wealth inequalities, and a rise in part-time, low-wage, unregulated, and temporary work.

While Bourdieu (2001b) comments on the 'precarious generation', Gill and Pratt's (2008) discussion on Autonomist Marxist writers, whom we will return to in Chapter Ten, provides a particularly useful theoretical explanation of precarity. They maintain that 'precariousness, precarity and precarization have recently emerged as a novel territory for thinking – and intervening in – labour and life' (Gill and Pratt, 2008, p 3). For them, precariousness 'refers to all forms of insecure, contingent, flexible work – from illegalized, casualized and temporary employment, to homeworking, piecework and freelancing' (Gill and Pratt, 2008, p 3). Precarity 'is a form of exploitation which operates primarily at the level of time, evaporating distinctions, between work and leisure, production and consumption' (Gill and Pratt, 2008, p 17). What is interesting in Gill and Pratt's interpretation, however, is that, for them, precarity also contains possibilities for hope and resistance:

> [it] signifies both the multiplication of precarious, unstable, insecure forms of living and, simultaneously, new forms of political struggle and solidarity that reach beyond the traditional models of the political party or trade union. This *double meaning* is central to understanding the ideas and politics associated with precarity: the new moment of capitalism that engenders precariousness is seen as not only oppressive but also as offering the potential for new subjectivities, new socialities and a new kind of politics. (Gill and Pratt, 2008, p 3, emphasis in original)

Consequently, precarity 'embodies a critique of contemporary capitalism in tandem with an optimistic sense of potential change' (Gill and Pratt, 2008, p 10). Moreover, precarity activism, and what they even dub the 'precarity movement', is a creative, frequently youthful, activism that often involves web-based subversion and organisation.[3] In this formulation, therefore, the 'precariat' is a 'neologism that brings together the meanings of precariousness and proletariat to signify both an experience of exploitation and a (potential) new political subjectivity' (Gill and Pratt, 2008, p 3).

Others such as Bourdieu and Harvey are far less optimistic about the progressive and radical possibilities connected to precariousness. For Harvey, the 'figure of the "disposable worker" now emerges as prototypical upon the world stage' (Harvey, 2005, p 169). His analysis, which is more clearly aligned with a classical Marxist perspective, is keener to stress how this development is related to what Marx called the 'industrial reserve army' and the usefulness for capital of workers who remain 'accessible, socialised, disciplined and of the requisite qualities (i.e. flexible, docile, manipulable and skilled when necessary)' (Harvey, 2010, p 58). Moreover, unemployment seeks to 'rediscipline labour to accept a lower wage rate' and inferior terms and conditions of employment (Harvey, 2010, p 60). Indeed, neoliberal theory maintains that 'unemployment is always voluntary. Labour, the argument goes, has a "reserve price" below which it prefers not to work. Unemployment arises because the reserve price is too high' (Harvey, 2005, p 53). In this context, it is apt to be maintained that this 'reserve price' is partly set by welfare benefits (within the neoliberal lexicon ordinarily referred to disparagingly as 'handouts').

A good deal of the 'welfare reform' and the wider *remaking* of welfare undertaken across a range of jurisdictions have been founded on this neoliberal perspective (Rutherford, 2007). Thus, the neoliberal rationality 'reaches beyond the market, extending and disseminating market values to all institutions and social action so that individuals are conceptualized as rational, entrepreneurial actors whose moral authority is determined by their capacity for autonomy and self-care' (Baker, 2009, p 277). The role of 'welfare reform' and 'welfare-to-work' initiatives becomes that of installing mechanisms that serve to orient the unwaged into the low-wage zones of the employment market. Thus, a panoply of employment 'activation' programmes introduce new means of surveillance to monitor and track 'job-seeking' activities, to mentor, coach and compel (Bunting, 2009). In this way, the unemployed are subjected – at the micro-level – to 'structural adjustments' to their lifestyles, hopes and aspirations:

> In general, across all levels of globalized labor markets, we see a trend toward short-term contract work, resulting in deepening employment instability and an overall demand for flexible workers who are ready and able to make repeated and rapid adjustments in their work schedules, relevant skills and knowledge, and place of residence. Workfare programs exemplify the co-ordering of activities and people by the state and economic markets. (Good Goodrich, 2010, p 108)

Such programmes 'serve to discipline the whole workforce', in that they operate to, for example, 'support and sustain the secondary, low-wage labor market through the steady supply of suitably flexible and compliant workers who have learned, out of necessity, to contend with instability, uncertainty and vulnerability' (Good Goodrich, 2010, p 131). In the UK, these programmes are also, following the US model, apt to involve outsourcing to private, profit-making providers such as Ingeus Deloitte, Serco and A4e (Toynbee, 2011a). What is more, across a range of jurisdictions, social workers are becoming incorporated into the management of 'labour market training programmes' targeted at particular groups, such as those with 'mental health problems' (see, eg, Roets et al, 2011).

As a number of feminist researchers have illustrated, this has specific consequences for women who are unemployed or low-waged (see Williams, 2011). Good Goodrich (2010), for example, has investigated single mothers' experience of workfare in Ontario. Consistent with previous research from the US, New Zealand, the UK and Europe, women interviewed 'described the intertwined procedures through which workfare is delivered to be: random and limiting employment programs; ambiguous and complex regulations; capricious and punitive service delivery; and managed precariousness' (Good Goodrich, 2010, p 111). While her findings are partly specifically related to specific trajectories of neoliberalisation in Canada, they also reveal how 'signature elements' of welfare-to-work programmes are common across national boundaries. In Ontario province, this includes: assisted job search; mandatory employment readiness programmes; compulsory 'volunteering'; short-term work preparation; and the threat of benefit withdrawal.

The idea that labour should be malleable, flexible and compliant is the core, recurring and unifying chord that echoes throughout Good Goodrich's 'signature themes'. Potential labour must be 'ready' and able to exhibit – in demeanours and dispositions – that it can add to processes of capital accumulation without destabilising them. In Foucauldian terms, this may hint at surveilled labour being reduced to a form of 'dressage' (Jackson and Carter, 1998). Expressed more baldly, workfare simply aims to 'put manners' on the working class (see Standing, 2011).

Renewing faith in the prison and the emergence of 'prisonfare'

Loïc Wacquant, using a 'single analytical frame' to observe the parallel developments in social welfare and crime control, reveals how 'precarious fractions of the urban proletariat' are now subject to the 'programmatic convergence and practical interlock' of workfare and the prison system: what he terms 'prisonfare' (Wacquant, 2009, pp xx–xxi; see also Wacquant, 2002). Despite Wacquant's perspective, most accounts of capitalism's trajectory since the early 1970s fail to consider neoliberalism's faith in the efficacy of the prison and wider strategies of containment (Harvey, 2005). Clearly relying on a strong, interventionist state, this expansion of the penal field clashes with previously mentioned readings of neoliberalism, which simplistically and unduly emphasise 'rollback'. Although the private sector is fulfilling a larger role in the penal sector, the 'doctrine of "small government" and the policy of downsizing public employment have not applied to penal confinement' (Wacquant, 2005a, p 9).

The tremendous increase of numbers in prison could, therefore, be interpreted as the 'hidden face' of the neoliberal model and the necessary counterpart to the restructuring of welfare. In this sense, it is legitimate to refer to the 'penalisation of poverty', designed to manage the effects of neoliberal policies at 'the lower end of the social structure of advanced societies' (Wacquant, 2001a, p 401). The sheer scale of the penal state in the US reveals how the growth in prison numbers is approximately coterminous with the rise of neoliberalism. After 1973, the confined population 'doubled in ten years and quadrupled in twenty' (Wacquant, 2001a, p 114). If it were 'a city, the carceral system of the United States would be the fourth-largest metropolis, behind Chicago' (Wacquant, 2001a, p 114).

While mostly concerned with developments in the US, Wacquant's analysis is applicable to the UK and elsewhere in Europe. Although the present Coalition is seeking to reduce the size of the penal estate as part of a programme of public sector spending cuts, the prison population grew by approximately 40% during the period of New Labour governments: by the summer of 2010, it had reached a record level of over 85,000.[4] The former Brown administration was also intent on creating three 1,500-place prisons as it prepared to increase capacity to 96,000 by 2016. In the Republic of Ireland, the number of people being sent to prison merely for failing to pay fines or debts continues to escalate and most of the prisons within the state are now operating at, or beyond, capacity. The population of serving prisoners is more than 4,000, twice the number behind bars 20 years ago.

As Wacquant suggests, we also need to be mindful of how the domains of 'prison' and 'welfare' are enmeshed in often complex and contradictory ways. As he suggests, the '"clients" of both assistantial and penitential sectors of the state fall under the same principled suspicion: they are considered morally deficient unless they periodically provide visible proof to the contrary' (Wacquant, 2001a, p 15). This was certainly apparent in terms of the New Labour approach to 'jobseekers', which endeavoured to extend the surveillance of claimants begun during the periods of Thatcher and Major. Moreover, the discursive presentation of 'welfare reform' under New Labour tended to gel with Wacquant's perspective. For example, an influential 'independent report' published by the Department for Work and Pensions published in late 2008 to envision 'a radically reformed welfare system between now and 2015', casually referred to some benefit recipients, 'found to be playing the system', as 'repeat offenders' (Gregg, 2008, pp 5, 8, 15).

A more socially pervasive 'new punitiveness' (Pratt et al, 2005) is also central to neoliberalism's mode of social regulation. This can be associated with the tendency to locate particular sections of the population (those regarded as ambiguously 'troublesome' or ambiguously out of place) within enclosures that may not in the ordinary sense of the word be 'prisons', but which remain zones of varying degrees of confinement and supervision (Guillari and Shaw, 2005). What is more, there is a related aspiration to use technology to track the troublesome in the 'community'. Indeed, it is now possible to detect a 'whole variety of paralegal forms of confinement ... including pre-emptive or preventive detention prior to a crime being committed' (Rose, 2000, p 335). These are targeted at, for example, *potential* paedophiles and *potential* terrorists – 'monstrous individuals', the 'incorrigibly anti-social' and other representatives of a 'new human kind' (Rose, 2000, p 333).

Being pragmatic and 'actually existing neoliberalism'

There is a need to be cautious and distinguish between 'neoliberalism as a system of thought and actually existing neoliberalism' (Munck, 2005, p 60). Certainly, a 'disjuncture' or discrepancy is detectable between the theory and rhetoric of neoliberalism and its pragmatics. First, the state has not been driven back in the way desired by ideologues such as Friedrich Hayek (Klein, 2007). Second, we are 'dealing here less with a coherently bounded "ism" or "end-state" than with a process ... neoliberalization' (Brenner and Theodore, 2002, p 6).

Neoliberals are rarely presented with a bare landscape on which to operate. Only after natural disasters or in post-war and post-invasion scenarios do we witness what Naomi Klein (2007) calls neoliberal-inspired 'disaster capitalism'. More frequently, however, neoliberal 'transformation' projects are 'path-dependent' (Brenner and Theodore, 2002, p 3) and are apt to falter due to their forced engagement with those ingrained cultural legacies and expectations, those ways of *seeing* and *doing*, which are averse to neoliberal 'common sense', its values and dominant orientations. Nevertheless, neoliberalism is resilient, has a 'dogged dynamism' and 'fails forward' (Peck, 2010). The willingness to be pragmatic and to reconfigure the 'state–finance nexus' is highlighted in the responses to the economic crisis that began to unfold from 2006.

The 'sucker could go down': a crisis for capital and neoliberalisation

In urging congressional leaders to pass the US$700 billion bailout plan 10 days after the Lehman Brothers' collapse, on 15 September 2008, President George W. Bush was reported to have confided: 'If money isn't loosened up, this sucker could go down' (quoted in Callinicos, 2010, pp 93–4).[5] In short, if Congress did not make available this massive package of aid to respond to the liquidity crisis, then the entire capital banking and financial system risked total collapse. The state had to act decisively and respond quickly to an unprecedented crisis. At the 'epicentre of the problem was the mountain of "toxic" mortgage-backed securities held by banks or marketed to unsuspecting investors all around the world' (Harvey, 2010, p 2). As Harvey (2010, p 1) notes:

> Something ominous began to happen in the United States in 2006. The rate of foreclosures on housing in low income areas of older cities like Cleveland and Detroit suddenly leapt upwards. But officialdom and the media took no notice because the people affected were low income, mainly African-American, immigrant (Hispanics) or women single-headed households…. It was only in mid-2007, when the foreclosure wave hit the white urban middle class … that officialdom started to take note…. By the end of 2007, nearly 2 million people had lost their homes and 4 million more were thought to be in danger of foreclosure.

The 'crash' began, therefore, as the bursting of a speculative bubble in the US housing market associated with the rapid growth of 'predatory lending' during the 1990s and 2000s. However, the expansion of the subprime market had deeper structural roots symbolising the process of 'financialization in advanced capitalist societies, as even the poorest became identified as worthwhile – that is, profitable – people to lend money to' (Callinicos, 2010, p 24).

By the autumn of 2008, the crisis had resulted – through change of status, forced mergers or bankruptcy – in the demise of all the major Wall Street investment banks. Most of the world was engulfed as the crisis 'cascaded from one sphere to another and from one geographical location to another, with all manner of knock-on and feedback effects that seemed almost impossible to bring under control, let alone halt and turn back' (Harvey, 2010, p 38).

'Nationalise to save the free market': reconfiguring the neoliberal project

This exhortation to nationalise came from *The Financial Times* on 13 October 2008. Indeed, a new 'common sense' quickly evolved for, as the banking system melted and the world slipped into recession, 'it was the state that came to the rescue with nationalizations, bailouts and fiscal stimuli' (Callinicos, 2010, pp 95–6). Moreover, supranational institutions, such as the International Monetary Fund (IMF) and the European Central Bank (ECB), also played a key role in recalibrating the 'state–finance nexus'.

The outgoing Bush administration enacted the Emergency Economic Stabilization Act 2008. In the UK, the Banking (Special Provisions) Act 2008 provided the government with the power to acquire failing banks and this legislation has been used to bring about the part-nationalisation of a number of banks and associated financial institutions. In France, President Sarkozy declared: 'Laissez faire is finished. The all-powerful market which is always right is finished' (quoted in Callinicos, 2010, p 5). Such statements and the measures being introduced to try and counter the crisis *seemed* to run entirely counter to the rhetoric of neoliberalism and would have been viewed as outlandish by the political mainstream only months previously. The 'very governments at the heart of the deregulated global markets organized mammoth rescues of institutions bankrupted…. These amounted to the greatest nationalizations in world history' (Callinicos, 2010, p 8). Do these developments signal, therefore, the end of the neoliberalism that encompassed most of the world for the 35 years spanning 1973–2008? Harvey's (2010, p 10) answer is instructive:

> The answer depends on what is meant by neoliberalism. My view is that it refers to a class project that coalesced in the crisis of the 1970s. Masked by a lot of rhetoric about individual freedom, liberty, personal responsibility and the virtues of privatisation, the free market and free trade, it legitimised draconian policies designed to restore and consolidate capitalism class power. The project has been successful, judging by the incredible centralisation of wealth and power observable in all those countries that took the neoliberal road. And there is no evidence that it is dead.

However, it is 'certain that the Anglo-American model of world economic development that dominated in the post-Cold War period of free market triumphalism in the 1990s was discredited' (Harvey, 2010, p 38). It is also possible to identify, one again, a cyclical movement that is integral to capitalism. That is to say, 'classical' market liberalism requires the forcible disembedding of economic relations from the social context, a move that proves unsustainable in the long run, provoking a reaction back to a measure of social protection. In this sense, neoliberalism can be interpreted as representing 'a reversion back to classical liberalism's attempt to disembed market exchanges from wider social relations'. Perhaps now, in a 'further swing of the pendulum', a reaction 'in favour of embedded liberalism' *may be* being generated (Callinicos, 2010, p 130, emphasis added). Indeed, what Hobsbawm (2008) has termed the 'most serious crisis of the capitalist system since 1929–33' has prompted some to argue that fundamental economic transitions may be under way and that we are witnessing a financial 'regime change' *within* capitalism (Wade, 2008). This is not to argue that the period of neoliberalism has ended. Rather, what is occurring is a reconfiguration of the neoliberal project and a rebalancing of the 'state–finance nexus' within and beyond sovereign states.

By mid-2009, many US and UK banks had:

> recovered their nerve, simultaneously demanding government austerity and promising their staff yet more bonuses. But the greater profits reported by stronger banks such as Goldman's, JP Morgan, Barclays and HSBC derived both from the elimination of rivals that had gone bust and from massive state support (for example, access to virtually free money from the central banks). (Callinicos, 2010, pp 92–3)

By 2011, many of the UK's wealthiest residents had recouped the losses they had suffered. According to *The Sunday Times'* annual 'Rich List', the UK's richest were worth £396 billion, a figure just below that recorded at the peak of the boom in 2008 ('Forget cuts and austerity. For the rich it's like the recession never happened', *The Guardian*, 9 May, 2011, p 3; see also Elliott, 2011).

Presently, the dominant approach appears to be one of 'macro-Keynesianism and micro-neoliberalism' (Callinicos, 2010, p 129). That is say, states are willing to intervene financially to safeguard and prop up the corporate banking sector, but workers and the unemployed continue to be targeted for punitive and coercive interventions. More generally, the aim is to privatise profits and socialise risks. This was the dynamic that prompted Dimitris Christoulas, a 77-year-old retired pharmacist, to shoot himself in the head in front of the Greek Parliament building in April 2012. This despairing, suicidal protest against neoliberal 'austerity' measures is now as tragically iconic as the self-immolation of Mohammed Bouazizi in Tunisia two years earlier (Smith, 2012).

Moreover, at the time of writing, it remains apparent that the economic crisis is not over. As Massey (2010, p 7) has maintained, for 'now, normality (the normality of the last thirty years)' appears to have been restored. However, this is likely to be a period of fragile and tenuous stabilisation. In just one week in August 2011, for example, almost £150 billion was wiped off Britain's top 100 companies. During the same period, with stock markets experiencing their worst week since the collapse of Lehman Brothers, US$2.5 trillion was eliminated from the value of global shares (Hutton, 2011). To differing degrees across the various states in the eurozone, the problems are apparent. Greece faces a financial meltdown and has been compelled to sell off state assets by the IMF/ECB/EU troika. A similar 'solution' is likely to be imposed on Italy and Spain. Meanwhile, in the Republic of Ireland, the first country in the eurozone to adopt a neoliberal-infused 'austerity budget', the unemployment rate is 14% and the ill-judged state bailout of the banks and acceptance of their liabilities – 'the greatest piece of social vandalism since Cromwell' (Browne, 2011) – is costing billions of euros.

A more general concern is the 'post-democratic turn' identifiable in parts of Europe. Thus, post-political forms of rule are emerging, with formerly democratic states beginning to be administered like corporations. Italy, for example, witnessed the installation of the administration of Mario Monti and his team of unelected 'technocrat' ministers in November 2011. In Greece, the similarly 'technocratic' government of Lucas Papademos came to power. However, while workers appeared initially stunned by the turn of events in 2007/08, popular protests against elite responses to the crisis have appeared across the globe. This has included strikes in a number of European capitals. In Africa, the trigger for the Tunisian revolution was also partly economic and related to the 'slow-motion aftershock of the 2008 crash', in that 'rising food prices and unemployment in the IMF poster-boy state, combined with declining workers' remittances from recession-hit Europe' (Milne, 2011, p 33).

The economic crisis and social work

The unfolding crisis has illuminated the interconnectedness of capitalism. A run of mortgage foreclosures in a US city can contribute to a revolutionary insurrection in Africa or a home-care worker being made redundant somewhere in Europe. In the UK, for example, it will be the very poorest – many of whom are in contact with social workers – who will suffer most on account of the cuts. Local councils now seem likely to come under pressure to 'outsource' more of their social work and social care services to the private sector to try and deal with massive spending cuts prompted by the Comprehensive Spending Review in October 2010. In the spring of 2012, for example, Virgin Care appeared poised to take over a number of children's social care services in Devon.

According to a report by the Low Pay Commission in 2011, the social care workforce is now one of the lowest paid in the economy with 9% of staff earning less than £5.93 per hour as of April 2010 (McGregor, 2011a). In the social work domain, the Unison trade union has denounced the increasingly widespread employment of 'cheaper' social work assistants to substitute for qualified professional practitioners (McGregor, 2011b). It has also been revealed that pressure is being put on front-line practitioners to reclassify 'child protection' cases as less serious – and financially demanding – 'child in need' cases (Cooper, 2011). As a result of these cuts, and following the example of local authorities such as Suffolk and Barnet, councils are also likely to introduce the 'easyCouncil' approach. Like the passengers on budget airlines, residents are charged levies or additional charges for a higher level of provision, with only a very basic service offered for those only able to afford to pay the minimum charge (Lombard, 2010).

These developments and the dramatic shifts in the distribution of income and wealth inescapably impact on a range of social work concerns: we can 'make the connections' between theorising neoliberalism and its practical impact – and playing out – within a number of fields. It is apparent, for example, in terms of the data highlighting how the economic crisis is adversely impacting on mental health. Indeed, many of those worst hit by the crisis are experiencing a health emergency. In Greece:

> There are signs that health outcomes have worsened, especially in vulnerable groups. We noted a significant rise in the prevalence of people reporting that their health was 'bad' or 'very bad'. Suicides rose by 17% in 2009 from 2007 and unofficial 2010 data quoted in parliament mention a 25% rise compared with 2009. The Minister of Health reported a 40% rise in the first half of 2011 compared with the same period in 2010. The national suicide helpline reported that 25% of callers faced financial difficulties in 2010 and reports in the media indicate that the inability to repay high levels of personal debt might be a key factor in the increase in suicides. Violence has also risen, and homicide and theft rates nearly doubled between 2007 and 2009. The number of people able to obtain sickness benefits declined between 2007 and 2009. (Kentikelenis et al, 2011, p 1)

As the authors of this piece in *The Lancet* observe, overall 'the picture of health in Greece is concerning. It reminds us that, in an effort to finance debts, ordinary people are paying the ultimate price' (Kentikelenis et al, 2011, p 2). What is more, the hardships being endured are clearly avoidable.

Elsewhere in the EU, there are not dissimilar findings, particularly in those countries where the social state is being subjected to the most severe attacks. In the Republic of Ireland the cuts in 'mental health services are taking an insidious form in that staff who leave or retire are not replaced. It is estimated that approximately 10% of psychiatric nursing staff left the mental health services in 2009' (Mental Health Commission, 2011b, p 10). Similar to Greece:

> economic adversity and recession specifically has been shown to result in an increase in suicide rates. Studies have also shown that factors in the current economic crisis, such as falling stock prices, increased bankruptcies and housing insecurity (including evictions and the anticipated loss of a home), and higher interest rates are all associated with increased suicide risk. People who are unemployed are two–three times more likely to die by suicide than people in employment. A recent Irish study has shown that during the boom years of the 'Celtic Tiger' male and female rates of suicide and undetermined death were stable during 1996–2006, while suicide among unemployed men increased. Unemployment was associated with a 2–3 fold risk

of suicide in men and a 4–6 fold increased risk in women. (Mental Health Commission, 2011b, p 14)

The Mental Health Commission (2011b, pp 14–15) also reported that by 'mid 2010 one in ten calls to the Samaritans in Ireland were described as "recession-related" and in June 2010 some 50,000 calls were received, up from an average of 35,000 in other months. The suicide rate in Ireland increased from 424 in 2008 to 527 in 2009, an increase of 24%'. Related to this, there has also been a steep rise in the prescribing of some anti-depressive drugs (Mental Health Commission, 2011b, p 16).

Conclusion

As Žižek (2008) argues:

> It is unlikely that the financial meltdown of 2008 will function as a blessing in disguise, the awakening from a dream, the sobering reminder that we live in the reality of global capitalism. It all depends on how it will be symbolised, on what ideological interpretation or story will impose itself and determine the general perception of the crisis. When the normal run of things is traumatically interrupted, the field is open for a 'discursive' ideological competition.... Consequently ... the main task of the ruling ideology in the present crisis is to impose a narrative that will not put the blame for the meltdown on the global capitalist system as such, but on its deviations – lax regulation, the corruption of big financial institutions etc.... The danger is thus that the predominant narrative of the meltdown won't be the one that awakes us from a dream, but the one that will enable us to continue to dream.

How states symbolise and ideologically interpret the crisis will be different in different national settings. Within neoliberal modernity, ruling elites deploy their slogans and sound bites to 'fix' and install dominant understandings. In the UK, as mentioned earlier, this has pivoted on ideas associated with Cameron's 'we're all in this together' and 'Big Society' constructs. In the Republic of Ireland, the blaming of public sector workers for the crisis is the core motif, along with the bogus notion that all must 'share the pain'. As we move into the second part of the book and an examination of the work of particular theorists, Antonio Gramsci's ideas are helpful in trying to understand such approaches to maintaining power and 'hegemony'.

|◀◀ Reflection and Talk Box 5 ▶▶|

- Does the theorisation of neoliberalism shed light on your experience as someone who may be working in or about to begin working as a social worker?

- In what areas in your work are you able to detect 'accumulation by dispossession'?

- Can you identify ways in which neoliberalism is 'playing out' in a specific way in your particular professional, local or national setting?

- Can you identify particular recurring or emerging patterns of 'precarious' working lives? How is this impacting on social work?

- How does incarceration and imprisonment impact on contemporary social work?

- What tensions are there in terms of social work ethics and neoliberalism?

Notes

[1] Some of the material featured in this chapter is derived from a couple of other sources and substantially revised: Chapter Two in my *'Transforming' children's services? Social work, neoliberalism and the 'modern' world* (Garrett, 2009); also 'Examining the "conservative revolution": neoliberalism and social work education', *Social Work Education*, vol 29, no 4, pp 340–55. I am grateful to the Open University/McGraw Hill and Taylor & Francis for allowing me to make use of my earlier work.

[2] The points in Table 5.1 are extracted from the encyclical issued to mark the 100th anniversary of the publication of *Rerum Novarum* by Pope Leo XIII in 1891. It has frequently been seen as merely supporting the rise of the *Solidarnosc* movement in the Pope's native Poland. More broadly, however, the encyclical can be read as a defence of social democracy and workers' rights during a period when both were subject to neoliberal assault. Signed by the Pope on 14 September 1981, it appeared one month after Reagan had launched his assault on trade union rights in the US by sacking 11,345 air traffic controllers who refused to end a strike.

[3] In their critical discussion, Gill and Pratt argue that the precarity movement is geographically and temporally specific. It originated in Western Europe and is associated with the politics of Turin in the 1970s. They suggest that the 'precariat is to post-Fordism what the proletariat was to the industrial age' (Gill and Pratt, 2008, p 11).

[4] What is often forgotten is that UK prisoners continue to work for some of Britain's best-known brands (such as Virgin Atlantic and Macmillan) for as little as £4 a week, see: http://www.prisonlabour.org.uk. During a period of 'austerity', a right-wing 'think-tank' has also called for greater exploitation of prison labour (Geoghegan and Boyd, 2011).

[5.] What was initially referred to as the 'credit crunch' commenced on 9 August 2007 when 'the French bank BNP Paribas suspended three of its investment funds that had been dabbling in US sub-prime mortgages' (*The Guardian*, 2011c).

Part Two

Theorists

CHAPTER SIX

Thinking with Gramsci

Introduction

Although Gramsci had been dead for 20 years before the first small selection of his writings were published in English, his work was, for a period, very influential across sections of the Left in Britain (Nairn, 1964; Williams, 1973; Hall et al, 1978). Gramsci:

> attracted attention outside Italy primarily as a communist thinker who provided a Marxist strategy for countries in which the October Revolution might have been an inspiration, but could not be a model – that is to say for socialist movements in non-revolutionary environments and situations…. Gramsci undoubtedly reached the peak of his international prominence in the years of 'eurocommunism' of the 1970s. (Hobsbawm, 2011, p 336)

Gramsci was an 'unapologetic' Marxist but rejected the notion that Marx's work provided a blueprint that had to be adhered to rigidly. Even in his now-neglected, pre-prison journalism, he asserted that the Bolsheviks were not 'Marxists' in the sense that they had:

> not used the Master's works to compile a rigid doctrine….They are living out Marxist thought….And this true Marxist thought has always identified as the most important factor in history not crude, economic facts, but rather men [sic, throughout] themselves, and the societies they create, as they learn to live with one another and understand one another. (Quoted in Bellamy, 1994, pp 39–40)

In Britain, the Thatcher administrations (May 1979–November 1990) triggered particular interest in Gramscian approaches. Indeed, the concept of 'Thatcherism' and the attempt to comprehend the 'great moving right show' were underpinned by an application of Gramsci's theorising during a period of radical transformation (Hall, 1993). A key figure in this regard was Stuart Hall, who was influential in bringing a Gramscian perspective to political analysis and cultural studies (Hall and Jacques, 1989). A frequent contributor to the British Communist Party publication *Marxism Today*, Hall called on the Left to think through problems in a Gramscian way and utilised some of Sardinian's formulations to better understand contemporary politics (see Hall, 1996, 1998, 2003). John Clarke, an associate of

Hall's from the late 1970s, brought a distinctly Gramscian-inflected perspective to analyse the politics of social policy and changes taking place inside the 'welfare' regimes that house social work and related forms of endeavour. More recently, it has been suggested that 'it is Cameron's Conservatives who have taken up the Gramscian method, by articulating concerns over the quality of life with their (still clearly anti-state and pro-marketisation) modernising conservatism' (Leggett, 2009, p 155). On an international scale, Gramscian approaches have proven useful in investigating the construction of a 'new world order' and how global hegemony is achieved.

Substantial obstacles confront those reading Gramsci. First, his web-like prose can appear fragmentary, even lacking coherence. This is particularly the case with the Prison Notebooks (PN), which 'consist of a massive series of notes and essays, sometimes rewritten and redeveloped with no single plan to give them structure' (Martin, 1998, pp 3–4). A second complicating factor is that Gramsci was constantly attentive to the need to evade censors and his work occasionally appears in coded form: most notably, the constant use of 'philosophy of praxis' for Marxism (Morton, 2003). Third, perhaps Gramsci's writings assume an understanding of the intellectual and political context in which he wrote: the struggle against fascism in Italy; the various competing political currents within the Italian Communist Party; and the shifts and turns of the Communist International. Good annotated editions of his work can, however, assist in this regard.[1] Fourth, related to his specific historical and cultural milieu, Gramsci can appear to present somewhat 'staid views on sexual morality, women and the family' (Forgacs, 1988, p 276). Similarly, his opinions on schooling can appear anachronistic to present-day readers.

Nevertheless, Gramsci's theorisation can be brought to bear upon the issues raised by Ferguson and Lavalette (2006, p 311), who, seeking to promote a 'social work of resistance', ask how 'can we begin to develop alternatives to the neoliberal social work that has brought us to our present impasse?' After a brief account of Gramsci's life, the chapter will address the most common arguments against the contemporary relevance of Gramsci's theorisation. The focus will then shift to a number of his signature themes: Americanism, Fordism and Taylorism; Hegemony; Common Sense; Intellectuals; and Critical Reflection. In the final section, the chapter will explore the use of such conceptualisations for contemporary social work and social policy.

Who was Gramsci?

After spending his first 20 years on the remote island of Sardinia, Gramsci arrived in Turin, 'the red capital of Italy' and 'home of its most advanced industry', in 1911 (Hoare and Nowell Smith, 2005, p xxv). It is difficult to conjure up the febrile atmosphere of this period but the two years of 1919 and 1920 'resulting from economic crisis and political upheaval after the First World War, together with expectations aroused by the Russian Revolution, created an environment in which it was widely felt that revolution was just around the corner' (Bellamy 1994, p xix).

In May 1919, Gramsci, along with Umberto Terracini (1895–1983), Angelo Tasca (1892–1960) and Palmiro Togliatti (1893–1964), founded the weekly *L'Ordine Nuovo*, which was to become the 'intellectual voice of a revolutionary movement' and the journal of the factory councils that formed the core organisational form for working-class opposition to capital during the period (Bellamy, 1994, p xiii).

After the defeat of the working-class movement in 1920, however, the shape of politics in Italy – and elsewhere in Europe – began to change rapidly. Industrialists moved onto the offensive, providing financial support and tacit approval to the emerging fascist squads. Indeed, by the end of the year, these roving bands of militia began undertaking 'punishment expeditions' against socialists and unions in the countryside and provincial towns (Martin, 2006). In October 1922, while Gramsci was in Moscow as the representative of the *Partito Communista Italiano* (PCI), Mussolini's 'March on Rome' ushered in the start of the fascist social and economic order. Having returned to Italy in December 1923, Gramsci became the leader of the PCI in 1924. However, on the evening of 8 November 1926, in defiance of his immunity as an elected deputy, he was arrested. At the ensuing 'trial', the fascist prosecutor who sent Gramsci to prison notoriously decreed that it was necessary to prevent his 'brain from functioning for 20 years' (quoted in Buttigieg, 1986, p 10).

The time he spent in prison was, for Gramsci:

> an eleven-year death-agony (Fiori, 1990). His teeth fell out, his digestive system collapsed so that he could not eat solid food, his chronic insomnia as so severe that he could go weeks without more than an hour or two of sleep at night; he had convulsions when he vomited blood, and he suffered from headaches so violent that he beat his head against the walls of his cell. (Hoare and Nowell Smith, 2005, p xcii; see also Gramsci, 1979)

Gramsci was to die under guard in a clinic in Rome at the age of 46. At his funeral, 'held as quickly as possible on April 28, 1937 the watchful police guards far outnumbered the mourners' (Buttigieg, 1986, p 2). The 'product of those years of slow death in prison were … 2,848 pages of handwritten notes which he left to be smuggled out of the clinic and out of Italy after his death' (Hoare and Nowell Smith, 2005, p xviii).

An important aspect of Gramsci's life is his status as an 'outsider' and this is apparent in at least four ways. First, he was from an island that 'held a relationship to northern Italy comparable to that of "underdeveloped" nations today' (Germino, 1986, p 24; see also Landy, 1986). Although Sardinians, such as Gramsci, were often regarded with disdain, his geographical and cultural location conferred on him certain advantages. Italy was a:

> microcosm of world capitalism inasmuch as it contained in a single country both metropolis and colonies, advanced and backward regions.

> Sardinia ... typified the backward, not to say archaic, and semi–colonial side of Italy ... [Gramsci was, therefore, in an] unusually good position to grasp the nature both of the developed capitalist world and the 'Third World' and their interactions, unlike Marxists from countries belonging entirely to one or the other. (Hobsbawm, 2011, p 317)

Second, from childhood, Gramsci was disabled and – throughout his life – periodically suffered from mental health problems (see, eg, Lawner, in Gramsci, 1979). Due to his 'hunchback', he suffered from 'the local superstition ... and often felt rejected as a consequence' (Bellamy, 1994, pp x–xi). His disability is often omitted in the pictorial imagery of him, which tends to promote a particular picture of revolutionary masculinity (perhaps suggestive of a somewhat more studious Che Guevara). However, Germino (1986, p 21) has contended that the fact that 'Antonio Gramsci was a *gobbo* (hunchback) helped make him enormously more attentive to the plight of individuals and groups at the "margins of history"'.

A third component of Gramsci's outsider status relates to the fact that for almost a quarter of his life, he was a prisoner of the Italian fascist state. During a period of turmoil and Stalinisation, a life *inside* provided Gramsci with the space to think *outside* the confines of formal party structures and review Marxism in the light of evolving economic, political and social circumstances. In the rest of the chapter, therefore, we will turn to look at some of the key ideas – or signature themes – which were to emerge as a result of his deliberations. Furthermore, how might some of the conceptualisations of this complex, tragic, intellectually brilliant figure contribute to social workers perhaps gaining a better understanding of their roles and the world that they inhabit?

Signature themes

Americanism, Fordism, Taylorism

Gramsci was preoccupied with 'modernisation' and what it meant to be 'modern'. In his time, the idea of modernity was bound up with industrialisation and the gradual introduction of mass production carried out in factories such as those established in Italy by the car manufacturer FIAT. Gramsci was particularly fascinated with the new regulatory practices, often originating from the US, which sought to manage and control the body of individual workers, the pace of their work, the extent of their productivity and their lives outside of the factory.

In a series of short articles from the early 1920s, he was already responding to the transformations under way in industrial centres such as Turin, a city that he saw gradually metamorphosing into 'one great factory' (quoted in Bellamy, 1994, p 137). In the cultural domain, he was increasingly attracted to Futurist art and its urge to declaim 'the age of big industry, of the large proletarian city and of intense and tumultuous life' (quoted in Bellamy, 1994, p 74). Gramsci himself tended to be rhapsodic in his praise for the factory:

> The working class … has been developing towards a completely new and unprecedented model of humanity: the factory worker, the proletarian who has shed all psychological traces of his agricultural or craft origins, the proletarian who lives the life of the factory, the life of production – an intense, methodical life. His life may be disorderly and chaotic where his social relations are concerned…. But within the factory, it is ordered, precise and disciplined. (Quoted in Bellamy, 1994, p 152)

The disciplining of the individual body is a recurring Gramscian theme and he was also alert to how the factory and the collective ordering of the workforce could help to promote workers' solidarity:

> The more the proletarian specializes in a particular professional task, the more conscious he becomes of how indispensable his companions are; the more he feels himself as one cell within a coherent body, possessed of an inner unity and cohesion; the more he feels the need for order, method, precision; the more he feels the need for the whole world to become like a vast factory organized with the same precision and method and order which he recognizes as vital in the factory where he works; the more he feels the need for order, precision and method which are the life-blood of the factory to be projected out into the system of relations than link one factory to another, one city to another, one nation to another…. Capitalism has become divorced from the sphere of production and the management of industry has fallen into inept and irresponsible hands; it is only the working class which retains a real love for labour and the machine. (Quoted in Bellamy, 1994, pp 152–3)

Although still committed to opposing capitalism, he looked favourably on some of the developments that were giving rise to a mechanised modernity (Martin, 1998). For him, the US was forging ahead and was not constantly dragged back by the 'leaden burden' of tradition that impeded the process of modernisation in Italy (quoted in Forgacs, 1988, p 277). In the US, the 'non-existence of viscous parasitic sedimentations left behind by past phases of history' allowed 'industry, and commerce in particular, to develop on a sound basis' (quoted in Forgacs, 1988, p 278). In Europe, it was, according to Gramsci, 'the passive residues that resist Americanism … because they have the instinctive feeling that the new forms of production and work would sweep them away implacably' (quoted in Forgacs, 1988, p 293).

Bound up with the creation of a new type of man suited to the new type of productive process was the demand for new modes of socialisation and the acquisition of new habits. These ruminations led Gramsci to comment on some of the innovations being introduced by Ford, in his car plants, and on the broader question of Fordism.

Seeking to retain workers and increase his profitability, Ford was determined to develop a new type of worker who was better suited to assembly line production. Acclaimed as a 'sociologist manufacturer' whose 'real business', according to the head of his employee relations office, was the 'making of men' (quoted in Grandin, 2010, p 34), Ford extended his control over his workers well beyond the factory limits. By '1919 [Ford's] Sociological Department employed hundreds of agents … asking questions, taking notes, and writing up personnel reports' to ensure Ford's workers possessed the prerequisite moral standards (Grandin, 2010, p 38).

Gramsci was particularly interested in the framework of coercion and consent in which Fordism was embedded:

> The enquiries conducted by the industrialists into workers' private lives and the inspection services created by some firms to control the 'morality' of their workers are necessities of the new methods of work. People who laugh at these initiatives … deny themselves any possibility of understanding the importance, significance and objective import of the American phenomenon, which is also the biggest collective effort to date to create, with unprecedented speed, and with a consciousness of purpose unmatched in history, a new type of worker and man. (Quoted in Forgacs, 1988, pp 289–90)

Unlike some on the Left, Gramsci was not scornful of such endeavours, nor did he place an emphasis on workers' organising to oppose what we might regard as a form of modernising capitalist paternalism:

> American industrialists are concerned to maintain the continuity of the physical and muscular-nervous efficiency of the worker. It is in their interests to have a stable, skilled labour force, a permanently well adjusted complex, because the human complex (the collective worker) of an enterprise is also a machine which cannot, without considerable loss, be taken to pieces too often and renewed with single new parts. (Quoted in Forgacs, 1988, p 291)

In this context, Gramsci argued that the history of industrialism had been:

> an uninterrupted, often painful and bloody process of subjugating natural (i.e. animal and primitive) instincts to new, more complex and rigid norms and habits of order, exactitude and precision which can make possible the increasingly complex forms of collective life which are the necessary consequence of industrial development. (Quoted in Forgacs, 1988, p 286)

These preoccupations were connected to Gramsci's interest in the method of labour management technique known, after its founder Frederick W. Taylor (1856–1915), as Taylorism. Famously, Taylor had maintained that if his techniques – which involved breaking the process of production down into a series of repetitive tasks devised by managers – were deployed, a 'trained gorilla' could undertake the work as efficiently as a human being could. Yet, for Gramsci:

> Taylor is in fact expressing with brutal cynicism the purpose of American society – developing in the worker to the highest degree automatic and mechanical attitudes, breaking up the old psycho-physical nexus of qualified professional work, which demands a certain active participation of intelligence, fantasy and initiative on the part of the worker, and reducing productive operations exclusively to the mechanical, physical aspect. But these things, in reality, are not original or novel: they represent simply the most recent phase of a long process which began with industrialism itself. The phase is more intense then preceding phases, and manifests itself in more brutal forms, but it is a phase which will be superseded by the creation of a psycho-physical nexus of a new type, both different from its predecessors and undoubtedly *superior*. A forced selection will ineluctably take place: a part of the old working class will be pitilessly eliminated from the world of labour, and perhaps from the world *tout court*. (Quoted in Forgacs, 1988, p 290, emphasis in original)

Taylorism and the increasing mechanisation of the worker and the stripping away of the 'human content' of work did not, however, result in the 'spiritual death of man' (quoted in Forgacs, 1988, pp 294, 295–6):

> Once the process of adaptation has been completed, *what really happens is that the brain of the worker, far from being mummified, reaches a state of complete freedom.* The only thing that is completely mechanized is the physical gesture; the memory of the trade, reduced to simple gestures repeated at an intense rhythm, 'nestles' in the muscular and nervous centres and leaves the brain free and unencumbered for other occupations. One can walk without having to think about all the movements needed in order to move, in perfect synchronization, all the parts of the body, in the specific way that it is necessary for walking…. [T]he worker remains a man and even during his work he thinks more, or at least has greater opportunities for thinking, once he has overcome the crisis of adaptation without being eliminated: and not only does the worker think, but the fact that he gets no immediate satisfaction from his work and realises that they are trying to reduce him to a trained gorilla, can lead him into a train of thought that is far from conformist. (Quoted in Forgacs, 1988, pp 295–6, emphasis added)

According to Gramsci, the ideas associated with Americanism, Fordism and Taylorism were rooted in notions about the direction the 'modernisation' was to take. This perspective can also be related to his ideas pivoting on hegemony because, for him, it was necessary for any ruling group to win consent for its *particular* vision of modernity.[2]

Hegemony

Given the existing social and economic conditions, it was not feasible to embark on a frontal assault against capital, what he called a 'war of manoeuvre'. He recommended instead, a 'war of position', a subtler form of confrontation, more conducive to the conditions in the West and focused on a more long-term and strategic struggle. According to Gramsci:

> In the East [where the Bolsheviks met with success] the state was everything, civil society was primordial and gelatinous: in the West, there was a proper relation between state and civil society, and when the state trembled a sturdy structure of civil society was at once revealed. *The state was only an outer ditch, behind which there stood a powerful system of fortresses and earthworks*: more or less numerous from one state to the next, it goes without saying – but this precisely *necessitated an accurate reconnaissance of each individual country*. (Quoted in Forgacs, 1988, p 229, emphases added)

In the West, therefore, the state was, for Gramsci, simply an 'outer ditch' and it was necessary for those seeking revolutionary change to gain consent within civil society to confront the powerful 'fortresses' and 'earthworks' that the bourgeoisie has at its disposal. This led Gramsci to emphasise the importance of the struggle to achieve hegemony (Nairn, 1964; Williams, 1973).

Derived from the word *hegemon*, literally meaning leader, the word tended to signify a combination of authority, leadership and domination (see Ives, 2004a, 2004b). The concept can be associated with the evolution of Marxism in Russia prior to the Bolshevik Revolution. As Perry Anderson (1976) observes, hegemony was one of the central political ideas in the Russian Social-Democratic movement from the late 1890s to 1917, and it was forged to theorise the role of the working class in a bourgeois revolution against a feudal order. Gramsci, however, used the notion of hegemony to understand the mechanisms of bourgeois rule over the working class in a *stable* capitalist society.

Even if throughout his writings Gramsci retains 'the language of base and superstructure, in practice he transcends this over-simple metaphor of stacked layers' (Crehan, 2002, p 72). During a period when Marxist theory was dominated by economic determinism, his recognition of the importance of 'superstructural' factors, such as politics, culture and ideology, shifted the emphasis away from an overly narrow focus on the economic basis of society (Joseph, 2006). Integral to a Gramscian approach is an understanding that the base–superstructure relation is far less static: more churning, more dynamic than the dominant, 'authorised' accounts of Marxism maintained. His:

> dialectical analysis proceeds from the assumption that everything in life is in constant motion, that everything is inter-related rather than rigidly schematic and systematic. In Gramsci's analysis of institutions, the church, schools, corporations, trade unions, and forms of 'entertainment', social structures are conceived of as a source of lived social relations and as sources of constant conflict. (Landy, 1986, p 53)

According to Gramsci, a movement does not become hegemonic simply because it manages to manipulate 'passive masses into supporting it, nor because it manages to construct cross-class alliances at the level of elite politics' (Robinson, 2006, p 82). For Gramsci, there existed no short cuts to achieving hegemony, and for a hegemonic project to be successful, it had to address and meaningfully respond to people's lived experiences of the world. Both hegemonic and counter-hegemonic projects need, in fact, to be embedded throughout 'civil society', a term Gramsci used to refer to:

> the sum of social activities and institutions which are not directly part of the government, the judiciary or the repressive bodies (police, armed forces). Trade unions and other voluntary organizations and political parties, when the latter do not form part of the government, are all part of civil society. Civil society is the sphere in which a dominant social group organizes consent and hegemony, as opposed to political society where it rules by coercion and direct domination. It is also the sphere where the dominated social groups may organize their opposition and where an alternative hegemony may be constructed. (Forgacs, 1988, p 420)

Hegemony also 'presupposes an active and practical involvement of the hegemonized groups, quite unlike the static, totalizing and passive subordination implied in the dominant ideology concept' (Forgacs, 1988, p 424). Furthermore, 'hegemonic power does not flow automatically from the economic position of the dominated group, rather it has to be constructed and negotiated' (Joseph, 2006, p 52). This is a complex task because, for Gramsci, 'classes are not homogeneous blocs, but are determined by a range of social, cultural, political and economic factors, creating various fractions and strata within classes' (Joseph, 2006, p 53).

Some writers, such as Said (2002), have recognised similarities in the approach of Gramsci and Foucault:

> Both see power as operating in complex ways in venues often not understood as political, strictly speaking. For them, politics as the

operation of power is not just about governments, elections or even the police and the army. Rather, politics occurs daily in everybody's lives, whether one is going to school, reading a novel or visiting [a social worker's office]. Some of the most crucial operations of power occur at the micro or molecular level.... Moreover, both Foucault and Gramsci see that power rarely operates in a simple unidirectional manner, with one person or group of people holding power and using it against another who is totally powerless. (Ives, 2004a, pp 142–3)

Nonetheless, there are also marked differences in the approach of these two European theorists, in that Gramsci provides:

not just a ruthless criticism of deconstruction of dominant hegemonies, but also a 'counter hegemony', a concrete alternative to oppression.... The most significant difference between Foucault and Gramsci is that Foucault does not concentrate on the mechanisms by which people could consciously mobilize to change a given 'discourse' in a progressive direction ... Gramsci places much greater emphasis on agency and how collective political action can topple, or at least alter, systematic inequality and oppression and lead to more equal power relations. (Ives, 2004a, pp 142–4)

Gramsci and 'common sense': 'everyone is a philosopher'

Unlike in English, the 'Italian notion of common sense (*senso comune*) does not so much mean good, sound, practical sense, rather it means normal or average understanding' (Ives, 2004a, p 74). Everyone:

has a number of 'conceptions of the world', which often tend to be in contradiction with one another and therefore form an incoherent whole. Many of these conceptions are imposed and absorbed passively from outside, or from the past, and are accepted and lived uncritically. In this case they constitute what Gramsci calls 'common sense' (or, in another context, 'folklore'). Many elements in popular common sense contribute to people's subordination by making situations of inequality and oppression appear to them as natural and unchangeable.... It is contradictory – it contains elements of truth as well as elements of misrepresentation – and it is upon these contradictions that leverage must be obtained in a 'struggle of political hegemonies'. (Forgacs, 1988, p 421)

This understanding was important to Gramsci because it clearly implied that Marxism should not simply present itself as an abstract philosophy, but 'should enter people's common sense, giving them a more critical understanding of their own situation' (Forgacs, 1988, p 421). Thus, Marxism should draw out and elaborate 'elements of critical awareness and "good sense" which are already present within people's "common sense"' (Forgacs, 1988, p 323). This, along with material changes, might then present the possibility of going beyond 'common sense' and onto a new plane of understanding. For Gramsci, Marxism – or what in the PN was cryptically referred to as 'philosophy of praxis' – must first of all 'demonstrate that "everyone" is a philosopher and that it is not only a question of introducing from scratch a scientific form of thought into everyone's individual life, but of renovating and making "critical" an already existing activity' (quoted in Forgacs, 1988, p 332).

Intellectuals

As early as 1916, in a piece titled 'Socialism and culture', Gramsci was beginning to sketch out his thoughts on intellectuality and intellectuals:

> It is essential to get out of the habit of conceiving culture as encyclopaedic knowledge, and, correspondingly, of man as a receptacle to be crammed with empirical data, with crude, unconnected facts which he must file away in his brain, as though in the columns of a dictionary, in order to be able to respond, on any given occasion, to the different stimuli of the world around him. This form of culture really is harmful especially to the proletariat. It can only serve to create misfits, people who believe themselves superior to the rest of humanity because they have amassed in their memory a certain quantity of facts and dates, which they trot out at any opportunity, setting up a kind of barrier between themselves and others. (Quoted in Bellamy, 1994, p 9)

According to Gramsci, this 'false conception of culture' served to create 'feeble and colourless intellectualism' (quoted in Bellamy, 1994, p 9). Gramsci shunned, therefore, the superiority complex that the dominant contemporary understanding of intellectuals generated. His emphasis was on the social location, role and function of 'intellectuals'. Underpinning his perspective was a democratising project aiming to extend 'the concept of the intellectual beyond the received notion of an elite intelligentsia' (Martin, 1998, p 44; see also Williams, 1983 [1976], p 169). In this context, he argued that although 'one can speak of intellectuals, one cannot speak of non-intellectuals, because non-intellectuals do not exist....There is no human activity from which every form of intellectual participation can be excluded' (quoted in Forgacs, 1988, p 321). Thus:

> [all] men are intellectuals, one could therefore say; but not all men have in society the function of intellectuals (thus, because it can happen that everyone at some time fries a couple of eggs or sews up a tear in

a jacket, we do not necessarily say that everyone is a cook or a tailor. (Quoted in Forgacs, 1988, p 304)

As he comes to redefine 'intellectual', it designates:

> anyone whose function in society is primarily that of organizing, administering, directing, educating or leading others. Gramsci is concerned both with the analysis of those intellectuals who function directly or indirectly on behalf of a dominant social group to organize coercion and consent and with the problem of how to form intellectuals of the subaltern social groups who will be capable of opposing and transforming the existing social order. (Forgacs, 1988, p 300)

Furthermore, the 'mode of being a new intellectual can no longer consist in eloquence ... but in active participation in practical life, as a constructor, organizer, "permanent persuader"' (quoted in Forgacs, 1988, p 321).

Historically, the 'most typical' of intellectuals' was that of ecclesiastics:

> who for a long time ... held a monopoly of a number of important services: religious ideology, that is the philosophy and science of the age, together with schools, education, morality, justice, charity, good works, etc. The category of ecclesiastics can be considered the category of intellectuals bound to the landed aristocracy. It had equal status juridically with the aristocracy, with which it shared the exercise of feudal ownership of land, and the use of state privileges with property. (Quoted in Forgacs, 1988, p 302)

Over time, we also find 'the formation ... of a stratum of administrators, etc., scholars and scientists, theorists, non-ecclesiastical philosophers, etc' (quoted in Forgacs, 1988, p 303). These 'various categories of traditional intellectuals ... put themselves forward as autonomous and independent of the dominant social group' (quoted in Forgacs, 1988, p 303).

One of the most important characteristics of any group that is 'developing towards dominance' is 'its struggle to assimilate and conquer "ideologically" the traditional intellectuals, but this assimilation and conquest is made quicker and more efficacious the more the group in question succeeds in simultaneously elaborating its own organic intellectuals' (quoted in Forgacs, 1988, pp 304–5, emphasis added).

Within this Gramscian framework, therefore, intellectuals (as we have seen, very broadly conceived) play a crucial role in helping to maintain or challenge a given economic and social order. That is to say, intellectuals (including social workers and social work educators) are potentially significant actors operating within civil society and are enmeshed in the exercise of hegemony. More expansively, for an oppressed group to challenge and ultimately usurp the existing order, it must cease being dependent on intellectuals from outside its own class and create its own 'organic' intellectuals. These 'organic intellectuals' of the new, emergent order would become, in Gramsci's well-known phrase, the 'whalebone in the corset' (quoted in Robinson, 2006, p 79). This, however, would be no easy task: 'If our aim is to produce a new stratum of intellectuals, including those capable of the highest degree of specialization, from a social group which has not traditionally developed the appropriate attitudes, then we have unprecedented difficulties to overcome' (quoted in Forgacs, 1988, p 320).

Gramsci believed that obstacles could be:

> surmounted in two complementary ways: through the mass political party, which functions as a 'collective intellectual' ... and through the school, which must be reformed so as to overcome the streaming of manual and mental skills and to enable a 'new equilibrium' between them to emerge. These two developments would also be part of a wider movement towards liberation and self-government. (Forgacs, 1988, pp 300–1)

Gramsci retained the idea that the Marxist political party – or 'modern prince' – was a vital and indispensable element in the struggle for socialism (Showstack Sassoon, 1986; see also Gill, 2000). However, instead of 'a Bolshevik vanguardism which would deliver to the ... working class an historical vision formulated from an Archimedean point populated by professional revolutionaries, at the core of Gramsci's project was a critical pedagogy' (Rupert, 2006, p 94). For Gramsci:

> [the] modern prince, the myth-prince, cannot be a real person, a concrete individual. It can only be an organism, a complex element of society in which a collective will, which has already been recognised and has to some extent asserted itself in action, begins to take concrete form. (Quoted in Hoare and Nowell Smith, 2005, p 129)

Critical reflection

Gramsci stressed the significance of the famous saying of Solon (later appropriated by Socrates) 'Know Thyself'. Solon, according to Gramsci, was not encouraging a narcissistic or intensively singular and insular inquiry. The saying was prompted by a much more political and democratising aspiration:

> Solon intended to provoke the plebeians, who believed themselves bestial in origin, while the nobles were of divine origin, to reflect on themselves and recognize themselves as being the same human nature as the nobles, and therefore to claim to be made equal with them in civil rights. And he identifies this consciousness of the shared humanity

of plebeians and nobles, as the basis and the historical reason for the rise of democracies in antiquity. (Quoted in Bellamy, 1994, pp 8–9)

Gramsci used this interpretation as a foundation for his own understanding, which connected the individual with the wider community:

> To know oneself means to be oneself, to be master of oneself, to assert one's own identity, to emerge from chaos and become an agent of order, but of one's own order, one's own disciplined dedication to an ideal. And one cannot achieve this without knowing others, knowing their history, the succession of efforts they have made to be what they are, to create the civilization they have created. (Quoted in Bellamy, 1994, p 11)

Thus, the 'ultimate aim' was 'to know oneself better through learning about others, and to know others by learning about oneself' (quoted in Bellamy, 1994, p 12). He returned to the same theme during the period of his confinement, insisting that there was a need to engage in:

> criticism of all previous philosophy, in so far as this has left stratified deposits in popular philosophy. The starting point of critical elaboration is the consciousness of what really is 'knowing thyself' as a product of the historical process to date which has deposited in you an infinity of traces, without leaving an inventory. Such an inventory must therefore be made at the outset. (Quoted in Forgacs, 1988, p 326, emphasis added)

In short, Gramsci's point was that if those seeking fundamental social change:

> were to develop a clear and coherent conception of the world they … should make a start by asking how people experienced the world as it was, how they got by and coped with it on a daily basis. And, 'people' and 'they' included 'me', 'us', the would-be world changers. (Brunt, 1989, pp 153–4)

All of his themes echo invocations for social workers to become more critically reflective (White et al, 2006). How, therefore, can we respond to some of Gramsci's ideas in the first quarter of the 21st century?

Social work inside the 'fortresses' and 'earthworks': engaging with Gramsci today

It is conceded that Gramsci's contributions on Americanism, Fordism and Taylorism are highly problematic. His perspective on the organisation of the factory is at odds with that of Marx, who tended to depict the factory as a place of exploitation and alienation (see Chapter Four), and other Marxian currents (such as the Frankfurt School) that were much more sceptical about modernity, mechanisation and the deployment of technology.

Pivoting on a simplistic body–mind dualism, the notion that 'modern' production techniques permit 'new and freer forms of thought' is unconvincing (Landy, 1994, p 229): Gramsci does not seems to recognise the harm that a worker's involvement in production can cause given that repetitious tasks can prove injurious to both body and mind (see Bellamy, 1994, p xxii). Specifically in relation to Fordism and forms of Taylorist working, he fails to realise that these were methods meant to control *alienated* labour, devised to discipline each worker's body, rendering it a mere 'part' in the process of production (Braverman, 1974). Strikingly, according to a union official in the United States in the early 1920s, the Ford workers enjoyed 'high pay, but they are not really alive – they are half dead' (quoted in Grandin, 2010, p 181). Such dehumanisation meant workers were not permitted to speak on the assembly line and had to develop a technique they referred to as the 'fordization of the face' – the ability to speak without moving the lips (Grandin, 2010, p 81). By the mid-1920s, Ford had, in fact, 'pretty much abandoned his liberal paternalism' (Grandin, 2010, p 69). He continued to pay better than most industrial companies, but he came to rely on very different – and intimidatory – tactics to increase productivity and enforce labour discipline (Grandin, 2010).

While it has been argued that Gramsci is 'under no illusions about the brutalizing effects of an application of the new technology and new organization of production under the hegemony of the present ruling class' (Showstack Sassoon, 1986, p 157), there is evidence to suggest that he tended to use organisation of production in the factory under capitalism as a model for the new society. Nevertheless Gramsci's observations on the incursion of technology in the workplace can add to debates about contemporary developments in social work. In this context some have complained that due to the deployment of computer technology and the greater use of centrally devised electronic templates, social work is becoming more Taylorised and deskilled (see, eg, Baines 2004a, 2004b; Carey, 2007). We may also be able to detect traces of Ford's approach in the new interest in monitoring social workers' private lives and activity outside of work (McLaughlin, 2007).

Gramsci also reminds us how seemingly private and personal aspects of daily life are politically important aspects of operations of power. He was deeply interested in the 'daily and molecular operations of power' and in how seemingly unrelated micro-practices can be rooted in more structurally embedded shaping mechanisms (Ives, 2004a, p 71). A similar attentiveness to the 'everyday' and the unquestioned could potentially steer social work in a more reflexive direction and move it into the orbit of anti-capitalism (see Trotsky, 1979). Emphasising that rule is constructed rather than given, his theorisation implicitly poses the question of how, within differing and specific national settings, social work academics, social workers and other social professions position themselves in a period of neoliberal hegemony. How does social work function in the context of specific hegemonic orders? How does this hegemony actually *look* and *feel* in concrete historical contexts, and how might it be overcome? This form of investigation might also prompt reflection on how social workers and those in receipt of welfare and social work services might act together to defend provision under threat or subject to commodification (Garrett, 2009).

A Gramscian questioning of social workers' professional 'common sense' would entail educators and practitioners becoming more analytical and defamiliarising 'official' discourses frequently riddled with taken-for-granted assumptions reflective of a particular and historically and economically determined conjuncture. This is apparent not only in the verbal categories that social workers are apt to use, promote and reify (eg the 'case'), but also in the documentation deployed and in recording practices (see, eg, Garrett, 2003).

Thinking about how hegemony works might also prompt social workers to reflect on how they engage with the ethical tensions inherent to their positioning within the 'outer ditches', 'fortresses' and 'earthworks' of civil society. More personally: to what extent do I, as an academic working on a social work programme, collude with commodifying hegemonic projects that diminish, stigmatise and exploit users of services while invoking their 'empowerment'? Such questioning further directs the attention to the use of language within micro-engagements involving social workers.

As Peter Ives (2004a, p 5) has noted, Gramsci 'pays great attention to language as a political issue'. Thinking more deeply and more politically about how language works within prevailing social work discourses and daily social work encounters may lead us to the question: what might particular words 'assume about a social totality or infrastructure, or the presumed characteristics of social actors?' (Barrett, 1992, p 202). Far from being an exercise in what is often caricatured as 'political correctness', such questions delve into a much deeper interrogation of how power relations operate through language and culture. The 'analyst of hegemonic control can – through a strategy of filtering, defamiliarizing, and X-raying – unmask a vast network of cultural minutiae which often becomes available for ideological use by virtue of its capacity for mediation, absorption, camouflage' (Hussein, 2004, p 174).

Keywords and phrases can continually – but often imperceptibly – contribute to the solidifying of neoliberal hegemonic order (see Williams, 1983 [1976]); hence the need to acknowledge that 'terms that are used to describe social life are also active forces in shaping it' (Fraser and Gordon, 1997, p 122). Entirely in tune with Gramsci's approach, Fraser and Gordon's interpretation assumes the development of a 'critical political semantics' (Fraser and Gordon, 1997, p 123): a practice rooted in a project to 'defamiliarize taken-for-granted beliefs in order to render them susceptible to critique and to illuminate present-day conflicts' (Fraser and Gordon, 1997, p 122). Indeed, failure to operate in this way could be highly problematic for social workers because 'unreflective' use of keywords might 'serve to enshrine certain interpretations of social life as authoritative and to delegitimate or obscure others' (Fraser and Gordon, 1997, p 123). This is generally to the advantage of other groups in society and to disadvantage of subordinate ones.

Engaging in such oppositional activity is, of course, a far from easy task because those in positions of structural power (and invested with the power of naming and defining) seek to maintain hegemony and identify what is permissible and what should be 'closed down'. Within academic institutions, educators are often constrained because programmes have curricula (mostly grounded in a neoliberal worldview or incessantly inflected in that direction) that are predetermined and mapped out by central 'authorities'. This is not to argue that there are no 'spaces' for a more critical engagement within social work education. Hegemony, in fact, is 'not a state of grace which is installed forever ... [it is] not a formation which incorporates everybody' (Hall, in Fischman and McLaren, 2005, p 430, emphasis added).

Attempts to promote more critical forms of intellectual engagement in professional education and practice are, of course, complex because social work is also constructed in different ways in different national settings. Indeed, although not specifically drawing on Gramsci's thinking, this is one of the themes at the core of Gudrid Aga Askeland and Malcolm Payne's (2006) remarks on a current within social work education that appears mistakenly intent on promoting a restrictive 'cultural hegemony'. For them, social work education:

> [has] become part of the global market in that those who have the resources to produce and market social work literature are able to disseminate their theoretical views and skills in social work throughout the world as the way of handling social issues in a professional way, ignoring the different local context in which it is produced and in which it should be read. (Askeland and Payne, 2006, p 734)

This dynamic can be seen in, for example, talk of the need for greater 'standardisation' and 'global standards', and in moves to ensure that there is one universal definition of 'social work'.

It needs to be stressed, however, that a Gramscian approach is not one preoccupied exclusively with words and discursive struggle, but one which is simultaneously committed to a more orthodox Left politics and looking for alternative bases (eg within trade unions, political parties and professional associations) from which to forge counter-hegemonic strategies to neoliberalism.

Conclusion

Gramsci's work contains no 'blueprints', nor is it embedded in notions associated in 'evidenced-based practice' or a fixation with 'outcomes'. Rather, his writing (and life) urges reflection on a range of interrelated questions: for example, does

Gramsci's theorisation aid our understanding of social work in our own specific time and place? How might his theorisation find expression in our everyday working (and personal) lives? How can he help us better understand those forces that constrain us and those forces that can potentially liberate us in these times of economic and social volatility? This chapter has tried, therefore, to encourage readers to 'think with' Gramsci because his work could enable us to consider such complex issues. This is not to argue that his conceptualisations should be 'literally or mechanically' applied (Morton, 2003, p 121). Instead, it is to maintain that there are key elements that we can distil from Gramsci's writings which might enable us to form a clearer view of social work, its constraints and possibilities.

The next chapter will concentrate on Pierre Bourdieu. Like Gramsci, Bourdieu is another European thinker, writer and – certainly in his later years – political activist (see Hobsbawm, 2007). Although Gramsci and Bourdieu, two very different theorists, are rarely 'brought into conversation', they frequently share similar thematic preoccupations. Abdirahman Hussein (2004, p 176) has suggested that hegemony – as we have seen, one of Gramsci's core concerns – is a:

> mode of living and intelligibility – a way of making sense of oneself and the world one lives in – which has evolved over a long period of time as a result of continual repetition and reinforcement. It has so effaced itself as to appear to be the absolutely logical view of things. Like the air we breathe, it is both invisible and all-enveloping, becoming part of the natural substance and rhythm of life. For all these reasons, its demystification is also absolutely necessary.

As we will see in the following chapter, this interpretation is closely related to Bourdieu's notion of 'habitus' in which individual subjects come to internalise and identify with dominant social institutions or structures.

◄◄Reflection and Talk Box 6: Looking at the 'Big Society' through a Gramscian lens►►|

The idea that Britain is a 'Broken Society' is central to the politics of the Conservative –Liberal Democratic Coalition government, which came to power in 2010. How the 'solution', the 'Big Society', was initially assembled and orchestrated is also important.

Through a Gramscian lens the 'Big Society' can be viewed as a potential hegemonic project:

- What were some of the main characteristics of the political and social landscape into which the 'Big Society' proposals were first introduced?

- What were the central, core ideas underpinning the introduction of the 'Big Society'?

- How was language deployed and manipulated? How was the 'official' discourse on the 'Big Society' constructed and 'put together'?

- How were attempts made to construct consent and 'win over' dissenting interests and voices to achieve hegemony for the 'Big Society' project?

- What was the role fulfilled by 'intellectuals' and 'experts' in promoting the 'Big Society' idea? In contrast, whose views and perceptions were rendered marginal? Were there any specific perspectives that were silenced, muted or 'reframed'?

- How was the role of social work and social workers delineated? What was the implicit trajectory being put in place for social work in the context of the 'Big Society'?

Notes

[1] The Prison Notebooks (PN), comprising 33 exercise books, were written between February 1929 and June 1935. Readers new to Gramsci can find English translations of his writings in Bellamy (1994), Forgacs (1988), Hoare (1988) and Hoare and Nowell Smith (2005). Edward Said (2002, p 9), however, has argued that Hoare and Nowell Smith tended, in their translations, to 'lop off bits of Gramsci'. Jones (2006) provides a short, accessible introduction laying particular emphasis on Gramsci's conceptualisations for cultural studies. Bambery (2006) has furnished a pithy, pocket-sized guide. The playwright Trevor Griffiths (2007) featured a dramatised Antonio Gramsci in his *Occupations*, first performed in 1970. This chapter is partly derived from two previously published articles: 'Thinking with the Sardinian: Antonio Gramsci and social work', *The European Journal of Social Work*, vol 11, no 3, pp 237–50; and 'The "whalebone" in the (social work) "corset"? Notes on Antonio Gramsci and social work educators', *Social Work Education*, vol 28, no 5, pp 461–75. I am grateful to Taylor and Francis for permitting me to draw on this earlier work.

[2.] Martin (2002) has provided a clear outline of how post-Marxists, particularly Laclau and Mouffe (1985), have attempted to develop the concept of hegemony by drawing on post-structuralist approaches (see also Smith, 1998). Žižek (2004, p 3) reminds us that hegemony is not simply related to words because an image can serve, in some instances, to hegemonise a field, and function as the paradigmatic image of an idea, a regime, a problem (see also Bren, 2010). See the job advert for vacant social work posts, and my interpretation of it, featured in Garrett (2003).

CHAPTER SEVEN

Thinking with Bourdieu

Introduction

Pierre Bourdieu, 'a philosopher turned anthropologist (and, later, sociologist)' (Callinicos, 1999a, p 288), was born the 'son of a postman in a remote peasant village in southern France' (Noble and Watkins, 2003, p 521). Drafted in 1955, he served as a conscript during the Algerian war of independence that had begun the previous year. While war continued, he started to work at Algiers University, carrying out the fieldwork he drew on throughout his career.[1] Upon his return to France, he went on to occupy a prestigious position within the higher education field and wrote more than 40 books and over 400 articles (Lane, 2000). For Fowler (2003, p 486), Bourdieu's 'magnum opus' was *Distinction* (Bourdieu, 2004 [1984]), published in 1979, the same year as Lyotard's (1984) immensely influential *The postmodern condition* appeared in France.

Beyond France, social work literature has tended to neglect Bourdieu, so much so that his name did not even feature in the index of Dominelli's (1997) *Sociology for social work*. This omission is most surprising given that Bourdieu is one of the very few high-profile social theorists – Bauman being a second notable exception – to have shown a keen interest in social work (see particularly, Bourdieu et al, 2002, pp 181–255). In the UK, Houston (2002) began to explore Bourdieu's relevance for social work (see also Emond, 2003). Less successfully, Fram (2004) and Emirbayer and Williams (2005) have pursued a similar endeavour in the US.

Renowned for his dense prose style and the vastness of his 'output', Bourdieu can often present challenges to first-time readers. After discussing some of these potential obstacles, the chapter will explain his 'conceptual arsenal' (Wacquant, 1998, p 220) and dwell on major theoretical 'tools', such as 'habitus', 'field' and 'capital'. Some of Bourdieu's theoretical shortcomings will also be examined: especially with regard to his problematic engagement with issues relating to multiculturalism, 'race' and ethnicity and his ideas on the function of the state.

Bourdieu did not exclusively inhabit the constrained and constraining environs of the university. Although 'repelled by Stalinist sectarianism', he was consistently 'a man of the left' (Wacquant, 2005b, p 11). The second part of the chapter will examine his perception of the role of intellectuals and particularly the function of sociology. Finally, the focus will turn to Bourdieu's understanding of social work, often broadly interpreted, during a period of neoliberal ascendancy.

Obstacles to understanding

Those unable to read French might be tempted to impute the awkwardness of Bourdieu's prose style to a faulty English rendition, but the translators are not to be blamed for such opacity, particularly given that the mainstream translations were approved by the author. Beyond the question of prose style, Jenkins (2002, p 26) refers to a 'kind of illusionary profundity which can make Bourdieu's work so irritating to read'. Others, such as Lemert (2000), are more impressed with Bourdieu's style. However, even Wacquant (1998, p 217), Bourdieu's loyal associate and frequent co-author, concedes that his friend's writing is often 'couched in a difficult technical idiom', which makes it 'on first sight daunting if not intractable'.

Whereas in his interviews and in more journalistic, polemical pieces, Bourdieu is relatively accessible, in his scholarly writing, the author shuns short sentences and pithy articulations, firmly maintaining that 'what is complex can only be said in a complex way' (Bourdieu, 1994, p 51). This deliberate stylistic choice is situated within a wider intellectual project aimed at 'break[ing] with naïve familiarity and the illusions of immediate understanding' (Bourdieu, 1996, p 2). As he elaborates in a compilation of interviews significantly titled *In other words*:

> My texts are full of indications meant to stop the reader deforming and simplifying things. Unfortunately, these warnings pass unnoticed or else make what I am saying so complicated that readers who read too quickly see neither the little indications nor the big ones and read more or less the opposite of what I wanted to say.... [W]hat is certain is that I am not out to make my writing clear and simple and that I consider the strategy of abandoning the rigour of technical vocabulary in favour of an easy and readable style to be dangerous. This is first and foremost because false clarity is often part and parcel of the dominant discourse, the discourse of those who think everything goes without saying, because everything is just fine as it is ... I am convinced that, for both scientific and political reasons, you have to accept that discourse can and must be as complicated as the (more or less complicated) problem it is tackling demands ... I don't believe in the virtues of 'common sense' and 'clarity'. (Bourdieu, 1994, pp 52–3)

This sociological aspiration, implicit in much of Bourdieu's work, to cast doubt on 'false clarity' is one that social work should perhaps share.

A second obstacle is that despite Bourdieu's resistance to misleading 'labels', some critics and commentators have insisted on 'pinning him down', or trying to 'pigeonhole' him. Some, such as Lash (1990), have viewed Bourdieu as a 'postmodernist' despite the fact that his work has consistently provided a 'conceptual antidote to postmodern voluntaristic politics' (Lovell, 2000, p 34). Others have dubbed him a 'Marxist', using the 'M'-word as a 'tactic of academic disqualification' (see Wacquant, 2001b, p 103). It is easy, though, to comprehend why Bourdieu would be tagged as a 'Marxist' in that he made frequent recourse to a terminology and vocabulary often associated with a Marxist analysis and was comfortable in referring to 'proletariat', 'cultural imperialism', 'class forces' and so on. Moreover, Bourdieu clearly associated himself with political causes generally backed by Marxists: for example, his trenchant opposition to market fundamentalism, job cuts and the commodification of all forms of cultural expression. His polemical and passionate attacks on unemployment also appear to hint if not to an adherence to Marxism, then to an orientation or worldview that is shared with Marxism.

In what follows, the aim is to concentrate on three of Bourdieu's main concepts: habitus, field and capital. Although a section will be devoted to each separately, these key ideas, like those of Gramsci discussed in Chapter Six, need to be viewed relationally and in dynamic interplay with one another.

Surveying Bourdieu: the 'conceptual arsenal'

Habitus

At the intersection between the two major intellectual currents of the 1960s and 1970s – existentialism and structuralism – Bourdieu's intellectual project can be interpreted as an attempt to locate his conceptualisations *between* the subjectivist emphasis of the former and the objectivist preoccupation of the latter. He saw structuralism, and the 'structuralist generation', as a response to the 'need to react against what existentialism had represented for them: the flabby "humanism" that was in the air, the complacent appeal to "lived experience"' (Bourdieu, 1994, pp 4–5). His habitus formulation, therefore, while being equally opposed to existentialism and other subjectivist visions, was seeking to:

> reintroduce agents that Levi-Strauss and the structuralists, among others Althusser, tended to abolish, making them into simple epiphenomena of structure…. Social agents, in archaic societies as well as in ours, are not automata regulated like clocks, in accordance with laws which they do not understand. (Bourdieu, 1994, p 9; see also p 20)

The problem, as he saw it, was that structuralists, such as Althusser, were producing a 'grand theory without agents' without ever seeing 'a worker, or a peasant, or anything' (Bourdieu, in Karakayli, 2004, p 359). In short, they left 'no scope for human agency' (Bourdieu, in Overden, 2000).

From Aristotle to Saint Thomas Aquinas, Hegel, Weber, Durkheim, Mauss and Husserl, the idea of habitus had currency within philosophical and sociological literature well before Bourdieu made it into his 'hallmark concept' (Shusterman, 1999, p 4). Yet, in his effort to oppose structuralist objectivism without relapsing into subjectivism, he completely rethought the meaning of habitus. 'As social life incorporated, and thus individuated', Bourdieu's habitus seeks to transcend the opposition between the individual and society. It represents the 'constraint of social conditions and conditionings, *right in the very heart* of the "subject"' (Bourdieu, 1994, p 15, emphasis added). It defines a person's 'whole manner of being' (quoted in Bourdieu et al, 2002, p 510; see also Bourdieu, 1994, 2002a, 2002b). In what Lemert (2000, p 101) describes as 'one of the most beautifully composed passages in the whole of sociological literature', Bourdieu characterises habitus as:

> structured structures predisposed to function as structuring structures ... practices and representations which can be objectively 'regulated' and 'regular' without in any way being the product of obedience to rules ... collectively orchestrated without being the product of the orchestrating action of a conductor. (Bourdieu, 2003b, p 72)

Furthermore, the practices produced by habitus are 'always tending to reproduce the objective structures of which they are a product, they are determined by past conditions' (Bourdieu, 2003b, p 72). Habitus can therefore be 'understood as a system of lasting, transposable dispositions which, integrating past experiences, functions at every moment as *a matrix of perceptions, appreciations, and actions*' (Bourdieu, 2003b, pp 82–83, emphases in original). Associated with habitus is what might be regarded as a self-censoring or self-editing trait because 'the dispositions durably inculcated by objective conditions ... engender aspirations and practices objectively compatible with those objective requirements, the most improbable practices are excluded ... as *unthinkable*' (Bourdieu, 2003b, p 77, emphasis in original).

Perhaps unsurprisingly given this conceptualisation, childhood is particularly important: habitus is 'laid down in each agent' in their 'earliest upbringing' and from then it continues to reverberate throughout a person's lifetime (Bourdieu, 2003a, p 81; see also Cronin, 1996; Circourel, 2003; Tomanovic, 2004). Moreover, Bourdieu was to maintain an interest in the function and role of education. Indeed, despite their different theoretical orientations, for both Althusser and Bourdieu, the school was 'the major modern ideological base' (Fowler, 1997, p 22). In the conversations reported in *The weight of the world: social suffering in contemporary society*, the school was frequently at the 'core of the suffering of the interviewees' (Bourdieu, in Bourdieu et al, 2002, p 507). Also relevant, for Bourdieu, is how 'materially secure children', with their 'casual ease' within education, are able to glide through this particular field, whereas working-class children and the children of the unemployed are likely to encounter obstacles and difficulties (Fowler, 1997, p 24). This is not to dismiss those miraculous exceptions (*les miraculés*), educationally highly successful children of the working class and unemployed who 'make it', thus allowing us to 'believe that the system is egalitarian and meritocratic after all' (Moi, 1991, p 1026). It is, however, to recognise along with Bourdieu that 'the education system is one of the principal agents of symbolic violence in modern democracies' (Moi, 1991, p 1023; see also Chapter Nine).

Two additional points are important in relation to Bourdieu's development of the habitus formulation. First, a number of commentators have noted the significance of the body within Bourdieu's theorisation (see, eg, Moi, 1991; Butler, 1999). Bridge (2004, p 62) has asserted that his 'understanding of class divisions is scripted around the body moving in space – the space it inscribes, its gait, the gestures of the arms and hands, inclination of the head and so on'. The 'bodily hexis', therefore – 'a durable manner of standing, speaking, and thereby of *feeling* and *thinking*' – was immensely important in the entire conceptual apparatus developed by Bourdieu (2003b, pp 93–4, original emphasis). Habitus is, in fact, 'society written into the body' (Bourdieu, 1994, p 63): the body 'does not memorize the past, it *enacts* the past, bringing it back to life' (Bourdieu, in Butler, 1999, p 115, emphasis in original). Similarly, habitus can be interpreted as 'history incarnate *in the body*' (Bourdieu, 1994, p 190, emphasis in original). A number of sociologists have subsequently done interesting work, much of it very relevant for social work, examining how the body might inform our understanding of dynamics associated with class and gender. Drawing on Bourdieu, Beverley Skeggs (1997, p 91) states that a body's 'use of space through movement and confidence [or lack of it] sends strong class signals'. More recently, the construction of the socially toxic 'chav' label, used to ridicule a section of the working class, is partly founded on a sense of scorn for the way this identified group are supposed to speak, or choose to adorn themselves (Haywood and Yar, 2006; Tyler, 2008; Jones, O., 2011; Toynbee, 2011b).

A second important point Bourdieu frequently emphasised was that habitus was not deterministic (although, at times, it can certainly appear so), since the 'social world may be uttered and constructed in different ways according to the different principles of vision and division' (Bourdieu, 2002a, p 237). This articulation of the concept is reminiscent of the famous comment of Marx that individuals 'make their own history, but they do not make it as they please; they do not make it under circumstances chosen by themselves, but under circumstances directly encountered, given, and transmitted from the past' (quoted in McLennan, 2000, p 329). Fowler (1997, p 23) maintains: 'Thus, people (agents), collectively or individually, transform or reproduce their social structures, but they do so within specific social conditions, including those that are internalised as part of the habitus even at the moment of revolution'.

For Bourdieu, a 'feel for the game' is what enables an 'infinite number of "moves" to be made' (Bourdieu, 1994, p 9; see also p 65). In Algeria, for example, the matrimonial strategies he examined were not simply the product of obedience to a rule but 'a feel for the game' that led people to 'choose' the best match possible given the game at their disposal. Similarly, Bourdieu maintains that habitus is:

> [N]ot something natural, inborn: being a product of history, that is of social experience and education, it may be changed by history, that is by new experiences, education or training.… Dispositions are long-lasting: they tend to perpetuate, to reproduce themselves, but they are

> not eternal....Any dimension of habitus is very difficult to change but
> it may be changed through the process of awareness and of pedagogic
> effort. (Bourdieu, 2002b, p 29)

He was, therefore, keen to contest the interpretation of some of his critics who placed, for him, too great an emphasis on the *entirely* constraining facets of the habitus (see, eg, Haugaard, 2002; Jenkins, 2002; Noble and Watkins, 2003). Thus, the 'model of the circle, the vicious cycle of structure producing habitus which reproduces structure *ad infinitum* is a product of commentators' (Bourdieu, 2002b, p 30). Even:

> in traditional societies or in specific sectors of modern societies, habitus
> is never a mere principle of repetition – that is the difference between
> habitus and habit. As a dynamic system of dispositions that interact
> with one another, it has, as such, a generative capacity. (Bourdieu,
> 2002b, p 30)

In the volume that he produced with Loic Wacquant, *An invitation to reflexive sociology* (Bourdieu and Wacquant, 2004), Bourdieu addresses this aspect of his thinking in some detail.

> Habitus is not the fate that some people read into it. Being the
> product of history, it is an open system of dispositions that is constantly
> subjected to experiences, and therefore constantly affected by them in
> a way that either reinforces or modifies its structures. It is durable but
> not eternal! Having said this, I must immediately add that there is a
> probability, inscribed in the social destiny associated with definite social
> conditions, that experience will conform to habitus, because most
> people are statistically bound to encounter circumstances that tend to
> agree with those that originally fashioned their habitus. (Bourdieu, in
> Bourdieu and Wacquant, 2004, p 133)

Indeed, 'the habitus goes hand in glove with vagueness and indeterminacy' (Bourdieu, 1994, p 77): it 'generates inventions and improvisations but within limits' (Bourdieu, 2002b, p 31). As Houston (2002, p 157) suggests, in an earlier examination of the relevance of Bourdieu for social work, the concept of habitus strongly implies that we 'are not automatons or mindless vehicles of our governing habitus. Rather, habitus acts as a very loose set of guidelines permitting us to strategize, adapt, improvise or innovate in response to situations as they arise'. The process of migration, family breakdown or the onset of an illness or disability may also give rise to a 'cleft habitus', which is 'inhabited by tensions and contradictions' (Bourdieu, 2007, p 100).

Similarly, in an interview shortly before his death, Bourdieu maintained that habitus:

is part of how society reproduces itself. But there is also change. Conflict is built into society. People can find their expectations and ways of living are suddenly out of step with the new social position they find themselves in....Then the question of social agency and political intervention becomes very important. (Quoted in Overden, 2000)

Eagleton (1991, p 50) also observes that a person's or a group's habitus is a 'practical ideology', which is a 'creative, open-ended affair, in no sense a simple "reflection" of dominant ideas'. The habitus, 'rather like human language itself, is an open-ended system which ... permits ceaseless innovation, rather than a rigid blueprint' (Eagleton, 1991, p 156).

Field

Bourdieu's conception of habitus exists in close relationship to his notion of field. A field, or *champ*, is 'a structured social space, a field of forces', with agents and groups of agents being defined by their relative positions in this space (Bourdieu, 1998b, p 40). Human beings are, therefore, 'situated in a site ... and they occupy a place. The *site* ... can be defined absolutely as the point in *physical space* where an agent or a thing is situated' (Bourdieu, in Bourdieu et al, 2002, p 123, emphasis in original). However, individuals are also 'constituted in, and in relationship to, a *social space* (or better yet, to fields)' (Bourdieu, in Bourdieu et al, 2002, p 124, emphasis in original).

The:

> space can also be described as a field of forces: in other words, as a set of objective power relations imposed on all those who enter this field, relations which are not reducible to all the intentions of individual agents or even to direct *interactions* between agents. (Bourdieu, 1991, p 230, emphasis in original)

Chopra (2003, p 427, original emphasis) has usefully elaborated that Bourdieu:

> employs the notion of field to explain the functioning and composition of social space *across* a society, as opposed to his theorization of habitus, which explains the functioning of social space in particular and homogeneous environments shared by groups of people. Social space can be understood as made up of different, and distinct (although overlapping) *fields*, which correspond to different spheres of activity and practice, such as the cultural, economic, social and political.

Such fields, including that of social work, have proliferated during the period of modernity (Cronin, 1996).

Every social field, therefore, is 'a *space of relations* which is just as real as a geographical space' (Bourdieu, 1991, p 232, emphasis in original). Moreover, every social field is 'necessarily structured by a set of unspoken rules for what can be validly uttered or perceived within it' (Eagleton, 1991, p 157). This aspect is important for those positioned inside a particular social field because within it, 'every discourse … has to observe the correct *forms* or risk exclusion as nonsense (in the case of the intellectual field, excluded discourses would tend to be cast as *stupid* or *naïve*) (Moi, 1991, p 1022, emphases in original). Even so, a field 'is not the product of a deliberate act of creation, and it follows rules or, better, regularities, that are not explicit or codified' (Bourdieu and Wacquant, 2004, p 98).

Fields can be interpreted as having at least three key characteristics. First, the field is crucial in terms of the evolution of the habitus of those operating within it. Second, a field seeks to maintain its autonomy. So, for Bourdieu, maintaining the autonomy of the fields of cultural and scientific production is to become increasingly important, indeed urgent, as forces of neoliberalisation attempt to penetrate and undermine their independence. A third characteristic of fields is the competition taking place within them. Here, his conceptualisation of capital is important.

Capital

Capital, for Bourdieu, does 'not exist and function except in relation to a field' (Bourdieu and Wacquant, 2004, p 101). Thus, in 'most fields, we may observe what we characterize as competition for accumulation of different forms of capital' (Bourdieu, in Bourdieu and Eagleton, 1994, p 271). Wacquant (1998, p 221) elaborates that the 'system of dispositions people acquire depends on the position(s) they occupy in society, that is, on their particular endowment in capital'. Importantly, only those who can mobilise the relevant resources are able to take part in the struggles which define a field. The position of an agent in the field is, therefore, 'characterised by the volume and type of capital it has access to' (Peillon, 1998, p 216). The 'right to speak, *legitimacy*, is invested in those agents recognized by the field as powerful possessors of capital' (Moi, 1991, p 1022, emphasis in original).

Bourdieu (1991, p 230) argues further that the different:

> kinds of capital, like trumps in a game of cards, are powers which define the chances of profit in a given field (in fact, to every field or sub-field there corresponds a particular kind of capital, which is current, as a power or stake in that field).

Elsewhere, he articulates capital as follows:

> At each moment, it is the state of the relations of force between players that defines the structure of the field. We can picture each player as

having in front of her a pile of tokens of different colors, each color corresponding to a given species of capital she holds, so that her relative force in the game, her position in the space of play, and also strategic orientation toward the game … the moves she makes, more or less risky or cautious, subversive or conservative, depend both on the total number of tokens and on the composition of the piles of tokens she retains, that is, on the volume and structure of her capital. (Bourdieu, in Bourdieu and Wacquant, 2004, p 99)

He identifies three main forms of capital. First, *economic capital*, which refers to material and financial assets, ownership of stocks and shares and so on. *Cultural capital* can be viewed as 'scarce symbolic goods, skills and titles' (Wacquant, 1998, p 221): for example, distinction within the fields of higher education. Bourdieu felt, moreover, that in the:

prosperous post-war societies of the West, 'cultural capital' – educational credentials and familiarity with bourgeois culture – was becoming a major determinant of life chances and that, under the cloak of individual talent and academic meritocracy, its unequal distribution was helping to conserve social hierarchy. (Wacquant, 1998, p 216)

A third form of capital, *social capital*, can be understood as resources or contacts 'accrued by virtue of membership of a particular group' or network (Wacquant, 1998, p 221). Drawing on Bourdieu's conceptual framework, Nowotny, among others, has also endeavoured to develop the concept of 'emotional capital', which she sees as a variant of social capital, but characteristic of the private, rather than public, sphere (see Reay, 2000, 2004). Parker (2000, p 88) has referred to the significance of 'imperial capital – the accumulated historical advantage of colonial power'.

Symbolic capital is best viewed as different to the three other forms of capital in so far as it can be *any* of these forms. As expressed by Bourdieu (1991, p 230), 'symbolic capital, commonly called prestige, reputation, fame, etc … is the form assumed by these different kinds of capital when they are perceived and recognised as legitimate'. In the 'symbolic struggle for the production of common sense or, more precisely, for the monopoly of legitimate naming as the official – i.e. explicit and public – imposition of the legitimate vision of the social world, agents bring into play' symbolic capital (Bourdieu, 1991, p 239). Those lacking 'appropriate' forms of symbolic capital can find themselves at a disadvantage within particular fields. They may even find themselves freighted with what Bourdieu terms 'negative symbolic capital' on account of 'their names, accent, and place of residence' (Bourdieu, in Bourdieu et al, 2002, p 185).

Disagreeing with Bourdieu

Bourdieu, multiculturalism, 'race' and ethnicity

Turning to analyse the problems with the content of Bourdieu's work, one difficulty is his somewhat unconvincing engagement with the related themes of multiculturalism, 'race' and ethnicity. In an attack on US 'cultural imperialism' in *Le Monde Diplomatique*, Bourdieu and Wacquant argued that 'multiculturalism' was – along with words such as 'globalisation', 'flexibility', 'governance', 'employability', 'underclass', 'exclusion', 'new economy', 'zero tolerance', 'communitarianism' – an example of what Orwell termed a 'strange Newspeak' (Bourdieu and Wacquant, 2001, p 2). 'North American "multiculturalism" is neither a concept nor a theory, nor a social or political movement', it is a 'screen discourse'. Bourdieu and Wacquant criticised terms such as 'minority', 'ethnicity' and 'identity' as being simply a facet of a 'new planetary vulgate – from which the terms "capitalism", "class", "exploitation", "domination" and "inequality" are conspicuous by their absence' (Bourdieu and Wacquant, 2001, p 2).[2] The two scholars were even more acrimonious in their invective against the field of Cultural Studies, which they described as a 'mongrel domain' (Bourdieu and Wacquant, 1999, p 47). They went on:

> Just as the products of America's cultural industry like jazz and rap, or the commonest food and clothing fashions, like jeans, owe part of the quasi-universal seduction they wield over youth to the fact that they are produced and worn by subordinate minorities, so the topics of the new world vulgate no doubt derive a good measure of their symbolic efficacy from the fact that, supported by specialists from disciplines perceived to be marginal or subversive, such as Cultural Studies, Minority Studies, Gay Studies or Women's Studies, they take on, in the eyes of writers from the former European colonies for example, *the allure of messages of liberation*. Indeed, cultural imperialism (American or otherwise) never imposes itself better than when it is served by progressive intellectuals (or by 'intellectuals of colour' in the case of racial inequality) who would appear to be above suspicion of promoting the hegemonic interests of a country against which they wield the weapons of social criticism. (Bourdieu and Wacquant, 1999, pp 50–1, emphasis added)

Specifically in terms of 'race', Bourdieu and Wacquant argued that the:

> American tradition superimposes on an infinitely more complex social reality a rigid dichotomy between whites and blacks [and] can even impose itself in countries where the operative principles of vision and

division of ethnic differences, codified or practical, are quite different.
(Bourdieu and Wacquant, 1999, p 44)

There is, of course, a good deal of truth in this charge. Within the discourse of
social work in the UK, for example, the deployment of this 'dichotomy' has served
to render Irish people invisible (Garrett, 2004). Likewise, it can be argued that
a rather shallow and, at times, merely rhetorical preoccupation with 'diversity'
and 'difference' has served to mask hardships rooted in social class and poverty
(Garrett, 2002). Indeed, this theme will be returned to in Chapters Nine and Ten.
Suffice to add here that the charge that a concern about multiculturalism is the
staple of the gullible, conned into participating in a 'screen discourse', is wide of
the mark, hinting at deeper problems in Bourdieu's engagement with issues of
'race' and ethnicity.

Jenkins (2002, p 92) has claimed that ethnicity is something Bourdieu 'rarely
considers except in his early research in North Africa'. However, this alleged
lacuna needs to be located within the 'field' of French cultural and political life.
As Werbner (2000, p 150) suggests, most 'commentators on France are agreed
that, given its republican ideals of individual equality in a culturally homogeneous
public sphere, a shift to more culturally pluralist concepts of national integration
has been deeply fraught for French intellectuals'. Within the wider political and
official discourse, when 'those who do not quite fit into the Republican imagery
mobilize, the principle of equality – otherwise strongly defended – gets displaced
by a preoccupation with "ethnic" origins and religious affiliations – otherwise
strongly criticised' (Dikec, 2006, p 163). This is particularly the case in terms of
the state-sanctioned 'Islamophobia' (Murray, 2006). The dominant Republican
model of integration has become vulnerable on account of the 'riots' taking place
in the *Banlieues* – suburbs inhabited by the unemployed and working poor – in
October and November 2005 (Dikec, 2006; Murray, 2006; Balibar, 2007; see also
MacCormaic, 2009). Debates generated by the ill-founded decision to ban the veil
also point to a more pervasive crisis of identity within the French polity (Liogier,
2010; see also the later discussion on Alain Badiou in Chapter Ten).

Bourdieu and Wacquant's orientation is, therefore, explicable (if less than
convincing) within a French milieu where 'Third Republic universalism' was, until
its recent destabilisation, the major paradigm for the understanding and analysing
of racism in France (Lane, 2000, p 200; see also Balibar, 2007). Nevertheless, the
whole notion of 'multiculturalism' is a good deal more complex than the pair are
prepared to concede (see Lewis, 2005; Lewis and Neal, 2005; Yuval-Davis et al,
2005). For example, debates centred on it are *not* simply a result of US dominance
of international intellectual fields. Research funding from the European Union, for
example, has encouraged comparative studies of ethnicity, racism and immigration
across Europe. Multiculturalism can also be interpreted as a 'travelling theory',
which 'disguises very different and fluid struggles in different countries, and
even in different cities and localities. This is because multiculturalism is always
mediated by pre-existing structures and policies already in place' (Werbner, 2000,

p 154). Neither is multiculturalism simply a 'top–down government-driven policy' because, on occasions, it is also a:

> response to grassroots demand for change, the product of local or national activism.... Critical multiculturalism – unlike corporate multiculturalism which exists in some European countries – is a mode of *dissent* adopted by excluded or marginalized minorities to attack old paradigms and desanctify tabooed discourses and sacred cows. (Werbner, 2000, p 154, emphasis in original)

Within social services in the UK and elsewhere, the promotion of 'multiculturalism' has, at least in part, been the product of the struggles of marginalised minority groups of workers and users of services.

Bourdieu does not, of course, entirely neglect issues rooted in 'race' and ethnicity and it has been argued that to reach the conclusion that he is 'against multiculturalism' is to lay a undue emphasis on merely one aspect of the *Le Monde Diplomatique* article (Puwar, 2009, p 373). It is clear that throughout his life, he remained an opponent of state-generated racism and xenophobia (see particularly, Bourdieu, 2008, pp 284–8). Following the 2005 'riots', he challenged the right-wing media in concluding that certain 'acts of delinquency or vandalism can be understood as an embryonic form of civil war' (Bourdieu, 2008, p 202).

On a more abstract and conceptual level, *The weight of the world* (Bourdieu et al, 2002) refers to the 'negative symbolic capital' of 'adolescents of foreign origin, notably North Africans' in the French school system. This is 'linked to the external signs of their body hexis that function as stigmata', along with their names, accent, and place of residence (Bourdieu, in Bourdieu et al, 2002, p 185). However, there are many instances where his analysis could be extended. For example, Bourdieu's reference to 'a habitus divided against itself' (Bourdieu, in Bourdieu et al, 2002, p 511; see also Bourdieu, 2002b, p 31) – a potentially useful notion in examining issues related to migration and displacement in contemporary Europe – could have been examined more fully (see Sayad, 2004). In this context, Parker (2000, p 82) has usefully evolved the idea of 'diaspora habitus', which refers to the 'scheme of perception, appreciation and action which governs everyday practices in diaspora'. This conceptualisation is important because habitus fails to capture 'the lived experiences of racialized hierarchy; its topology of social space prioritises mapping of class positions'. The 'diasporic social location adds an extra element which he [Bourdieu] cannot accommodate in his model: the stubborn commitments and resistances resulting from the differentially racialized embodiment of social inequalities' (Parker, 2000, pp 83–4).

Bourdieu's 'left' and 'right' hands

Bourdieu writes impressively on the role of the state, especially in shaping public perceptions:

> In modern societies, the State makes a decisive contribution towards the production and reproduction of ... social reality. In particular ... it imposes all the fundamental principles of classification – sex, age, 'competence', etc. – through the imposition into social categories.... [It] sets up durable and often definitive symbolic differences, universally recognized within its area of authority.... Through the structuring it imposes on practices, the State institutes and inculcates common symbolic forms of thought, social frames of perception or memory, State forms of classification or, more precisely, practical schemes of perception, appreciation and action. (Bourdieu, 2000, p 175)

Wacquant (2005b, p 17) further develops this perspective, asserting that the:

> state does not exist only 'out there', in the guise of bureaucracies, authorities, and ceremonies: it also lives 'in here', ineffaceably engraved in us in the form of state sponsored mental categories acquired via schooling through which we cognitively construct the social world, so that we already consent to its dictates prior to committing any 'political' act.

Bourdieu's (2001b, p 5) depiction of the state is nonetheless problematic, especially in its distinction between what he calls the 'left hand' and the 'right hand' of the state. According to him, the state's 'left hand' is composed by social workers, youth leaders and secondary and primary school teachers, in other words, 'the set of agents of the so-called spending ministries which are the trace within the state of the struggles of the past' (Bourdieu, 2001b, p 2). Conversely, the 'right hand' is comprised of Treasury and bank technocrats who, 'obsessed by the question of financial equilibrium, knows nothing of the problems of the left hand, confronted with the often very costly social consequences of "budgetary restrictions"' (Bourdieu, 2001b, p 5). In some respects, this description of the state's internal fracturing is persuasive. Yet, while acknowledging tensions between particular ministries and significant state actors, it is preferable to consider the state as a complex totality. Here, the activities of the 'left hand' cannot be viewed as unambiguously benign because doing so would mask their potentially regulatory intent. If Bourdieu's dichotomy were accurate, how could we understand, for example, the abuses committed in 'care' settings discussed in Chapter Three? Not only can the 'left hand of the state' also be a *punishing* hand, but – historically and in a more contemporary context – it performs a key ideological role, distinguishing between the 'deserving' and the 'undeserving' poor.

One can also criticise Bourdieu's faith in the emerging 'supranational' states, such as the European Union, despite the fact that these more territorially expansive formations are, as discussed in Chapter Five, also neoliberal in character and trajectory (see Callinicos, 1999b, pp 92–3; see also Harvey, 2010).

Bourdieu and the working class

A third criticism of Bourdieu strikes at the foundations of his conceptual apparatus. Surveying his work, Fowler (2001), one of his most informed and enlightening commentators, maintains that the force of habitus can be resisted by the use of reflection. Nonetheless, Bourdieu can on occasion appear far too deterministic, unduly emphasising the dulled passivity of social actors and particularly of dominated groups. He observes, for example:

> Once an object of pride, rooted in traditions and sustained by a whole technical and political heritage, manual workers as a group – if indeed it still exists as such – are thrown into demoralization, devaluation and political disillusionment, which is expressed in the crisis of activism or, worse, in a desperate rallying to the themes of quasi-fascist extremism. (Bourdieu, 2001b, p 100)

Discussing key passages in Bourdieu's work with working-class respondents in Rotherham, Yorkshire, Charlesworth found that they 'were fascinated by the ideas and knew precisely what Bourdieu was expressing'. He maintains that these 'people passionately seize Bourdieu's interpretations of their way of living' (Charlesworth, 2000a, p 27; see also Charlesworth, 2000b). Despite this apparent endorsement, Bourdieu's approach remains problematic. As Noble and Watkins (2003, p 524) point out, Bourdieu 'asserts that habitus is not fate, but an open system of dispositions that shape and are shaped by experience, but [he still] focuses on its inert and conservative nature'. For example:

> People are not fools ... they have internalized, through a protracted and multisided process of conditioning, the objective chances they face. They know how to 'read' the future that fits them, which is made for them and for which they are made (by opposition to everything that the expression 'this is not for the likes of us' designates) ... what unquestionably imposes itself as that which 'has' to be done or said (and which will retrospectively appear as the 'only' thing to do or say). (Bourdieu, in Bourdieu and Wacquant, 2004, p 130)

Thus, habitus tends to be presented as a rather static entity, which risks undermining Bourdieu's theorisation of practice as interactive, strategic and relational. Friedmann (2002), for example, has identified five areas where habitus is susceptible to change: instances of social mobility; migration, which can involve a 'massive readjustment of migrants' habitus', with migrant children often opting for the 'habitus of the metropolis' (Friedmann, 2002, p 302); the impact of the social movements, notably the feminist movement, on shared, collective habitus; accelerated change of habitus during a period of late capitalism; and the breakdown of habitus in societies where social order has collapsed (Rwanda, Kosovo, etc), 'but also in such reputedly stable societies such as the Japanese' (Friedmann, 2002, p 304).

From a feminist perspective also, reference has been made to Bourdieu's 'alleged determinism' and some 'have seen Bourdieu's sociology as drawing an illegitimate emphasis on women's complicity with masculine domination' (Fowler, 2003, p 485), yet he always insists that his theory of practice is not a theory of total determination (see Adkins, 2004a, 2004b; Lovell, 2004; Skeggs, 2004a, 2004b, 2004c).[3] Thus, *Pascalian meditations* (Bourdieu, 2000):

> restates the view that agents possess a 'margin of freedom'. Resigned hopelessness can always be broken through in a crisis, 'civilized routines' can – at least temporarily – be cast aside. So there is always a potential for the lack of a match between objective structures and internal cognitive categories. In crises, in particular, there is a sudden nerve-racking sense of openness. (Fowler, 2003, p 485)

Nonetheless, Bourdieu *does* frequently seem 'eager to explain the inertia of habitus ... not its dynamism' (Noble and Watkins, 2003, p 524; see also Adkins, 2004a, 2004b). Moreover, his analysis can seem to lend insufficient weight to the hard *ideological* work taking place to maintain – what we have seen Gramsci refer to in Chapter Six as – hegemony and bolster the worldview of the dominant (Friedman, 2009). As Noble and Watkins (2003, p 525) observe, there is 'little sense of the acquisition of habitus which is construed as transmission, internalization, inculcation and conditioning': Bourdieu 'forgets the tedious processes of learning the second nature' (Noble and Watkins, 2003, p 527). Similarly, how habitus 'works out' and varies between individuals similarly 'remains under-theorized by Bourdieu' (Lau, 2004, p 373).

Bourdieu's discussion on the unemployed sub-proletariat in Algeria suggests that their poverty imposes 'on them with a necessity so total that it allows no glimpse of a reasonable exit' (quoted in Jenkins, 2002, p 28): an idea bearing 'more than a passing resemblance to Oscar Lewis's much-criticised notion of the "culture of poverty"' (Jenkins, 2002, p 28). As Lane (2000, p 16) highlights, if:

> traditional Algerian society were indeed as static as Bourdieu suggested, as inherently resistant to initiative or innovation, it was difficult to see how he could account for the emergence of an indigenous liberation movement which was to prove powerful enough to provoke the downfall of a French Republic and the end of colonial rule in Algeria.

Similarly, Bourdieu fails to take into account the transcultural nature of Algerian society. For example, Algerian nationalism 'drew on both Western Marxism, which Algerian labourers had first encountered in French factories between the wars, and indigenous traditions, notably Islam' (Lane, 2000, p 17).

Bourdieu's perspective on working-class life and of the capacity (or lack thereof) of the working class to drive social change is also connected to such criticisms (see Calhoun, 2003). For him, a profound realism characterises the worldview of the dominated:

> I know perfectly well that those who are dominated ... oppose and resist this domination.... But at a certain period, the struggles of the dominated were so romanticized (to such an extent that 'in struggle' has ended up working as a sort of Homeric epithet, liable to be stuck on anything that moved – women, students, the dominated, workers, and so on) that people finally forgot something that everyone who has seen it from close up knows perfectly well: the dominated are dominated in their brains too. (Bourdieu, 1994, p 41)

It could be countered that in seeking to combat the bogus optimism of some sections of the Marxist Left, Bourdieu is simply succumbing to an opposite and equally misleading conceptualisation: one that is apt to lay far too great an emphasis on the compliance of the downtrodden and dominated.[4] Thus, it has been maintained that he 'presents a model of the working-class in *Distinction* [Bourdieu, 2004 [1984]] in a particularly quaint and romantic way but with dignity – but in *Weight of the world* [Bourdieu et al, 2002] as racist, pathetic, useless and abused' (Skeggs, 2004a, p 87). In the latter book, the:

> working-class habitus is absolute and complete lack.... But what about elements of working-class culture that we know have value not just for the working class: the creative hedonism; the anti-pretentious humour, the dignity, the high ethical standards of honour, loyalty and caring?... What about all the working-class dispositions that the middle class crave and appropriate whenever they can? (Skeggs, 2004a, p 88)

Bourdieu's perspective on working-class life is also reflected in his comment that workers 'know a lot: more than any intellectual, more than any sociologist. But in a sense they don't know it, they lack the instrument to grasp it, to speak about it' (quoted in Bourdieu and Eagleton, 1994, p 273). In conversation with Terry Eagleton, Bourdieu was asked about the lack of room for dissent, criticism and opposition:

> That is a very good question. Even in the most economistic tradition that we know, namely Marxism, I think the capacity for resistance, as a capacity for consciousness, was overestimated. I fear that what I have to say is shocking for the self-confidence of intellectuals, especially the more generous, left-wing intellectuals. I am seen as pessimistic, as discouraging the people, and so on. But I think it is better to know the truth; and the fact is that when we see with our own eyes people

living in poor conditions – such as existed, when I was a young scholar, among the local proletariat, the workers in the factories – it is clear that they are prepared to accept much more than we would have believed. That was a very strong experience for me: they put up with a great deal, and this is what I mean by doxa – that there are many things people accept without knowing.... It doesn't mean that the dominated individuals tolerate everything; but they assent to much more than we believe and much more than they know. (Quoted in Bourdieu and Eagleton, 1994, pp 268–9)

Commenting on this dimension of Bourdieu's work, Callinicos (1999a, p 295) maintained that the French sociologist 'does not offer those at the bottom of society any prospect of a collective escape from structures of class domination and cultural distinction'. Most fundamentally, at the time of Bourdieu's death, there remained a striking gap between his political activism and the 'conceptual apparatus he sets to work in response to the neoliberal challenge' (Callinicos, 1999b, p 88). From a similar position, Wolfreys (2000) argues that Bourdieu's concept of habitus is so 'saturated with the lifeblood of structures ... that the chances of breaking out of the cycle of reproduction seem subject to interminable constraints'.[5] There is a striking:

> absence of any real sense either of what drives the system to reproduce itself, besides the mechanical process of reproduction itself, or of what may subvert or revolutionise this process, which makes the otherwise fruitful concept of habitus appear trapped in a circular process. (Wolfreys, 2000)

Thus, for Bourdieu, 'the protest movement of the unemployed' could only appear a 'social miracle' (Bourdieu, 2001b, pp 88–91). Such comment led Schinkel (2003, p 86) to criticise Bourdieu's failure to acknowledge 'the emancipatory potential in people themselves', arguing that although 'most emancipatory movements do not find their origin in sociology, to Bourdieu it was a "miracle" for one to appear without its guidance'.

Underpinning criticisms such as these is also the feeling that parts of Bourdieu's work seem to 'evoke a naïve scientism where only (properly sensitised) sociologists are able to fully understand social relationships' (Devine and Savage, 2005, p 16). Similarly, Bohman (1999, p 142) claims that implicit in Bourdieu's approach is the belief that 'only the sages and sayers – sociological theorists – somehow possess the reflexivity necessary for radical change and the articulation of novelty'. Perhaps what is most troubling is that in:

> its continued reliance on the opposition between science, the preserve of the detached sociological observer and the doxic, pre-reflexive immediacy inhabited by other agents, Bourdieu's sociology finds

it difficult to theorise the possibility of a genuinely participatory democracy and, albeit unintentionally, implies a certain elitism. (Lane, 2000, p 197)

The critical intellectual and activist

Critical intellectuals challenging doxic understandings

Bourdieu (quoted in Bourdieu and Eagleton, 1994, p 272) referred to himself as a 'first generation intellectual', one of those social 'miracles' who had 'made it' within the field of higher education. Partly as a consequence of this, his critical engagement with sociology was, intensely personal and autobiographical:

> My main problem is to try and understand what happened to me. My trajectory may be described as miraculous, I suppose – ascension to a place where I don't belong. And so to be able to live in a world that is not mine I must try to understand both things: what it means to have an academic mind – how such is created – and at the same time what was lost in acquiring it. For that reason, even if my work – my full work – is a sort of autobiography, it is a work for people who have the same sort of trajectory, and the same need to understand. (Quoted in Bourdieu and Eagleton, 1994, p 272)

As Stabile and Morooka (2003, p 327) maintain, in many ways, at 'the heart of Bourdieu's project lay a very special vision of what it means to be an intellectual'.

More specifically, what did it mean for him to be a *critical* intellectual who was politically active in the public sphere? Prior to exploring this aspect of his role, it is important to briefly consider his comments on doxa because these provide the intellectual foundation for his activism.

In *Outline of a theory of practice* (Bourdieu, 2003b), which concentrates on his fieldwork in Algeria, Bourdieu observed that every 'established order tends to produce (to very different degrees and with different means) the naturalization of its own arbitrariness' (Bourdieu, 2003b, p 164). However, within doxa, the 'world of tradition [is] experienced as a "natural world" and taken for granted'. That is to say, 'the established cosmological and political order is perceived not as arbitrary, i.e. as one possible among others, but as a self-evident and natural order which goes without saying and therefore goes unquestioned' (Bourdieu, 2003b, p 166): 'what is essential *goes without saying because it comes without saying*: the tradition is silent, not least about itself as a tradition' (Bourdieu, 2003b, p 167, original emphasis).

Bourdieu uses doxa, as 'opposed to ideology or common sense, not only to convey a certain level of volition among players, but to avoid the Althusserian usage of the term "ideology"' (Stabile and Morooka, 2003, p 242). Somewhat similar to Gramsci's 'hegemony', doxa:

operates as if it were the objective truth – across *social space* in its *entirety*, from the practices and perceptions of individuals (at the level of habitus) to the practices and perceptions of the state and social groups (at the level of fields). (Chopra, 2003, p 421, emphasis in original)

Furthermore, doxa 'is habitus-specific, thus, implying that what is doxa for inhabitants of one habitus need not necessarily be *doxa* for the inhabitants of another' (Chopra, 2003, p 426, emphasis in original).

Within a doxic society, there appears to be no space for social transformation. Thus, entirely 'doxic social power rules without opposition: this is a universe in which the very question of legitimacy does not even arise' (Moi, 1991, p 1027). However, it is questionable whether *any* society or dominant power can ever achieve a degree of control so complete as to be able to shut out *all* challenge. Bourdieu himself recognises that it is possible to question or oppose doxa and that moments or times of crisis can provide an opportunity for movement and change and 'provoke a redefinition of experience' (Moi, 1991, p 1027).

Bourdieu was of the view that although derived from his empirical work in a 'traditional' or peasant society, his sociological insights on doxic or taken-for-granted knowledge may shed light on some of the social dynamics present within capitalist societies. More specifically, his analysis has implications for those operating in the academic or intellectual fields where a key division exists between doxosophers, expounders of 'legitimate' or doxic knowledge – 'technicians of opinion who think themselves wise' – and critical intellectuals (Bourdieu, 2001b, p 7). In *Homo Academicus* (Bourdieu, 2001a), Bourdieu derides these spokespersons for the doxa as 'consecrated intellectuals', establishment figures, heavy with symbolic capital and a sense of their own worth, who are 'crowned with scholastic glory ... the ultimate product of the dialectic of acclaim and recognition which drew into the system those most inclined to reproduce it without distortion' (Bourdieu, 2001a, p 83).

In contrast, Bourdieu defends above all 'the possibility and necessity of the critical intellectual', arguing that 'there is no genuine democracy without genuine opposing critical powers' (Bourdieu, 2001b, p 8). In 'his view, a questioning of doxa, intellectual or otherwise, is the foundation for intellectual work' (Stabile and Morooka, 2003, p 335). The critical intellectual fosters, maintains and protects 'freedom with respect of those in power' and is prepared to formulate 'the critique of received ideas, the demolition of either-ors' and is attentive to the complexity of problems (Bourdieu, 2001b, p 92). These intellectuals are detached and informed scholars who 'are unconcerned with winning traditional honours' and prepared to interrogate and challenge established 'truths' and conventions (Fowler, 1997, p 32). This is the 'civic mission of intellectuals' (Wacquant, 1998, p 227) and of all those 'who are willing to and capable of investing their intellectual weapons in political struggles' (Stabile and Morooka, 2003, p 334). The critical intellectual:

incorporates into a political struggle their specific competence and authority, and the values that are involved in exercising his [sic] profession, such as the truth or disinterestedness; in other words, someone who enters the political terrain without abandoning his research-obligations and competences. (Bourdieu, in Schinkel, 2003, p 80)

Thus, '"scholarship" and "commitment" go hand in hand' (Schinkel, 2003, p 80; see also Poupeau and Discepolo, 2005).

It has been suggested that Bourdieu's project constitutes an attempt to create a new type of 'traditional' intellectuals (Hoare and Nowell Smith, 2005, pp 7–8; see also McLennan and Squires, 2004, p 92). Autonomous and independent of the dominant social group, these figures would be wedded to progressive causes and social struggles but, unlike Gramsci's 'organic intellectuals', would not be associated with any political party (see Bourdieu, 2008, p 216). However, Bourdieu felt that there was an urgent need for 'critical networks that bring together "specific intellectuals" (in Foucault's sense of the term) into a veritable collective intellectual' (Bourdieu, 2003a, p 20). The task of the 'collective intellectual' was to help to create, even be the 'midwife' for, the social conditions for the collective production of realistic utopias' (Bourdieu, 2003a, p 21). He elaborated:

The whole edifice of critical thought is in need of reconstruction. And this work of reconstruction cannot be effected, as some have thought in the past, by a single great intellectual, a master thinker endowed with the sole resources of his singular thought, or by the authorized spokes-person for a group or an institution presumed to speak in the name of those without a voice. (Bourdieu, 2003a, p 21)

If, like Foucault, Bourdieu acknowledged that the social sciences are 'deeply implicated in modern forms of power', unlike Foucault, he maintained that there remained a 'qualified autonomy' that potentially enabled academics to fulfil 'a role in facilitating resistance to power' (Cronin, 1996, p 76). This autonomy had to be constantly defended against the corrosive impact of neoliberal encroachment and the disastrous proliferation of the media, even if such defence may verge on professional and scholarly elitism. He castigated 'organic intellectuals of the technocracy' who 'monopolize public debate' (Bourdieu, 2008, p 215) and 'the stranglehold of a media–intellectual complex … seeking to introduce into intellectual life and the public space the logic of show business, a cynical quest for visibility at any price and a traffic in symbolic capital' (Bourdieu, 2008, p 240). In response to these developments, he helped to establish a number of publications, such as *Liber*, and was involved in the foundation of an 'international of intellectuals' with the inauguration of an International Writers' Parliament in 1993 (Bourdieu, 2008). During a period of neoliberal hegemony, this was committed to independence from 'political, economic and media powers, as well as from any other kind of orthodoxy', a 'new internationalism, based on knowledge and recognition of the diversity of historical traditions', and on the desire to foster and promote 'new kinds of activism' (Bourdieu, 2008, pp 238–42).

Sociology and sociologists

Fundamental to Bourdieu's understanding of the role of the critical intellectual was his perception of the role of sociology and sociologists. In a remarkable passage in *An invitation to reflexive sociology* (Bourdieu and Wacquant, 2004), purposely saturated with the spirit of primitive Christianity and echoing St Paul's appeal to Christians not to conform to the world, Bourdieu and Wacquant (2004, p 251) assert that sociology:

> [d]emands a *conversion of one's gaze* and one can say of the teaching of sociology that it must first 'give new eyes'… The task is to produce, if not a 'new person', then at least a 'new gaze', *a sociological eye*. And this cannot be done without a genuine conversion, a *metanoia*, a mental revolution, a transformation of one's whole vision of the social world. (Emphases in original)

This 'new gaze' would enable sociology to unveil the 'self-deception, the collectively entertained and encouraged lying to oneself which, in every society, is at the foundation of the most sacred values and, therefore, all social existence' (Bourdieu, 1994, p 188). This was not, claimed Bourdieu (1994, p 181), to argue that a sociologist is able, like the 'impartial arbiter or the divine spectator', to simplistically report, in an uncomplicated way, the 'truth'. However, s/he 'is the one who strives to speak the truth about struggles whose stakes include, among other things, the truth'.

Two factors are crucial if the sociologist is to fulfil this role. First, there is a need for incessant scrutiny of the self. Thus, sociology has to be used 'as a weapon against yourself, an instrument of vigilance' (Bourdieu, 1994, p 27). This would involve reflecting on one's own habitus and field. Second, there needs to be a constant struggle to maintain the 'extraordinary autonomy' that sociology confers (Bourdieu, 1994, p 27). Bourdieu (1994, p 178) was to argue, therefore, that one 'does not enter sociology without severing all the adherences and adhesions by which one is ordinarily bound to groups, without abjuring the beliefs constitutive of membership and without renouncing all ties of filiation or affiliation'. In France, he feared that sociology was neglecting a concern with problems of deprivation, poverty and class and becoming incorporated into the so-called 'modernisation' drive (Lane, 2000). He was especially critical of those sociologists who placed themselves at the disposal of the state. On many occasions, therefore, he produced scathing criticisms of the complicity of 'leading intellectuals' in the promotion of neoliberalism. Bourdieu and Wacquant (2001, p 5) identify two key figures who are 'increasingly crowding the autonomous and critical intellectual born of the Enlightenment tradition out of the public scene':

> One is the *expert* who in the shadowy corridors of ministries ... or in the isolation of think-tanks prepares highly technical documents, preferably couched in economic or mathematical language, used to justify policy choices made on decidedly non-technical grounds.... The other is the *communication consultant to the prince* – a defector from the academic world entered into the service of the dominant, whose mission is to give an academic veneer to the political projects of the new state and business nobility. (Bourdieu and Wacquant, 2001, p 5, original emphasis)

In an article originally published in *Le Monde Diplomatique* in 2000, they became even more specific and turned their fire on Anthony Giddens, whose 'life politics' notion was, as we have seen in Chapter Two, espoused by Harry Ferguson as a new template for social work theory and practice (see Chapter Two). Giddens, 'the globe trotting apostle of the "Third Way"' was, in fact, a 'planetary prototype' of the 'communication consultant to the prince' (Bourdieu and Wacquant, 2001, p 5). In a French television documentary screened in 2001, Bourdieu lambasted 'lackeys' of the establishment and referred to sociologists who put themselves at the service of the state as 'scabs' (quoted in Wolfreys, 2002). In contrast, Bourdieu's sympathy with the unemployed and socially and economically marginalised was very clear. This critique of Giddens was not simply mud-slinging, it illustrated two recurring and interrelated themes in Bourdieu's later writings: the danger posed by neoliberal economics; and the threat to partly autonomous spheres of culture, such as art, literature and science (Bourdieu, 2008).

For example, in comments made with reference to France, but equally applicable elsewhere in Europe and beyond, he specifically criticised the role that some intellectuals fulfilled in promoting so-called 'modernisation':

> [B]y associating efficiency and modernity with private enterprise, and archaism and inefficiency with the public sector, they seek to substitute the relationship with the customer, supposedly more egalitarian and more effective, for the relation to the user; finally, they identify 'modernization' with the transfer into the private sector of the public services with the profit potential and with eliminating or bringing into line subordinate staff in the public services, held responsible for inefficiency and every 'rigidity'. (Bourdieu, in Bourdieu et al, 2002, pp 182–3)

Comments such as the above have led a number of writers to argue that in Bourdieu's later contributions, there is something of a 'political turn'. For Wolfreys (2000, 2002), for example, it was the abandonment of reformism by French social democracy and increased neoliberalisation that led Bourdieu to adopt a more radical stance. It should be noted, however, that some of Bourdieu's earliest contributions, a number of which are unfortunately unavailable in English, were already critical, political pieces (see Lane, 2000; see also Bourdieu, 2008). Perhaps what changed in his later years 'was the directness with which the critique was put forward' (Schinkel, 2003, p 69; see also Bourdieu, 2008).

Politics

To which particular social and political causes did Bourdieu lend his support? Not surprisingly, given his remarks above, the key struggle was to be waged against the 'scourge' of neoliberalism, which has come to 'be seen as an inevitability' (Bourdieu, 2001b, pp vii, 30). The kinds of precarious and temporary work referred to in Chapter Five marked, for Bourdieu, a return to the 'worst moments of nascent capitalism' (Bourdieu, 2008, p 202). In response, he called for a return to a more Keynesian state-regulated market and appealed for the need to restore a human dimension to economic planning:

> All the critical forces in society need to insist on the inclusion of the social costs of economic decisions in economic calculations. What will this or that policy cost in the long term in lost jobs, suffering, sickness, suicide, alcoholism, drug addiction, domestic violence, etc. all things which cost a great deal, in money, but also in misery? (Bourdieu, 2001b, p 39)

We are now witnessing the 'destruction of the economic and social bases of the most precious gains of humanity' (Bourdieu, 2001b, p 37). It is vital that the 'critical efforts of intellectuals [and] trade unions ... should be applied as a matter of priority against the withering away of the state' (Bourdieu, 2001b, p 40). Unlike voguish social theorists, such as Beck (2000a), for whom trade unions are to be derided and ridiculed as 'zombie categories', Bourdieu recognised the vital role that they fulfil within social democracies. Indeed, he argued that a European social movement would only be effective if it integrated 'trade unions, social movements and scholars'. If this counter-hegemonic alliance was to be constructed, there had to be an end to 'union-phobia' (Bourdieu, 2008, pp 282–3). During the wave of public sector strikes sweeping across France in December 1995, Bourdieu made numerous interventions, speaking, for example, at a large meeting of striking railway workers. His active engagement led Wolfreys (2000, p 13) to consider him 'a vigorous optimistic antidote to the pessimism which has gripped sections of the Left'. Shortly before his death in early 2002, Bourdieu claimed that he was 'more optimistic about the future than at any time in the last three decades, despite the seeming triumph of global capital' (quoted in Stabile and Morooka, 2003, p 338).

In terms of international affairs, Bourdieu opposed NATO's intervention (and bombing campaign) in the Balkans and championed the cause of a new internationalism, opposed to 'nationalist division ... an international movement to fight against global capital' (Bourdieu, in Ovenden, 2000). Indeed, he viewed it as crucial to combat the 'myth of globalization' (see particularly, Bourdieu, 2001b, pp 28–9). Today, it is:

> accepted with resignation as the inevitable outcome of national evolution. [However, an] empirical analysis of the trajectory of the advanced economies ... suggests, in contrast, that 'globalization' is not a new phase of capitalism, but a 'rhetoric' invoked by governments in order to justify their voluntary surrender to the financial markets. [In reality, however, it is] *domestic political decisions* [that are] tipping the balance of class forces in favour of the owners of capital. (Bourdieu and Wacquant, 2001, p 4, emphasis in original)

One final dimension of Bourdieu's role as a critical intellectual, alluded to earlier, is his analysis and critique of the 'cultural imperialism' of the US. For Bourdieu and Wacquant (1999, p 41), this was founded on the:

> power to universalize particularisms linked to a singular historical tradition.... [T]oday numerous topics directly issuing from the intellectual confrontations relating to the social particularity of the American society and its universities have been imposed, in apparently de-historicized form, upon the whole planet.

This process, often masquerading within the social sciences as benign and simply indicative of 'policy transfer' (Dolowitz, 2000), could be viewed as a form of 'symbolic violence' (Garrett, 2007b; see also Chapter Nine). For Bourdieu and Wacquant (1999, p 54), there was ample evidence available to support this analysis. For example, the 'diffusion of the scientific myth of the "underclass" as a result of high-profile media interventions of Charles Murray ... and of its counterpart, the theme of the "dependency" of the disadvantaged upon the public aid'.

Pileggi and Patton (2003, p 313) have referred to Bourdieu's 'poor reception in the USA'. However, his (and Wacquant's) critical interventions on 'cultural imperialism' should *not* be interpreted as crudely anti-American: a charge increasingly levelled at those even timorously critical of aspects of public and foreign policy emerging from the new 'symbolic Mecca' (Bourdieu and Wacquant, 2001, p 3). Certainly, Bourdieu *does* pinpoint an important aspect of this 'policy transfer' dynamic. For example, initiatives, such as those centred on 'zero tolerance', prominent again in England following the 'riots' during the summer of 2011, can be related to policy discourses in the US. The whole 'tough love' ambiance detectable in both New Labour and the Conservative–Liberal Democratic administrations' policy and rhetoric with regard to families in contact with social services is also largely lifted from inside the Washington beltway (Jordan, 2001; see also Swanson, 2000; Prideaux, 2005).

Admittedly, matters may be a good deal more complex than Bourdieu and Wacquant maintain given that the US is not 'the sole locus of celebratory liberalism' and that some of the 'strongest critiques of neo-liberalism are also from the USA' (Friedman, 2000, p 140). Moreover, in spite of US military power, the world system has become decentralised in terms of capital accumulation, with significant regional poles of accumulation as well. However, the key point remains that Bourdieu was alert to – and horrified by – the way in which capital is continuing to transform the US and he was fearful that Europe risked being transformed in a similar way (Bourdieu, 2008). This specifically relates to his concern about the impact of neoliberalism on the socially and economically marginalised in contact with social workers. The ghettos of the US were now 'abandoned sites that are fundamentally defined by an absence – basically that of the state and of everything that comes with it, police, schools, health care institutions, associations, etc' (Bourdieu, in Bourdieu et al, 2002, p 123). Indeed, in some US cities, 'public authority has turned into a war machine against the poor' with social workers only able to see 'clients' in their offices (Wacquant, in Bourdieu et al, 2002, pp 137–8).

Against 'apparatus' social workers and social work educators

Bourdieu viewed social workers as 'agents of the state' who are 'shot through with the contradictions of the state' (Bourdieu, in Bourdieu et al, 2002, p 184). In *The weight of the world* (Bourdieu et al, 2002), he pays particular attention to the 'real institutional dilemmas haunting "street-level" bureaucrats' (Stabile and Morooka, 2003, p 337), recognising that many social workers are likely to 'feel abandoned, if not disowned outright, in their efforts to deal with the material and moral suffering that is the only certain consequence of rampant neoliberalism' (Bourdieu, in Bourdieu et al, 2002, p 183). One of the chief problems faced by practitioners is that they:

> must unceasingly fight on two fronts: against those they want to help and who are often too demoralized to take a hand in their own interests, let alone the interests of the collectivity; on the other hand, against administrations and bureaucrats divided and enclosed in separate universes. (Bourdieu et al, 2002, p 190)

Bourdieu is alert to the 'antinomy between the logic of social work, which is not without a certain prophetic militancy or inspired benevolence, and that of bureaucracy, with its discipline and its prudence' (Bourdieu et al, 2002, p 190). Here, a key paradox is that:

> the rigidity of bureaucratic institutions is such, that ... they can only function, with more or less difficulty, thanks to the initiative, the inventiveness, if not the charisma of those functionaries who are the

least imprisoned in their function. If bureaucracy were left to its own logic ... then bureaucracy would paralyse itself. (Bourdieu, in Bourdieu et al, 2002, p 191)

Moreover, this type of contradiction 'opens up a margin of maneuver, initiative and freedom which can be used by those who, in breaking with bureaucratic routines and regulations, defend bureaucracy against itself' (Bourdieu, in Bourdieu et al, 2002, p 191).

Perhaps there is a need if not for a Bourdieusian social work, then for a social work *informed* by Bourdieu's theoretical insights and by his opposition to neoliberalism and the imposition of so-called 'austerity' measures. Furthermore, there are at least two significant ways in which he might aid the reconfiguring of a critical and 'radical' social work in the first quarter of the 21st century.

Bourdieu's work emphasises how neoliberalism is more than an abstract consideration because on a daily basis, it *bites into* social work practice and related fields. First, it is particularly important for social workers to defend the autonomy of the field. Practitioners in a field are 'liable to two masters: the practices and norms of the discipline and the practices and norms of the market' (Pileggi and Patton, 2003, p 318). Given this tension– this competition for the allegiance of social workers – individual practitioners are confronted with a choice as to which 'master' to follow. In his later interventions, one of Bourdieu's main concerns was that a number of previously autonomous or quasi-autonomous fields may be corroded by rampant neoliberalisation. Thus, the transformation from field to apparatus occurs when 'under certain historical conditions ... the dominant manage to crush and annul the resistance and reactions of the dominated, when all movements go exclusively from the top down' (Bourdieu, in Bourdieu and Wacquant, 2004, p 102). In other words, apparatuses are 'the *pathological* state of fields' (Bourdieu in Bourdieu and Wacquant, 2004, p 102, emphasis added). Nevertheless, some are keen to comply with the doxic understandings and more than willing to take on the role of 'apparatus intellectuals' (Bourdieu, 2008, p 387). Furthermore, it is likely that there exists an equivalent category of 'apparatus' social workers and social work educators.

Second, Bourdieu's theorisation – what has been described as his 'conceptual arsenal' – might assist social workers in evolving better forms of practice. His contribution could help practitioners to reflexively *fold inwards*, with social workers and social work academics scrutinising their individual habitus and professional field. Indeed, Bourdieu's originality lies in his development of a micro-theory of social power in which habitus constitutes, what we can perceive as, an individual's personal, hegemonised space. This is also the space in which social work functions. In the welfare field, the concept of habitus becomes particularly relevant at the point of contact between practitioners and those using (or being denied) services. Bourdieu's theoretical contribution can assist social workers working with children and families to gain greater insight into doxic ideas on 'good enough parenting' (Polansky et al, 1983). Perhaps particularly relevant for social work and its day-to-day interpersonal dimension is the emphasis Bourdieu places on the body. For him, subtle, yet immensely important, forms of cultural capital include 'body mannerisms and pronunciations (accents)' (quoted in Bourdieu et al, 2002, p 28). The body is seen, therefore, as 'an instrument of cultural capital' and for the middle class, 'the long process of education' tends to inscribe 'a particular bodily manner' (Gunn, 2005, p 60). This can be observed in the demeanour of middle-class participants at, say, child protection case conferences. In this frequently highly charged context, professionals and (less commonly present, of course) middle-class parents are likely to act like 'fish in water' and exhibit a self-certainty, confidence and ease that may well be lacking in working-class participants (see Bourdieu, in Bourdieu and Wacquant, 2004, p 127). An awareness of how habitus is embodied may also aid practitioners' understanding of the restrictions, constraints and limitations faced by the ill body. In this context, although she does not use a Bourdieusian framework, Havi Carel (2008) has provided an evocative account of when a body becomes 'broken' with the onset of unpredictable and serious illness.

Through a Bourdieusian lens, often reified categories such as 'child protection' and 'family support' need to be viewed with a reflective and wary caution. Inscribed within the assessment schedules, questionnaires and scales promoted by the UK government is a preoccupation with the stock of cultural capital displayed by families (Garrett, 2003); hence the references to various types of middle-class distinction, such as well-maintained gardens, country fetes and good manners (Department of Health, 1988; Department of Health, Department for Education and Employment, and Home Office, 2000). In term of social work practice and social work assessments, an awareness of habitus, field and capital might help social workers counter such class bias. The way cultural capital is deployed is also the focal concern of social workers involved in the assessment of the 'parenting capacity' of prospective adoptive parents. In this context, professionals are encouraged to examine how capital is implicitly marshalled within child adoption processes, and, more specifically, how the differential access to capital(s) might impact on, even determine, the outcomes both for the 'birth parents' and those seeking to adopt children. Are the differing positions that they frequently occupy in social space a crucial yet insufficiently examined factor?

Clearly, the fact that social workers themselves operate in a field with political capital can produce 'stigma, negative symbolic capital for their clients' (Peillon, 1998, p 223). The profession often has to work with people who lack capital – not only economic capital, but also the other types of capital adumbrated by Bourdieu. It is also possible to see how, in political and media discourses, particular geographical localities can become associated with deficits in capital. In this way, social and geographical spaces become enmeshed to produce symbolic locations that are then presented as loci of crime and other assorted threats and troubles. In England, particularly during the period of the Thatcher administrations in the 1980s, Liverpool often fulfilled this role (Lane, 1987). In the Republic of Ireland, Limerick has served a similar function (Hourigan, 2011). Within each of these urban locations, specific impoverished neighbourhoods are constructed as pariah zones within the wider city: for example, in Liverpool this has been Toxteth; in Limerick it has been Moyross and Southill. Attentiveness to these doxic biases is crucial to a progressive and critical social work practice.

The field of social work can be perceived as relatively lacking in symbolic capital when viewed alongside other professions. Here, the media has frequently played a key role in presenting its alleged shortcomings (Gaughan and Garrett, 2011). However, institutions may also possess sufficient symbolic capital to withstand critique or impede or censor the public airing of damaging revelations. This was apparent in the Republic of Ireland, where because of the volume of symbolic capital held by priests, nuns and other associated religious figures in the Roman Catholic Church, information about clerical abuse in industrial schools and similar institutions was either suppressed or withheld (see Anderson, 2010). The children incarcerated in such establishments had neither economic capital nor the reserves of other forms of capital identified by Bourdieu. The fact that these children were mostly, but not exclusively, from the families of the urban and rural poor is likely to have contributed to their being especially vulnerable to abusive and criminal practices. As the report investigating the abuses committed in industrial schools (Commission to Inquire into Child Abuse, 2009) confirms, the 'predatory nature of sexual abuse including the selection and grooming of socially disadvantaged and vulnerable children was a feature of the witness reports' pertaining to 'special needs services, Children's homes, hospitals and primary and second-level schools'. Children with impairments of sight, hearing and learning were also 'particularly vulnerable to sexual abuse' (Commission to Inquire into Child Abuse, 2009, p 26). Moreover, as we saw in Chapter Three, a secular form of symbolic capital – that possessed by 'experts'– further aggravated the plight of the detainees.

Bourdieu's work can also serve to emphasise the profession's more benign characteristics and map its future direction. Important in this respect is Bourdieu's recognition of the centrality of 'talk' for social work (see Parton and O'Byrne, 2000). Thus, his theorising might assist in combating the damage caused by the increasing use of centrally devised schedules and tick lists, a development deepened and embedded since the introduction of the immensely damaging LAC materials in the UK. In contrast, Bourdieu's approach is pluralistic and open to hearing many 'voices'. As he states, 'we must relinquish the single, central, dominant, in a word, quasi-divine, point of view.... We must work instead with the multiple perspectives that correspond to the multiplicity of coexisting, and sometimes directly competing points of view' (quoted in Bourdieu et al, 2002, p 3). Although Bourdieu's commitment to 'active and methodical listening' – as opposed to 'half-understanding' based on 'distracted and routinized attention' (quoted in Bourdieu et al, 2002, pp 609, 614) – chimes with social work's traditional emphasis on the 'respect for persons', such practice is becoming oddly subversive in a field increasingly subjected to the pressures of nervous and edgy neoliberal regimes demanding 'time discipline', 'fast thinking' and tangible 'outcomes' (Bourdieu, 1998b, pp 28–30).

Conclusion

When Bourdieu died in January 2002 it was as if the world had lost one of that rare and 'perhaps most endangered species: a prominent university intellectual who was also … coolly and passionately and scientifically and politically engaged with the world around him' (Stabile and Morooka, 2003, p 326). As Callinicos (2000, pp 118–19, original emphasis) observes, because his early work 'focused on how class is *lived*, on how social differences inhabit the grain of everyday life', Bourdieu was 'especially sensitive to the scale of socially unnecessary suffering – what he … called *la misere du monde*' (see also Robbins, 2002). By the time of his death, he was considered 'the unofficial ideologue of the anti-globalization movement(s)' (Schinkel, 2003, p 81; see also Grass and Bourdieu, 2002). Predictably, on account of the critical and oppositional stance that he took in the public sphere, he was 'demonized by that section of the French intelligentsia which, twenty years ago, made its peace with liberal capitalism' (Callinicos, 1999b, p 87).

Bourdieu's work frustrates, confuses, annoys, enlightens – like many of the social theorists examined in this book, he *unsettles*. He compels his readers to return to read him again and again and to 'take away' different or refined understandings of aspects of his mammoth contribution. Most importantly, within the discourse of social work, Bourdieu's theorisation and his nagging insistence on the relevance (and sheer *stickiness*) of social structure provides a useful counterweight to those contributions that unduly inflate the role of individual agency within neoliberal modernity (Ferguson, 2001). Bourdieu's disruptive, insistent interrogation of established 'truths' and his 'refusal to compromise with institutions' (Bourdieu, 1994, p 4), which are increasingly steered, directed and shaped by demands for 'austerity', can serve as a guiding light for a renewed 'radical' social work (Lavalette, 2011a). Bourdieu's probing into *why* people might tolerate oppressive circumstances and his empirical and theoretical examination of the underlying dynamics that contribute to the solidification of existing social relationships are core contributions to the field of social work. More fundamentally, reading his work might stimulate social work to develop a keener and more penetrating 'sociological eye' (Bourdieu, in Bourdieu and Wacquant, 2004, p 251).

The next chapter will turn to examine the work of Habermas. Again working within a modernist framework, his social theory contains, it has been argued, important considerations for social work.

> **◀◀ Reflection and Talk Box 7 ▶▶**
>
> - How helpful are Bourdieu's concepts in aiding our perceptions of social work?
>
> - What are the key characteristics and doxic understandings within the 'field' of social work?
>
> - How useful are the concepts of 'habitus', 'field' and 'capital' in enabling us to grasp some of the difficulties in multidisciplinary working?
>
> - How is technology impacting on the sense of 'habitus' of social workers?
>
> - How can social workers defend the field of social work from neoliberal incursion?
>
> - What do you perceive as some of the main difficulties with Bourdieu's theorisation?

Notes

[1] For accessible pieces on Algeria, see Bourdieu (2008, pp 3–31). *Sociological Review*, vol 57, no 3, published in 2009, is an excellent special issue providing insights into Bourdieu's sociology, and colonialism, derived from his photography in Algeria. See particularly the articles by Back (2009), Haddour (2009), Loyal (2009), Puwar (2009), Schultheis et al (2009) and Sweetman (2009). This chapter is partly based on two of my earlier articles drawing critical attention to Bourdieu: 'Making social work more Bourdieusian: why the social professions should critically engage with the work of Pierre Bourdieu', *European Journal of Social Work*, vol 10, no 2, pp 225–43; and 'The relevance of Bourdieu for social work: a reflection on obstacles and omissions', *Journal of Social Work*, vol 7, no 3, pp 357–81. I am grateful to Taylor & Francis and Sage for letting me refer to the pieces once again.

[2] Vulgate refers to an ancient Latin version of the Scriptures made by St Jerome and others in the 4th century.

[3] Terry Lovell (2000, p 36) states that women feature:

> in his schema of the social field, primarily as social objects, repositories of value and capital, who circulate between men and who serve certain important functions in the capital accumulation strategies of families and kinship groups. While class penetrates right through his diagrammatic representations of the social field, like the lettering in Brighton rock, gender is largely invisible, as is 'race'.

[4] On occasions, Bourdieu's depiction of the working class, amid the 'monotonous drab daily life in the inner city' (Bourdieu, 1998b, p 21), can also be regarded as somewhat patronising.

[5.] In a footnote, in one of their collaborative contributions, Wacquant adds that habitus:

> can also be transformed via socio-analysis, i.e., via an awakening of consciousness
> and a form of 'self work' that enables the individual to get a handle on his or her
> dispositions…. The possibility and efficacy of this kind of self-analysis is in itself
> determined in part by the original structures of the habitus in question, in part by
> the objective conditions under which the awakening of self-consciousness takes
> place. (Wacquant in Bourdieu and Wacquant, 2004, p 133; see also Bourdieu, 2007)

CHAPTER EIGHT

Thinking with Habermas[1]

Introduction

Jürgen Habermas was born in 1929 in Dusseldorf, Germany. As a teenager, he 'joined the Hitler youth along with many of his peers' (Houston, 2009, p 13). His subsequent professional and intellectual career has, however, been rooted in the thematic concerns of the Marxist left and, more recently, social democracy. Some have argued that 'his thought and especially his frequent interventions into public debate should be seen as dedicated to providing the philosophical arguments that might protect democratic societies from his own nation's past' (Neilson, 1995, p 809). In terms of his theorisation of modernity, Habermas distances himself from the pessimism of Weber – and his 'iron cage' perception of its dominant rationalising impulse (Roberts, 2004) – and the Frankfurt's School's disdain for popular or mass culture. For him, meaningful communication provides a possible counter to the damaging and corrosive tendencies associated with modernity. Indeed, his 'leitmotif' is the notion of 'unconstrained, open debate amongst equals' (Baert, 2001, p 85). Perhaps paradoxically, he has a 'dense, heavy and discouraging writing style' (Scambler, 2001, p 1).

More expansively, Habermas remained 'one of the most coherent and persuasive defenders of the project of the Enlightenment' during a period when postmodernism became increasingly the focal-'ism' within academic and cultural settings (Baert, 2001, p 89). It 'seems to be rarely recognized' that Habermas has also been as 'damning of the *unreconstructed* Enlightenment project' as any postmodernist. However, 'whereas postmodernists have judged the Enlightenment project to be flawed beyond redemption, Habermas has committed himself to its necessary and compelling reconstruction' (Scambler, 2001, p 9, emphasis in original). Since the 1970s, the commitment to a defence of this reconstructed version of the Enlightenment project, and against those he regards as advocates of counter-Enlightenment, has been increasingly apparent in his work.

Habermas's influences include not only the German intellectual tradition. 'Unfashionably and ambitiously', he seeks, for example, to identify and articulate connections between the evolution of individuals and societies (Scambler, 2001, p 11). He draws on theorisation associated with Jean Piaget (1886–1980), the Swiss developmental psychologist, and Lawrence Kohlberg (1927–87), the American developmental psychologist. Such figures have also been central within the mainstream discourse of social work education in the West and this facet, along with Habermas's interest in communication, may have resulted in some social work academic commentators emphasising the usefulness of his ideas for practitioners. Hayes and Houston (2007) have argued that his conceptualisations could aid social workers' abilities to engage in family group conferences (FGCs) and so enhance opportunities for 'empowering' dialogue between the participants involved in such fora. While welcoming their thoughtful contribution and willingness to stress the relevance of social theory for social work, this chapter will suggest that there are problems attached to Hayes and Houston's promotion of Habermasian social work.

The first half of the chapter provides a resume of the argument of Hayes and Houston (2007), who provide a lucid lens through which to view some of Habermas's focal themes and intellectual preoccupations: the work of other commentators on Habermas, such as Finlayson (2005), will also be referred to (see also Outhwaite, 1996). It will then be maintained that a more complex understanding of power relations than that furnished by Habermas destabilises his analysis. Habermas's views on the welfare state can also be perceived as presenting difficulties. In pursuing this line of critique, Gramsci and Bourdieu will be 'brought into dialogue' with Habermas. As well as referring to feminist criticisms of his work, the chapter will draw attention to Mikhail Bakhtin (1895–1975) and the Bakhtin Circle.[2]

Habermasian social work?

Hayes and Houston (2007, p 988), in articulating their case that Habermas is of significance for social work, maintain that the 'unifying thread' in his entire 'corpus of work' is the 'power of unconstrained dialogue'. Related to this, the German social theorist wants to 'highlight distortions within human communication to promote and safeguard what he saw as a natural human tendency to forge co-operation, understanding and consensus' (Hayes and Houston, 2007, p 989).

Part of the conceptual foundation for the Habermasian paradigm is the relationship between what he termed the 'lifeworld' and the 'system', which is adumbrated most clearly in the second volume of *The theory of communicative action* (Habermas, 1987). Edmund Husserl (1859–1938) was the first to use the term 'lifeworld' to 'contrast the natural, pre-theoretical attitude of ordinary people to the world with the theoretical, objectifying, and mathematized perspectives of the natural science' (Finlayson, 2005, p 51). For Habermas, the 'lifeworld' is the 'name for the informal and unmarketized domains of social life: family and household, culture, political life outside of organized parties, mass media, voluntary organizations, and so on' (Finlayson, 2005, p 51). These 'unregulated spheres of sociality provide a repository of shared meanings and understandings, and a social horizon for everyday encounters with other people' (Finlayson, 2005, p 52). The 'lifeworld' is a 'force for social integration', which is 'conservative of social meaning' (Finlayson, 2005, p 53). Every time a 'successful communicative action takes place, a consensus is reached that feeds back into the lifeworld and replenishes it': in this way, the 'lifeworld' is able to 'function as a kind of bulwark against social disintegration, resisting the fragmentation of meanings and preventing the eruption of conflicts' (Finlayson, 2005, p 53).

What Habermas refers to as the 'system' can be divided into two different subsystems – money and power – which 'cut deep channels into the surface of social life, with the result that agents fall naturally into pre-established patterns of instrumental behaviour' (Finlayson, 2005, p 54). Although he does not have entirely negative views of the 'system', he is, however, fearful that it tends to encroach upon, to displace and even destroy the 'lifeworld':

> The notion of the colonization of the lifeworld refers to a complex of eventually harmful historical and social processes. To begin with, the steering media of money and power become uncoupled from the lifeworld.... As the networks of instrumental action increase in their density and complexity, so they gradually intrude into the lifeworld and absorb its functions. Strategic decisions are left to the markets, or placed in the hands of expert administrators. The transparency of the lifeworld is gradually obscured and the bases of action and decision are withdrawn from public scrutiny and from possible democratic control. As the domain of the lifeworld shrinks, a whole gamut of what Habermas calls 'social pathologies' arise, which include, but are not limited to the negative effects of markets on the non-market domains they colonize. (Finlayson, 2005, p 56)

Thus, for Habermas, 'instrumentality, rationality, money, bureaucracy and power – the trapping of the "system" – usurp *the time-honoured processes of consensual communication* that exist in the "lifeworld"' (Hayes and Houston, 2007, p 990, emphasis added). More broadly:

> [a] colonization of social life has taken place in modern society bringing with it all manner of social problems including: (i) a decrease in shared meanings; (ii) the erosion of social bonds; (iii) a lack of belonging; (iv) a sense of demoralization; and (v) the destabilization of social order. (Hayes and Houston, 2007, p 990)

However, in charting the work of Habermas, Hayes and Houston (2007, p 988) maintain that it is possible to detect a change of course. They suggest that *The theory of communicative action* volumes (Habermas, 1984, 1987) 'emphasized the polarized relationship between the state and civil society under advanced capitalism', yet in his later contributions, such as *Between facts and norms* (Habermas, 1996), he 'refines his views on the interrelationship between "lifeworld" and "system". What is depicted forcibly in this re-worked position is the need for a constructive *mediation* or conciliation between the two spheres' (Hayes and Houston, 2007, p 991, emphasis in original). In this way, 'a complementary, rather than adversarial, relationship between "lifeworld" and "system" begins to unfold. What we see then is a retreat from the older colonization thesis to a more affirmative sense of the possibilities of mediation between the two spheres' (Hayes and Houston, 2007, p 992). Some commentators, such as Cook (2001), have argued that 'this apparent shift in his thinking represented a significant departure from his earlier allegiance to critical social theory towards a more liberal-reformist position' (Hayes and Houston, 2007, p 988).

It is argued that the FGC model lends itself to Habermasian analysis because his 'central idea that the "system" and "lifeworld" must come together in a collaborative set of exchanges finds a practical, if coincidental, expression in the FGC' (Hayes and Houston, 2007, p 1003). FGCs are contrasted with child protection case conferences (CPCCs) and we are told that these emerging fora differ significantly from traditional CPCCs in the UK and case review meetings held in the US. CPCCs are, we are advised, 'dominated, or colonized (to use the Habermasian term), by the voice of the "system" with social work professionals chairing and minuting the meetings, and largely taking responsibility for making and implementing the decisions' (Hayes and Houston, 2007, p 994).

Echoing earlier remarks by Houston (2003, p 62) that Habermas's ideas on 'moral discourse provide a framework for making decisions' in 'formal social work meetings more systematic and fair', it is asserted that the conduct of FGCs can be enhanced if those involved are willing to have recourse to Habermas's discourse ethics. This, for Hayes and Houston (2007, p 1000), is important because of the current 'absence of explicit, moral rules for reaching agreement over the welfare plan for the child'. Thus, to deal with this 'significant gap', they lay out six imperatives derived from Habermas's (1990) *Moral consciousness and communicative action* (Hayes and Houston, 2007, p 1000): everyone affected by the issue in question is included in the dialogue, provided they have the communicative ability to converse meaningfully with others; each of the participants is allowed to introduce, question and criticise any assertion whatsoever; participants are permitted to express their attitudes, desires and needs without restrictions; participants must have genuine empathy for others' perspectives, claims and frames of reference; power must be in check so that the only legitimate force is the force of the better argument; and participants must (i) strive to achieve consensus in relation to the matters under discussion based on reasoned argumentation and (ii) abandon strategic forms of communication where there is a lack of transparency in articulated goals and coercion is present. They also add a seventh imperative derived, as we shall see in Chapter Nine, from the work of Axel Honneth on the philosophy of recognition: participants must confirm each other's identity through different forms of recognition that (i) demonstrate positive regard, (ii) acknowledge the other's individual and social rights, and (iii) value the other's abilities and traits.

Examining the 'lifeworld' and 'system'

Hayes and Houston's piece invites a range of specific questions. How can the ideas associated with 'lifeworld' and 'system' inform our understanding of social work and, more broadly, 'welfare'? Would Habermas's 'system' be more appropriately named and articulated as a historically specific *capitalist* system? Does this body of theorisation fail to address questions related to the deployment of power in encounters involving individuals and wider social forces? Does, in fact, Habermas's emphasis on 'procedure' fail to incorporate a satisfactory understanding of how power operates in social work and associated fields? Does the promotion of Habermasian ideas risk conferring a spurious and false harmony on social and economic relationships that are, in truth, riddled with conflict and disharmony?

In this context, the 'lifeworld' can, perhaps, be interpreted as an overly idealised and harmonious social space. Operating with a somewhat crude binary, Hayes and Houston (2007, p 993) maintain, for example, that in 'Habermasian terms, familial networks constitute a particular constellation emerging from the "lifeworld" whereas the social work professionals are representatives of the "system"'. This understanding is implicitly critical of social work's bureau-professionalism and implies that power exercised by agents (in this case, social workers) on behalf of a particular state formation is more likely to be injurious to children and families than that prompted by those operating in the private sphere ('familial networks'). Aside from being rooted in a form of familism (Barrett and McIntosh, 1982), this interpretation lends itself to a distinctly neoliberal form of reasoning because it gels with assertions that 'private is better than the public', that there is 'too much bureaucracy', and that there is too much of the 'nanny state'. Over 20 years ago – as we saw in Chapter Two – Osborne and Gaebler (1992) provided an example of this neoliberal critique of the public sector, which was influential in the US and, subsequently, Europe.

A more fundamental problem is (if we are to use this terminology) that the 'lifeworld' and 'system' conceptualisation is too simplistic because these are *not* truly separated, enclosed and discrete zones. In his huge corpus of work, Habermas has little to say about gender and this underpins his misreading of the 'family' and his locating of it inside the 'lifeworld'. Specifically, in terms of the feminist perspective, Nancy Fraser, whose theorisation will be explored in more detail in Chapter Nine, has mounted a substantial scholarly critique of Habermas's failure to incorporate a satisfactory analysis of gender and the operation of patriarchy within capitalism's dynamic matrix of social relations (Fraser, 1999). She argues that feminists:

> have shown through empirical analyses of contemporary familial decision making, handling of finances, and wife battering that families are thoroughly permeated with, in Habermas's terms, the media of money and power. They are sites of egocentric, strategic, and instrumental calculation as well as sites of usually exploitative exchanges

of services, labor, cash, and sex – and frequently, sites of coercion and violence. But Habermas's way of contrasting the modern family with the official capitalist economy tends to occlude all this. It overstates the differences between these institutions and blocks the possibility of analyzing families as economic systems, that is, sites of labor, exchange, calculation, distribution, and exploitation. (Fraser, 1989, pp 119–20)

Fraser's comments are significant for social workers and remind us that it is important – as argued in Chapter One – to incorporate feminist analysis into the profession's knowledge base and to integrate this into the assessment of abuse and harm caused to children *within* families (White, 2006). More emphatically, a 'critical social theory' of capitalist modernity *demands* 'gender-sensitive categories' (Fraser, 1989, p 128; see also Goode, 2005, ch 2). However, a Habermasian approach appears, at best, to dilute a gender-sensitive way of *thinking* and *working*. What is more, it may be possible to detect, in some of Habermas's work, an implied and nostalgic longing for a previous era prior to what he refers to as the dismantling of 'paternal authority' (Habermas, 2006, p 156). Moreover, in the contemporary world, the family retains only 'the illusion of an inner space of pseudo-privacy' (Habermas, 2006, p 157). For Habermas, there has been a 'hollowing out of the family's intimate sphere' and all that is left is a type of 'floodlit privacy' (Habermas, 2006, pp 157, 159). This perspective might, however, be challenged by those who have suffered abuse and who have not been believed when they tried to illuminate abusive practices within their own families (McKay, 1998).

Elsewhere, Habermas's (2001a, pp 131–71) focus on an 'asymmetrical distribution of power amongst family members' and 'systematically distorted communication' serves to amplify some of these criticisms. His reflections on 'communicative pathology' within 'conflict-ridden families' pays only passing attention to the issue of patriarchy (or wider structuring social class factors). In a typically positivistic and functionalist fashion, Habermas resorts to contrasting 'pathological' or 'dysfunctional families' with, what he terms, 'normal families' (Habermas, 2001a, pp 162–3). Although he concedes that the 'system of power and the lifeworld can and do interpenetrate, this does not amount to a recognition of the ways in which core domains of the lifeworld', such as the family, are themselves structured by power relations. As Amy Allen (2008, p 104) asserts, the 'elephant in the room' here is a failure to interrogate how these 'normal families' may themselves provide fora for relations of 'dominance and subordination'. She continues:

> the smouldering conflicts that arise from gender power asymmetries will serve to systematically distort communication between men and women in *most* families; such distortions will in turn suppress conflicts so that they continue to smoulder beneath the surface of apparently communicative interaction.... [I]t becomes apparent that the scope of systematically distorted communication ... is much broader than

Habermas seems to assume; indeed, it appears pervasive. (Allen, 2008, p 104, emphasis added)

Habermas's flawed interpretation of the role fulfilled by state welfare is of particular significance for social workers. Hayes and Houston (2007, p 990) maintain that he:

> explores the role of the modern welfare state, viewing it as a key arm of the state's colonization of the 'lifeworld'. In other words, by offering a raft of bureaucratized interventions to people in need, bureau-professionals erode earlier traditions of care, such as are found in neighbourhoods and social networks.

That is to say, Habermas tends to perceive the impact of 'welfare states' as deeply ambivalent. Writing in the early 1960s, he observed that the 'classical risks, especially of unemployment, accident, illness, age, and death are nowadays largely covered by welfare state guarantees' (Habermas, 2006, p 155). Reflecting an overly complacent appraisal of the role played by Western democracies in alleviating poverty, he confidently asserted that the family itself was not 'expected to provide subsidiary support to any considerable extent' because the 'individual family member today is publicly protected' (Habermas, 2006, p 155). Aside from being historically questionable, Habermas's analysis fails to appreciate that as products of the shifting balance of social and economic forces at particular historical conjunctures, 'welfare states' are not stable but, rather, changeable, likely to be *different* in *different* times (see Coates and Silburn, 1970; Hall and Jacques, 1989; Clarke, 2004, 2005). As John Saville (1957, p 2) observed over a half a century ago, the welfare state came about as a consequence of the 'interaction of three main factors': the struggle of the working class against their exploitation; the requirements of industrial capitalism for a more efficient environment in which to operate and, in particular, its need for a highly productive labour force; and the recognition by property owners of the price that had to be paid for political security.

However, since the inception of neoliberalisation and the demise of the Soviet bloc, diminished welfare provision has become more prevalent, with the introduction of social security cutbacks, more 'time-limited' and 'conditional' welfare support, and the introduction of 'user fees' for services, including access to third-level education. Such an approach penetrated deep into the policy approach of New Labour in the UK. In early 2008, the then Housing Minister, Caroline Flint, located the council estate question at the forefront of the government's 'modernising' policy agenda, suggesting that unemployed tenants should be compelled to sign 'commitment contracts' attesting to their desire to find work:

> It would be a big change of culture from the time when the council handed over someone the keys and forgot about them for 30 years. The question that we should ask of new tenants is what commitment

they will make to improve their skills, find work, and take the support that is available to them. (Quoted in Fabian Society, 2008)

Similar sentiments were expressed more recently by the Labour leader Ed Miliband (2011), who argued that when decisions are being made on who should have access to 'social housing', priority should be 'given to those who contribute – who give something back.... It is about rewarding people who do the right thing in their communities'. Related to this perspective, in November 2011, the Conservative-controlled London Borough of Wandsworth agreed to introduce a pilot project demanding that new council tenants should actively seek work, undergo training or commit to local volunteering; otherwise, they could lose their homes (Hennessy, 2011).

Policy departures such as this indicate that even within social-democratic thinking, welfare – in this instance in the form of social housing provision – is becoming more 'conditional', a reward for those who do the 'right thing'. There are, in fact, no 'welfare *guarantees*' of the type identified by Habermas. Moreover, dominant discourses now hold 'welfare', recoded as 'dependency', as responsible for misshaping people, leaving them unsuited for their slots within neoliberal modernity (Standing, 2011).

Reviewing the 'utopia of perfectly transparent communication'

It would be wrong, despite the emphasis that he places on dialogue, to suggest that Habermas feels that all contentious questions can be resolved by means of dialogue taking place within a transparent procedural framework. In terms of international geopolitics, for example, he found the use of military force acceptable during the first Gulf War in the early 1990s and supported the bombing of Yugoslavia (Habermas, 1997, 2001b, 2003; see also Anderson, 2005). The next part of the chapter, however, will argue that Habermas's theorisation does not provide social workers with an adequate basis for thought and praxis because it fails to acknowledge how power differentials are apt to *complicate*, even undermine, his discourse ethics and elaborate procedural framework. It is apparent that Hayes and Houston, Habermas's advocates within the profession, recognise the 'under-cutting, pervasive and subliminal effects of ideology', acknowledging that 'intra-familial dialogue' in FGCs 'should not be considered as completely free from the influence of power, competing interests and structural allegiances' (Hayes and Houston, 2007, p 1001). The problem, however, is that the difficulties with the Habermasian approach to FGCs and related fora are insufficiently interrogated, even obscured.

Although *Social work and social theory* does not seek to promote a Foucauldian perspective, it would seem that Foucault provides a more nuanced, although still problematic, understanding of power relations (see also Chambon et al, 1999; Skehill, 2004). As he maintained, one 'impoverishes the question of power if one poses it solely in terms … of the state and state apparatus. Power is quite different from and more complicated, dense, and pervasive than a set of laws or a state apparatus' (Foucault, 1980, p 158). Thus, for him, 'power relations … are multiple; they have different forms, they can be in play in family relations, or within an institution, or an administration' (Foucault, 1988d, p 38). That is to say, power relations are more fluid and omnipresent than Habermas suggests. Neither is it so easy to screen out, bracket or nullify differential power relations by erecting procedural rules to govern discourse in fora such as FGCs. Perhaps unsurprisingly given this critique, Foucault criticised Habermas for the undue emphasis he placed on a 'utopia of perfectly transparent communication' and the notion that 'there could be a state of communication … without obstacles, without constraint and without coercive effects' (Foucault, 1988a, p 18).

In what follows, the aim will be to outline issues connected to power differentials and suggest that despite Habermas's emphasis on the possibility for unconstrained dialogue, social 'inequalities in stratified societies can "infect" deliberation even in the absence of formal exclusions' (Asen, 2000, p 428).

Returning to Gramsci and Bourdieu

One of the weaknesses of Hayes and Houston's Habermasian perspective is that it fails to adequately examine the contemporary economic and political context. There is no questioning of neoliberalism and the imperatives, ways of seeing and organizational structures that this economic *and* cultural project is producing. As a consequence of this omission, individual participants in FGCs risk being torn from the totality of their social relations: perhaps especially, there is a failure to acknowledge how 'the silent compulsion of economic relations' exerts pressure *on* and *inside* the lives of families (Marx, 1990, p 899).

A number of Habermas's critics deny that his social theory is critical at all and 'see his analysis as a long-winded justification of a mixed economy' (Finlayson, 2005, p 57). Indeed, it could be argued, as Gardiner (2004, p 43) has observed, that Habermas's position:

> is idealist in both the philosophical and everyday senses of the word, because it supposes that material conflicts of a socio-economic nature can be effectively transcended or at least effectively sublimated into a rational discourse that can suspend ingrained power differentials.

In contrast, the work of Gramsci prompts us to ponder how changes within the sphere of welfare, such as those relating to the management of meetings relating to children and families, can be connected to more encompassing social forces and how a particular ruling bloc in a given social formation maintains 'hegemony'. A Gramscian way of thinking about FGCs might, therefore, stimulate social work and social policy research agendas seeking to historicise and investigate the reasons for the promotion of FGCs as a mechanism of intervention in the present conjuncture. Do FGCs appear to be configured differently in different national settings and if so *why*? How can we seek to try and comprehend keywords, such as 'empowerment' and how are they *put to work* in the discourse pivoting on FGCs? What might be the focal, yet unexamined, ideas underpinning FGCs? If FGCs implicitly provide a critique of social work practices, how are these critiques being shaped and who are the primary definers? Whose 'voices' are rendered subaltern, silent or marginal within the discourse centred on FGCs and why is this so? How might FCGs be altering the *work* in social work and related forms of activity? How, moreover, given the centrality of independent sector projects frequently involved in FGC facilitation, might the new structures be promoting a form of privatisation?

This form of critical reflection – and a deeper interrogation of *specific* professional roles, within *specific* structures in *specific* places at *specific* moments in time – might aid social workers involved in FGCs and other fora with children and families. The type of rigorous intellectual interrogation suggested by Gramsci is preferable to merely reifying structures, such as FGCs. Unlike Habermas, whose work can often appear arid, schematic and procedural, Gramsci appears better able to prompt a deeper and more political appraisal of how wider social forces infiltrate or deflect child welfare practices. This becomes apparent in the way micro-technologies of practice – such as assessment schedules, other forms and e-templates – not only seek to structure communicative encounters, but also often implicitly reinforce, or simply fail to question, existing patterns of economic and social relations. For example, how do child welfare professionals '*interpret* the law, policy and procedures in ways which are in keeping with the best interests of the child' (Houston, 2010a, p 1749, emphasis in original)? What is meant by '*sincere*' arguments? How might social workers and others 'promote *partnership*' (Houston, 2010a, p 1749, emphases added)? How does this language and these fluid concepts function when located within hegemonic orders in particular locations?

Here, again, Gramscian ideas are useful, for although language itself is 'not a source of hope for Gramcsi, nor is it a vehicle for rescue' (Ives, 2004b, p 164), he was, at the time he was writing, 'Europe's most linguistically orientated revolutionary' (Hirschkop, in Ives, 2004b, p 55). More fundamentally, as Peter Ives (2004b, p 136) argues:

> Gramsci's insights into language show that all debate is framed by political relations and that even perfectly 'reasonable' and often necessary statements such as 'What did you mean to say?' 'What do you mean?' and 'Make yourself clearer' are forms of censorship and monitoring, replete with power dynamics among the speakers.... Thus, Gramsci shows us that all meaning production, distribution, and reception takes place within socio-political contexts outside any 'universal' frameworks of ethical behaviour.

As we read in the previous chapter, Bourdieu, much more attentive to the impact of neoliberalism than Habermas, has provided a helpful articulation of this point by highlighting how inequalities impact on the tone and tenor of social interactions. Bourdieusian conceptual tools, in fact, illuminate the complexities of communication and exchanges in settings such as FGCs. A Bourdieusian approach erodes the notion that the deployment of a set of procedural rules can supply a 'technical fix' and dissolve impediments to communication that are rooted in power differentials. Indeed, a Habermasian perspective appears to pay little attention to the social location of individual participants in FGCs and similar fora. Is it possible to truly have untrammelled, open, transparent communicative engagement given that individuals – family members and 'professionals' – are located in different social fields and have differential access to the various types of capital outlined by Bourdieu? In posing this question, it is not implied that a Bourdieusian approach *entirely* undermines the Habermasian proposals of Hayes and Houston. Rather, it is to suggest that Bourdieu's form of analysis *complicates* their perspective.

Some of the complications become apparent when Hayes and Houston discuss the role of the FGC 'Independent Coordinator' who fulfils a pivotal role, acting as a 'kind of invigilator patrolling the boundary between the "lifeworld" and "system" domains, harnessing their respective perspectives and encouraging collaboration'. It is argued:

> Critically, they [the Independent Coordinators] are in a primary position to monitor and regulate the … dialogue between the family and the professionals. This is a matter of them policing the boundary of the "lifeworld" and "system" assiduously, protecting and nurturing *power-free communication and unrestrained argumentation*. In doing so, co-ordinators might act as mediators, spanning the different interests and needs of each of the parties. (Hayes and Houston, 2007, p 1002, emphasis added)

This would seem to imply that the 'Independent Coordinators' are socially neutral and that their 'patrolling' and 'policing' activity (to use the rather masculine imagery conjured up by Hayes and Houston) exists *outside* or *beyond* power relations. Within a Bourdieusian framework, however, the activity of Independent Coordinators is inevitably influenced by their sense of habitus, which is manifested in the way they dress, speak and act in the meeting. Independent Coordinators will, in fact, perform in a manner regarded as 'appropriate' by their field, using 'professional' language to define, shape and represent the core issues for the FGC and judging what is legitimate to discuss and what is peripheral or warranting exclusion. In a neoliberal context, for example, questions related to resources and the financial circumstances of the family are likely to be viewed as largely beyond the purview of the meeting. In short, there are a plethora of micro-sociological factors that seem to 'get lost' within the Habermasian perspective.

Introducing Bakhtin: open dialogue and *against* transparency

Described as the 'patron saint of open dialogue' (Emerson, in Irving and Young, 2002, p 19), the late Russian literary theorist Mikhail Bakhtin would seem to share some of Habermas's theoretical aspirations. However, his work is at variance with that of the German theorist because Bakhtin was also 'acutely sensitive to the potential for domination in abstract reason, and throughout his work he favored the marginal, the contingent, and the unofficial' (Irving and Young, 2002, p 25). Such preference relates to Bahktin's emphasis on unfinalisability:

> Against all thought that tends towards finality, closure and systems, throughout his work he constantly invoked the term 'unfinalizability', which captured his conviction that the world was not only a messy place but always an open place. The word unfinalizability signifies a structure of values at the core of his thinking: innovation, astonishment, discovery, the genuinely new, openness, potentiality, freedom and creativity – values that give us a more hopeful and expansive vision than the usual house of values that social workers dwell in. (Irving and Young, 2002, pp 20–1)

Although Irving and Young, Bakhtin's chief advocates within the social work literature, are too confident that his work lends itself to a 'postmodernist' approach to social work, they do perform a useful service in highlighting some of the key aspects of Bakhtinian thought. They maintain that one of his most important contributions to social work understanding was his theory of dialogue (or dialogism):

> The single adequate form for *verbally expressing* authentic human life is the *open-ended dialogue*. Life by its nature is dialogic. To live means to participate in dialogue: to ask questions, to heed, to respond, to agree, and so forth. In this dialogue a person participates wholly and throughout his [sic] whole life: with his eyes, lips, hands, soul, spirit, with his whole body and deeds. He invests his entire self in discourse, and the discourse enters into the dialogic fabric of human life, into the world symposium. (Bakhtin, in Irving and Young, 2002, p 22, emphasis in original)

This more existentially grounded, perhaps even mystical, approach to communicative practices is, therefore, very different to the procedural approach of Habermas, mapped out by Hayes and Houston. Differences are also apparent on account Bakhtin's writing on the 'carnival':

> Everything that was completed, fixed, determined, and too narrowly defined was for Bakhtin dogmatic and repressive; on the other hand,

> the carnival sense of the world is one in which the highest values are
> openness and incompletion ... it involves a mockery of all serious,
> closed attitudes about the world and an inversion of top and bottom
> in any given structure, a 'discrowning'. (Irving and Young, 2002, p 25)

This preoccupation with carnival and the disruptive reveals that the approach of
Bakhtin fundamentally differs from that of Habermas despite their shared interest
in how communicative practices are embodied. What is more, his emphasis on the
'open-ended' dialogue and carnival (with its strategic ridiculing of officialdom and
'official' discourses and practices) might seem to place Bakhtin beyond the reach of
'official' contemporary social work with its willed emphasis on the 'practical' and
'evidenced-based theory' (Webb, 2006).[3] Specifically in relation to social work's
micro-practices, Bakhtin might help in comprehending some of the dynamics in
fora such as FGCs: here, a key facet of Bakhtin's work pivots on his wariness about
ideas such as 'transparency', which, as we have seen, are so central to Habermasian
discourse ethics. In this context, one of the critical commentaries on Bakhtin refers
to his 'hard-nosed rejection of the idea of transparency' (Garvey, 2000, p 377). In
'practical terms transparency is much more closely associated with tyranny, and
Bakhtin is much more interested in ways of using language to destabilize and
subvert institutions that work to undermine autonomy' (Garvey, 2000, p 379).
Certainly, in comparison to Habermas, Bakhtin is far 'less confident about the
ability of speakers to achieve transparency, and thus he is more preoccupied with
exploring the way that impulses toward consensus and transparency contribute
to processes of ideological centralization that undermine autonomy' (Garvey,
2000, p 371). Thus, for him, 'opacity and ambiguity play the same liberating role
in Bakhtin's thought that transparency and clarity play' in Habermas's (Garvey,
2000, p 370).

Bakhtin's suspicion of 'transparency' in communication might initially appear
obtuse and provocative, even at odds with a social work approach to communication
and working in 'partnership'. However, his thoughts are – like those of Bourdieu
– far more attentive to the kind of power differentials that undermine the
Habermasian procedural framework promoted by Hayes and Houston. Perhaps
Bakhtin's scepticism about notions concerned with 'transparency' might also serve
to shed light on why users of services are, at times, fearful of the *reach* of the state
and its panoply of surveillance and tracking mechanisms, and are reluctant to
give voice to their experiences or even to surrender 'information' for assessments
(Garrett, 2003, 2009).

Arguably, Bakhtin provides a much better sense that *real* people in *real* situations
are the core issue for practitioners. Indeed, it has been maintained that Habermas's
'thoughts on rational dialogue and the public sphere do not in any substantive way
concern themselves with, much less address, *the embodied experiences and activities
of actual people in the context of everyday lives*' (Gardiner, 2004, pp 30–1, emphasis
added). In a similar fashion, Agnes Heller (1982, pp 21–2) has correctly observed
that the Habermasian subject lacks:

the sensuous experiences of hope and despair, of venture and humiliation ... the creature-like aspects of human beings are missing. [It is a subject with] no body, no feelings; the 'structure of personality' is identified with cognition, language and interaction ... one gets the impression the 'good life' consists solely of rational communication and needs that can be argued for without being felt. (See also Goode, 2005, p 48)

With Habermas, this absence of 'fleshiness' and a rather flat and sober perspective on the way in which people come together seeking to resolve or ameliorate hardships can be viewed as a further potential problem eroding the utility of social work approaches influenced by his theorisation.

Conclusion

This chapter has attempted to provide a critical commentary on Hayes and Houston's (2007) articulation of how Habermasian theorisation might assist social workers involved in FGCs and similar fora. It has been suggested that the work of Habermas is problematic because of the 'lifeworld'–'system' binary and on account of his failure to appreciate the complexity of power differentials. In the next chapter, we examine the work of Axel Honneth, a former student of Habermas, and one of his main intellectual critics, Nancy Fraser. Both of them have received some attention within the social work literature because of their theorisation of recognition.

> ## |◀◀ Reflection and Talk Box 8 ▶▶|
>
> - How can the ideas of Habermas associated with 'lifeworld' and 'system' inform our understanding of social work? Are the concepts of 'lifeworld' and 'system' convincing?
>
> - Can you provide any instances of where you may have seen or used (a) communicative action or (b) strategic action in your social work practice? How, moreover, do these ideas relate to your experience of supervision?
>
> - Does the procedure of Habermas fail to incorporate a satisfactory understanding of how power operates in social work and associated spheres?
>
> - Can we identify any forces of *monologism* within social work?
>
> - How can Bakhtin help us to make better sense of working within social work bureaucracies?
>
> - What happens *after* the 'carnival'?

Notes

[1] This chapter substantially reworks an article previously published as 'Making social work more Habermasian? A rejoinder in the debate on Habermas', *British Journal of Social Work*, vol 40, no 6, pp 1517–33. I am grateful to Oxford Journals for allowing me to have recourse to this material once again.

[2] For commentaries on Bakhtin, see Brandist (1996), Brandist et al (2004), Gardiner (2004), Hirschkop (1999, 2000, 2004), Hirschkop and Shepherd (2001), Neilson (1995; 2002), Pollard (2008), Smith (2004) and Vice (1997). A number of these contributions note the similarities and differences in the theoretical preoccupations of Habermas and Bakhtin (see, eg, Roberts, 2004). The latter's most notable collaborators were V.N. Voloshinov, a philosopher of language, and P.N. Medvedev, a literary theorist. Disputes exist as to which of the triumvirate was responsible for specific pieces of work; hence the preference of many scholars for 'Bakhtin Circle' as opposed to simply Bakhtin.

[3] There are more sceptical readings of the carnivalesque. During a period in which the 'dominant mechanism of escape is privatized hedonism', carnivalisation as 'commodity … now sustains global capitalism' (Langan and Ryan, 2009, pp 472, 479). In short, the carnivalesque has been *incorporated* into the hegemonic order of neoliberalism.

CHAPTER NINE

Thinking with Honneth and Fraser[1]

Introduction

> Among the few things I took in during my stint in the Philosophy
> Department at Humboldt was the idea – I forgot whose – that the
> underlying motive for all human action is the desire for *recognition* –
> recognition of one's worth and dignity as a human being, without
> which one was a nonperson; a slave. The concept had articulated very
> precisely the obscure cravings of my soul, and it had lodged itself in
> my imagination. It had felt incontrovertible. (Lasdun, 2007, p 133)

Like the central character in James Lasdun's (2007) novel, *Seven lies*, a number
of writers located within the field of social work appear to have become fixated
with the ethics and politics of recognition. Moreover, they have made thoughtful
contributions stressing the relevance of this theorisation for practitioners' day-
to-day encounters with the users of social services (see, eg, Froggett, 2004; Webb,
2006, 2010; Houston, 2008, 2010b; Houston and Dolan, 2008; Marthinsen and
Skjefstad, 2011).

Within philosophy, 'recognition designates an ideal reciprocal relation between
subjects in which each sees the other as its equal ... one becomes an individual only
in virtue of recognizing, and being recognized by, another subject' (Fraser, 2003,
p 10). In this sense, due 'recognition is not just a courtesy we owe people. It is a vital
human need' (Taylor, 1992, p 26). The German philosopher Hegel (1770–1831)
coined the phrase the 'struggle for recognition' (*Kampf um Anerkennung*), but it
was the early 1990s that marked a resurgence of academic interest in this theme.

The 'two most prominent main contemporary theorists of recognition' are the
neo-Hegelian philosophers Charles Taylor and Axel Honneth (Fraser, 2003, p 28).
Here, Taylor's (1992) *The politics of recognition* – variously referred to as a 'catalytic
essay' (Markell, 2003, p 2) or 'signal essay' (McNay, 2008, p 2) – probably remains
the single most influential work on the theme in contemporary political theory.
His intervention, preoccupied, in part, by his own engagement in Canadian
politics, and more specifically with the status of Quebec and its francophone
community, had a much wider resonance. In the same year (1992), Honneth's
focal intervention, *The struggle for recognition*, was first published in Germany
(Honneth, 1995). There are significant differences between Taylor and Honneth
but, along with the American feminist philosopher Nancy Fraser, they are united
in a foundational – and contestable – belief that 'contemporary politics has seen
a shift away from ideas of class, equality, economy and nation towards those of

identity, difference, culture and ethnicity' (Thompson, 2006, p 3). For them, 'the idea of recognition' is now situated at the 'heart of what justice means today' and, consequently, a 'just society would be one where everyone gets due recognition' (Thompson, 2006, p 3).

Due to the technical, even obscure, language deployed by recognition theorists, the politics of recognition has, save for a handful of social work academics, been mostly neglected in the profession's literature. This chapter cannot provide a detailed overview of the expansive and frequently conceptually complex contemporary literature on recognition theory (see Thompson, 2006), but will seek to extend the parameters of social work interest by examining and critically engaging with the work of Honneth and Fraser. The discussion will begin by focusing on Honneth's contribution, which – owing to its 'philosophical and political comprehensiveness' (Houston and Dolan, 2008, p 462) – has been hailed by some commentators as a new theoretical bedrock for social work and associated spheres. After highlighting a number of substantial problems and elisions connected to Honneth's theorisation, it will be suggested that the work of Fraser – who has been involved in sustained exchanges with Honneth – provides a more convincing set of ideas related to recognition.[2] It will, however, be argued that most proponents of recognition theory, including Fraser, fail to adequately address the crucial impact of the neoliberal state on contemporary social relations (see also Chapter Five). Mirrored by social work's chief advocates of recognition theory, this lacuna is especially damaging given that most social workers, in the UK and Ireland for example, are employed by the state and fulfil professional roles that are mapped out, ordered and regulated by the state.

Theorising recognition: Axel Honneth and Nancy Fraser

Although, as mentioned, the philosopher Charles Taylor was the first to elaborate on the notion of recognition, within social work theory, it is Honneth's account of recognition that has been afforded the most attention and, indeed, endorsement (see Houston, 2008, 2010b; Houston and Dolan, 2008). For Honneth, there are three key factors that impact on and shape individuals' lifelong capacity to fruitfully engage with others: the sense of basic *self-confidence* (related to how we were, and are presently, situated within loving relationships), *self-respect* and *self-esteem*. Arguing that the initial love relationship precedes, both conceptually and genetically, every other form of reciprocal recognition, Honneth relies heavily on early childhood 'object-relations theory' and, particularly, on Donald Winnicott's (1896–1971) conviction that the 'development of children cannot be abstracted from the interactive relationships in which the process of maturation takes place' (Anderson, 1995, p xiii).

Winnicott (1965, p 161) regards the relationship of a child to her/his mother as particularly important during the early months and years, perceiving the father as merely 'the protecting agent who frees the mother to devote herself to her baby'. Although Honneth is prepared to use the term 'mother' to refer to a role that can be fulfilled by persons other than the biological mother, he is adamant that 'all love relationships are driven by the unconscious recollection of the original experience ... that characterized the first months of life for "mother" and child' even if this occurs *'behind the back of the subject and throughout the subject's life'* (Honneth, 1995, p 105, emphasis added).

Honneth argues that this particular 'psychoanalytical' perspective is 'especially well suited to the purposes of a phenomenology of recognition' (Honneth, 1995, p 98). He is of the view that 'the intuitions of the young Hegel are confirmed to a surprising degree' by Winnicott (Honneth, 1995, p 98). In this context, the English paediatrician and psychoanalyst emphasises the idea that a 'successful relationship between mother and child' can establish the foundation or 'pattern' of subsequent interactions and relationships rooted in reciprocal recognition (Honneth, 1995, p 104). Honneth is also keen to stress that his abstract theorisation is evidence-based and informed by empirical studies. Here, he refers to what he terms the 'path-breaking studies' by John Bowlby (1907–90), a British developmental psychologist, on the 'good enough' conditions for the socialisation of young children and his 'conclusion that human infants develop an active willingness to produce interpersonal proximity, which provides a basis for all later forms of affectional bonds' (Honneth, 1995, p 97). This 'theoretical conclusion was supported on the therapeutic side by the discovery', we are told, that a 'growing number of patients suffered from mental illnesses that could ... be traced back to ... interpersonal disturbances' in the process of the child's development (Honneth, 1995, p 97). In contrast, infants responded to with loving concern by the primary carers will acquire a 'body-related *self-confidence*' (Honneth, in Thompson, 2006, p 26, emphasis in original).

Only when an individual possesses the 'self-confidence', born out of, engendered by and maintained in loving relationships, will they be able, it is argued, to then acquire self-respect. As Honneth understands it, self-respect has 'less to do with whether or not one has a good opinion of oneself' than it does of one's sense of possessing the 'universal dignity of persons' (Anderson, 1995, p xiv). Related to this, being accorded rights is also 'crucial to self-respect' (Anderson, 1995, p xv). Whereas 'self-respect is a matter of viewing oneself as entitled to the same status and treatment as every other person, self-esteem involves a sense of what it is that makes one special, unique' (Anderson, 1995, p xvi). What 'distinguishes one from others must be something *valuable*. Accordingly, to have the sense that one has nothing of value to offer is to lack any basis for developing a sense of one's own identity' (Anderson, 1995, p xvi, emphasis in original).

As previously noted, Honneth's theorisation on recognition has received more attention within social work than any other theorist. One reason for this may be that his approach is partly rooted in the social psychology of Winnicott and Bowlby, whose work was central to the mainstream discourse on child care social work in the 1950s and subsequent years. Like Honneth, the feminist philosopher Nancy Fraser agrees that 'recognition's salience is now indisputable' and is happy to reject the 'economistic view that would reduce recognition to a mere epiphenomenon of distribution' (Fraser and Honneth, 2003, pp 1, 2). However, of the three key theorists associated with the politics of recognition, she is the one who is most intent on distancing herself from psychological reductionism or 'psychologisation' (Fraser, 2003, p 31): the transfer, or displacement, of what are fundamentally social and economic issues and problems to a solely psychological domain. Indeed, 'psychologisation' would appear to be a key facet of Honneth's approach. Fraser maintains that recognition theory needs to eschew 'psychologisation' in order to avoid reducing the injustice of misrecognition to a matter of individual psychological shortcomings or failings. More seriously, for her, when misrecognition is identified with 'internal distortions in the structure of the self-consciousness of the oppressed, it is but a short step to blaming the victim' (Fraser, 2003, p 31). Furthermore, it could be argued that many people experience severe forms of hurt, rejection and loss, yet do not find themselves permanently 'scarred' and 'injured' in the way that more psychologically oriented accounts of recognition would have us believe (Honneth, 1995, p 135; Markell, 2003, p 18). Some individuals in contact with social work and related services, subjected to social suffering and (mis)recognition, have responded by collectivising their experiences and forming 'survivor' and campaign groups. This understanding would seem to be especially important in social work given that practitioners frequently work with individuals and groups, such as children and young people 'looked after', whose lives have been impaired by problematic early relationships with their parents. However, this need not always result in irretrievably blighted lives. Neither can we assume that acquiring 'self-confidence' early in life provides an uncomplicated foundation for the dynamics of mutual recognition because even seemingly 'well brought up' and 'secure' individuals have the potential to be part of fraught interpersonal relationships. What is more, 'confident' people can, of course, be highly exploitative, predatory, racist and misogynist. Equally important, people ostensibly lacking in confidence may live and act in ways that provide esteem and recognition to others. In short, what seems to be 'missing in Honneth's model is the concept of mediations' (Alexander and Lara, 1996, p 131).

Although Fraser herself does not dwell on it, Honneth's intellectual indebtedness to the Western European, more specifically British, social psychology of the 1950s and 1960s remains vulnerable to the criticism that the 'scientific' insights of that period are redolent of the dominant social, economic and gender ordering of the Cold War era (see, eg, Winnicott, 1965, ch 18). More specifically, perhaps, Honneth's 'unqualified reliance' (McNay, 2008, p 132) on the theorisation of figures such as Winnicott and Bowlby fails to pay due regard to the critiques of feminist scholars (McNay, 2008). Notably, Bowlby's work was particularly influential in the 1950s, providing an intellectual basis for regulating and disciplining 'deviant' mothers positioned outside dominant constructions of 'normality' (Bowlby, 1990): for example, 'unmarried mothers' (Spensky, 1992). Related to this is the emphasis Honneth places on the 'mother'–infant dyad. More fundamentally, underpinning his approach to recognition is a certain psychological determinism that grants too much prominence to early interactions and insufficient attention to the 'habitus' of the child and their more encompassing and fuller sense of their place in the world (Lovell, 2007; see also Chapter Seven).

Fraser's own and very specific approach to the question of recognition is grounded in what she refers to as the 'principle of parity of participation' and the promotion of embedded social arrangements that permit all (adult) members of society to interact with others as peers (see, eg, Fraser, 1989, 1997, 2000, 2003; Fraser and Honneth, 2003). The aim, therefore, should be to preclude 'institutional norms that systematically depreciate some categories of people and the qualities associated with them' (Fraser, 2003, p 36). Her formula on participatory parity is also able to 'exclude opportunistic and destructive claims' such as those of racists and xenophobes (McNay, 2008, p 149).

While remaining situated within political theory debates on recognition, Fraser is distinctive in that she is perturbed that the rise of the 'politics of recognition' has been at the expense of what she calls the 'politics of redistribution'. For Fraser, there is the continuing danger that the politics of 'difference' – discursively preoccupied with questions of 'identity' and often associated with the demands of social movements representing particular 'minority groups' – might lead to the marginalisation, or displacement, of a politics of equality grounded in an attentiveness to class and focused on economic inequality and campaigns for economic justice. Similarly, it can be argued that, for a period, the dominant discourse of social work in the US and, perhaps to a lesser extent, the UK was responsible for prioritising questions connected to 'diversity' and 'difference' over matters of class inequality and economic exploitation (Garrett, 2002; see also the related discussion on Badiou in Chapter Ten). Fraser suggests that some reject the politics of recognition outright because of the global increase in poverty and mass inequalities. For them, claims for the recognition of 'difference' are an obstruction to the pursuit of social justice. Conversely, some of the promoters of recognition are sceptical about the politics of redistribution and disdain the failure of difference-blind economic egalitarianism to bring about justice for women and minority ethnic groups. Thus, it can appear that we are 'effectively presented with an either/or choice: redistribution or recognition? Class politics or identity politics? Multiculturalism or social democracy?' (Fraser, 2003, p 8). In contrast, her own carefully argued claim is that these are false antitheses and that neither 'alone is sufficient' (Fraser, 2003, p 9). Thus, instead of endorsing either one of these paradigms to the exclusion of the other, she seeks to develop a 'two-dimensional' conception of justice. Without 'reducing either dimension to the other, it encompasses both of them within a broader overarching framework' (Fraser, 2003, p 35).

Consequently, Fraser advocates a theory of social justice in which redistribution *and* recognition play equal and interwoven parts. Fraser rejects approaches that tilt conceptually too far in the direction of either economism or culturalism. More specifically, she asserts that the injustices confronting individuals and groups are rooted in economy *and* culture; that is to say, economy and culture are intertwined and interpenetrating social spaces. No zone of society can be purely economic or purely cultural since '*every* practice' is 'simultaneously economic and cultural, albeit not necessarily in equal proportions' (Fraser, 2003, p 63, emphasis in original). She argues, therefore, that in 'all societies economic ordering and cultural ordering are mutually imbricated' (Fraser, 2003, p 51). Perhaps alert to more Gramscian approaches to the maintenance (and instability) of hegemony, she maintains that this requires us to assess just 'how precisely they relate to each other in a given social formation' (Fraser, 2003, p 51).

Fraser's approach clearly diverges from Honneth's 'doggedly monistic' belief that recognition theory 'can underpin an account of justice which can deal with *all matters* of recognition' (Thompson, 2006, p 104, emphasis added). Thus, Honneth deems recognition to be the '*fundamental* overarching moral category', considering 'the socialist ideal of redistribution as a *subvariety* of the struggle for recognition' (Fraser and Honneth, 2003, pp 2–3, emphases added). Fraser's analysis pivots instead on the core idea that the '*two* categories are *co-fundamental and mutually irreducible* dimensions of justice' (Fraser and Honneth, 2003, p 3, emphases added). Her perspective is more convincing than that of Honneth because of a willingness to articulate how questions of recognition – and (mis)recognition – can only be examined satisfactorily if fused with questions related to the economy and patterns of redistribution. In short, individuals are 'nodes of convergence for multiple, cross-cutting axes of subordination' (Fraser, 2003, p 57). This understanding highlights the complexities inherent in engaging, as social workers do, with people whose lives (and life chances) are determined by their positioning within a grid of intersecting forms of stratification.

What is required, therefore, is a conceptualisation that is equipped to 'theorize the dynamic forms of status subordination characteristic of late-modern globalizing capitalism' (Fraser, 2003, p 8). Fraser terms this 'perspectival dualism' (Fraser, 2003, p 63). She then goes on to try to illuminate her approach by, for example, focusing on gender because the 'two-dimensional character of gender wreaks havoc on the idea of an either/or choice between the paradigm of redistribution and the paradigm of recognition' (Fraser, 2003, p 22). Indeed, historical accounts of the installation of capitalist regimes provide evidence to support Fraser's theorising. Primitive patterns of capital accumulation, for example, were not simply an accumulation and concentration of exploitable workers and capital. They were also an accumulation of differences and divisions with the working class, 'whereby hierarchies built upon gender, as well as "race" and age, became constitutive of class rule and the formation of the modern proletariat' (Federici, 2004, pp 63–4). Federici also argues, because of these 'imposed divisions – especially between women and men – that capitalist accumulation continues to devastate life in every corner of the planet' (Federici, 2004, pp 63–4).

A similar point can be made in terms of the social divisions rooted in 'race', given that racist norms are 'wired into the infrastructure of capitalist labour markets' (Fraser, 2003, p 58). More fundamentally, Fraser argues that a 'genuinely critical perspective ... cannot take the appearance of separate spheres at face value. Rather, it must probe beneath appearances to reveal the hidden connections between distribution and recognition' (Fraser, 2003, p 62).

'Perspectival dualist' approaches should, therefore, be founded on helping to create the conditions for, what we have observed she terms, the 'parity of participation'. Such analyses are, for Fraser, not merely describing and interpreting the world, they are part of a more encompassing political aspiration to *change* the world. Thus, she stresses the need to go beyond 'affirmative strategies' – reflected in mainstream multiculturalism – for 'redressing injustice which aim to correct inequitable outcomes of social arrangements without disturbing the underlying social structures that generate them' (Fraser, 2003, p 74). What is required, she affirms, are 'transformative strategies' that seek to 'correct unjust outcomes precisely by restructuring the underlying generative framework' (Fraser, 2003, p 74). Moreover, genuine 'transformative strategies' aim to painstakingly construct a 'counter hegemonic bloc of social movements' (Fraser, 2003, p 86). While acknowledging the validity of Fraser's critique, the following sections will draw on recent debates in political theory to question the core assumption of recognition theory.

Alternative conceptualisations

A number of contributions made in recent years have used recognition theory as a foundation from which to articulate a range of counter-perspectives. Oliver (2004), for example, has argued that the 'need for recognition from the dominant culture or group' is actually 'a symptom of the pathology of oppression' given that oppression 'creates the need and demand for recognition' (Oliver, 2004, p 79). Thus, she explains, the 'internalization of stereotypes of inferiority and superiority leave the oppressed with the sense that they are lacking something that only their superior dominators have or can give'. Implied in this 'diagnosis is the conclusion that struggles for recognition and theories that embrace those struggles may indeed presuppose and thereby perpetuate the very hierarchies, domination, and injustice that they attempt to overcome' (Oliver, 2004, p 80).

According to Markell's (2003) insightful critique, the politics of recognition tends to divert 'attention from the role of the powerful, of the *misrecognizers* … focusing on the consequences of suffering misrecognition rather than on the more fundamental question of what it means to commit it' (Markell, 2003, p 18, emphasis in original). Furthermore, recognition theory is apt to present a rather static, stable perception of culture and has, more generally, an insufficiently nuanced grasp of what it means to be human. As an alternative, he proposes an existentially inclined 'politics of acknowledgement', which 'involves coming to terms with, rather than vainly attempting to overcome, the risk of conflict, hostility, misunderstanding, opacity, and alienation that characterizes life among others' (Markell, 2003, p 38).

In another elegant critique of recognition theory, McNay (2008) has also drawn attention to a number of theorists who maintain that 'far from being authentic indicators of oppression or injustice, recognition claims derive their legitimacy from a certain sentimentalized discourse of suffering' (McNay, 2008, p 10). Some 'go further and argue that the politics of recognition is essentially a middle-class phenomenon since it is only privileged groups that have the disposition required to manage a rhetoric of personal suffering and distress to personal advantage' (McNay, 2008 p 10). The 'desire for recognition might be a far from spontaneous and innate phenomenon [and more] the effect of a certain ideological manipulation of individuals' (McNay, 2008, p 10). She then furnishes a useful summary of an alternative Foucauldian perspective on recognition theory, with the assertion that the 'pervasive desire for recognition' can be interpreted as 'a manifestation of an encroaching governmental power that controls individuals by manipulating the type of relation they have with themselves' (McNay, 2008, p 133). This inculcation in individuals of a preoccupation with the self is not only compatible with an individualised consumerism, it also 'diffuses energies that might otherwise be directed towards more radical forms of social transformation' (McNay, 2008, p 133). From this perspective, therefore, what Honneth regards as 'the spontaneous and innate nature of the desire for recognition is an example of how, in late modernity, disciplinary structures have been so thoroughly internalized by individuals that they become self-policing subjects' (McNay, 2008, p 133).

Given the weight of these varied and critical interventions, how can the recent attempts to locate the politics of recognition at the core of social work theory and practice be assessed?

Taking recognition theory into social work

Clearly, members of marginalised and subaltern groups have been, and are, systematically denied dignity, self-esteem and recognition either as persons or on account of their way of life and culture. Such processes of denial and disrespect extend into the practices of social work and into the lives of children and their families seeking out interventions, or having interventions imposed upon them. Shortcomings, failings and abusive 'care' practices can, in part, be attributed to a failure to accord meaningful recognition to specific groups and individuals (Wardhaugh and Wilding, 1993). The dynamics of (mis)recognition may, for example, be associated with the response of UK social services to Victoria Climbié and Peter Connelly (Secretary of State for Health and Secretary of State for the Home Department, 2003; Ofsted, Healthcare Commission and HMIC, 2008; see also Garrett, 2009). In Ireland, we can also connect some of the ideas related to recognition theory to the findings of a number of inquiries that have examined clerical abuse in institutional settings (Murphy et al, 2005; Commission of Investigation, 2009, 2010; Commission to Inquire into Child Abuse, 2009).

Much of this would, therefore, seem to support the notion that social workers need to become familiar with the ethics and politics of recognition: if this new engagement occurs, it is implied, practices are likely to be unambiguously enhanced. Moreover, the way in which recognition has been articulated within the discourse of social work, usually drawing exclusively – and rather uncritically – on Honneth, suggests that it is entirely aligned with the ethics of the profession, which emphasise notions of 'respect' for persons and the relational aspects of life. Social work's interest in questions of 'diversity' and 'difference' might also be interpreted in terms of recognition ethics. More fundamentally, this theorisation has the potential to appeal to the 'common sense' of the profession – its sense of 'mission' – and it seems congruent with its 'sacred' lexicon (see Beckett, 2003).

Recognition theory's person–centred politics would seem to be completely at odds with and oppositional to neoliberalism (Webb, 2006). We are also advised that the provision of social support for children and their families is a practical expression of recognition (Houston and Dolan, 2008). According to its proponents within the sphere of social work, recognition theory can provide the ethical core and conceptual bedrock to enable practitioners to *reclaim* social work and to inject a fresh, reinvigorated and more 'human' approach to the *work* in social work. Such an approach, it is maintained, gains particular resonance and meaning in the light of what has been denounced as the sterile and arid nature of some contemporary social work practices (see Chapter Four). Nevertheless, despite the theorisation of recognition being a diverse field with numerous internal debates and disagreements, its main theorists tend to neglect or under–theorise the role of the neoliberal state. This 'gap' tends, in fact, to unite its proponents, and becomes particularly problematic given that social work is mostly an activity undertaken at the behest of the state. This *disappearing* of the state also risks mistakenly casting social work as existing *outside* of the dominant social and economic relations that characterise the times in which we live. We will now turn to examine this lacuna.

Recognition theory and the disappearing neoliberal state

Most theorists of recognition (including Nancy Fraser's more persuasive analysis) fail to acknowledge that the state, primarily intent on maintaining patterns of capital accumulation, can be a substantial source of oppression and hardship in itself. It is striking that many theorists of recognition, as well as the promoters of recognition in social work, do not explicitly even refer to the state (Houston and Dolan, 2008): the state is seemingly *lost* as an object of analysis, critique and comment. This then enables these theorists to 'implicitly treat institutionalized forms of recognition as expressions of, and ultimately reducible to, more elementary and unmediated exchanges of recognition among persons' (Markell, 2003, p 26). In this way, the state simply appears to melt away like ice cream on a hot summer's day.

An alternative approach, on the part of some recognition theorists, is to cast the state 'in a far more important role, depicting it as a mediating institution that has the capacity to resolve struggles for recognition, *transcending* the conflicting dynamics that characterize social life' (Markell, 2003, p 26, emphasis added). This latter approach is also problematic because the state – perceived here as a 'neutral delivery system' (Feldman, 2002, p 418) – is summoned to resolve struggles for recognition that are, seemingly, beyond 'the social' and 'miraculously transcending its conflicts' (Markell, 2003, p 26). What this fails to acknowledge is that state formations, at particular times and places, are never *outside* social and economic relations, but are *products* of class struggles.

This under-theorising of the state is connected to the suggestion from recognition's promulgators in social work that it is merely *interpersonal* (mis) recognition that is largely responsible for conflict. Thus, it is implied that if – what we might term – a deficit of recognition was addressed, via face-to-face encounters, a diminution in conflictive relationships would follow. More generally, within recognition theory, oppression tends to be perceived as a form of 'interpersonally engendered misrecognition' rather than as a form of exploitative interaction that is '*systematically* generated' (McNay, 2008, p 9, emphasis added). As McNay has lucidly maintained, this is:

> not to deny that inequalities are created through personal interaction, but, by focusing principally on this mode, the idea of recognition obscures the extent to which identity and subjectivity are penetrated by structural dynamics of power which often operate *at one remove from the immediate relations of everyday life.* (McNay, 2008, p 9, emphasis added)

This emphasis on the 'face-to-face' encounter is emphasised by Houston, who, in an otherwise closely reasoned contribution, asserts that 'sectarianism is fuelled by a *misconception* about the other's identity, whether it takes place in Belfast, Baghdad or Beirut' (Houston, 2008, p 38, emphasis added). According to Houston (2008, p 38), contemporary and historical conflicts in these locations – in truth, rooted in colonisation and imperialism and not simply 'sectarianism' – can be solved by 'contact', which provides an 'opportunity for commonality to emerge'. Occluded here is the role that powerful structural forces play in promoting division and partitioning communities: generating and bolstering structuring relations of (mis)recognition and social difference. Such comments also provide evidence of the '*inclusive inflexion* that thinkers of recognition give the dialogical constitution of the subject' in that individuals are perceived as having 'the capacity', or even the predisposition, 'to empathize with the other rather than being locked in antagonistic relation with them' (McNay, 2008, p 7, emphasis added). Not only does Houston's observation disconnect the domain of personal interactions from underlying structural dynamics, it also seems to disregard the possibility that in a situation of conflict, the parties involved may have arrived at a considered and accurate assessment of their respective interests and of the nature of their struggle. Integral to the 'inclusive inflexion' is a rooted and normative assumption that successful recognition is possible and desirable, whereas this notion can be contested: should, for example, those subject to occupation 'recognise' and seek 'commonality' with an invading army?

Most observers would concede that Northern Ireland provides an example of a state having routinely functioned as a steering mechanism for promoting and sustaining patterns of (mis)recognition, oppression and hardship. The state in Northern Ireland, created following the Government of Ireland Act in 1920, promoted and maintained class and protestant sectarian hegemony until the signing of the Belfast Agreement in April 1998. Unavoidably, this structurally rooted discrimination impacted on social work education and practice (Garrett, 1999). Historians of social policy have also highlighted thay the British Empire fostered and promoted 'difference' and religious identifications as a strategy to divide and rule potentially insurgent nationalism. Here, the administration of welfare played a key strategic role in sifting and managing populations (Midgley and Piachaud, 2011). Within India, for example, British rule significantly expanded and sharpened caste norms and conventions. Indeed, this 'colonial essentialization of caste' has 'haunted India since Independence' (Jayaram, 2011, p 93). More recently, in the UK, social sorting processes now in place to combat 'terrorism' have 'led to the crude profiling of groups, especially Muslims, that has produced inconvenience, hardship and even torture' (ICO, 2006, p 8). As Guru (2010) bravely noted – given the absence of discussion on this topic – these processes are bound to have a negative impact on social work practice in a range of professional specialisms.

Symbolic violence: the neoliberal state as an engine of (mis)recognition

In most contemporary neoliberal societies, the state is able to divide and segregate people in at least two intertwined, and not easily separable, ways. First, the neoliberal state can be regarded as *a literal builder and consolidator of 'difference'*. This is achieved via spatial and territorial separating practices, in the disciplining of space and the arranging of architecture (see also Jones, 2012). In Northern Ireland, the construction of 'peace' walls provides a good example of this process. More routinely, it is detectable in terms of the control of 'borders' and in how housing, education and the transport infrastructure is plotted, built and configured so as to ensure differential access patterns. In an American context, Hayward (2003, p 502) refers to the role of the state 'not simply in responding to extant social differences, but in making, re-making and reinforcing relations of identity/difference' (see also Balibar, 2007). This tendency, she asserts, is apparent in the urban planning of American cities, where state actors 'helped forge the black American ghetto' (Hayward, 2003, p 503).

Second, the state is responsible for *the discursive promulgation of categories and labels attached to particular groups*. States:

> have not only attempted to monopolize physical force, taxation, and the means of movement, but also the legitimate use of symbolic force, including the power to name, to categorize, and define objects and events by giving them an official seal of approval. (Loyal, 2009, p 420)

The state possesses the 'power to (re)make reality by preserving or altering the categories through which agents comprehend and construct the world' (Loyal, 2009, p 420). State actors, in their naming and classifying practices, can be perceived as primary definers and generators of (mis)recognition. Historically, social work shares complicity in facilitating these dividing practices, which can humiliate, overlook or render invisible those 'cases' receiving services or being dispensed 'care'. This collusion may stem from an uncritical or unwitting adoption of the state's 'categories, schemes of perception, ideology and organizing principles' (Loyal, 2009, p 420). State classifications are also 'crucial in determining ... differential allocations and access to material resources, and thereby in shaping ... lives' (Loyal, 2009, p 421). For Bourdieu (2000, p 175) this is bound up with what he terms 'symbolic violence' and the role that the state, and its functionaries, play in instituting and inculcating 'common symbolic forms of thought, social frames of perception or memory ... forms of classification ... practical schemes of perception, appreciation and action' (Bourdieu, 2000, p 175).[3] This, in turn, contributes to the 'formation of doxic understandings and 'unquestioned background assumptions' (Loyal, 2009, p 420).

Symbolic violence may be found in the ambiguous labels attached to various categories of users of welfare services, for example, 'jobseekers' or 'problem families'. In a contemporary context, the vocabulary used by governments is saturated in contempt for families who are chided and condemned for 'welfare *dependency*' (Fraser and Gordon, 1997). Table 9.1, taken from a 'benefits' office in the Republic of Ireland, highlights how those seeking financial aid from the state are positioned within pernicious, dominant discourses. Although imbued with the language of managerialism ('customer', 'quality'), the 'charter' provides an example of symbolic violence, whereby the state enforces discriminatory 'forms of classification' and 'social frames of perception'. In a country whose economy has been wrecked by bankers, property developers and a compliant political class, it is benefit claimants who find themselves framed as an unpredictable, transient and troublesome population. Volatile others, temporarily located in 'our' offices, are implicitly and explicitly presented as foul and vulgar, and prone to racist behaviour, violent outbursts, drunkenness and drug use.

How claimants are treated serves to instil a particular patterning of relationships, which fosters segregation, social division and (mis)recognition. For welfare claimants, this dynamic can be identified not only in the 'Customer Charter', but in the most mundane and recurrent scenarios: for example, that of waiting to be interviewed by a welfare officer or to learn the outcome of an assessment of entitlement. 'Waiting is one of the privileged ways of experiencing the effect of power, and the link between time and power' and this is reflected in '... adjourning, deferring, delaying, raising false hopes, or, conversely rushing, taking by surprise' (Bourdieu, 2000, p 228). Indeed, according to Bourdieu (2000, p 228), waiting 'implies submission'.

Table 9.1: Customer Charter: rules of conduct, Department of Social Protection

We aim to give a quality service to our customers. To help to do this, please treat our staff, our other customers and our public offices with respect. In particular please obey the following rules:

1. Do not act in any way that disrupts others and interferes with their use of the office
2. Do not harass any staff or members of the public by using abusive, racist, obscene or threatening language
3. Do not use violence, threaten violence to staff or members of the public. If you do we will report you to the Gardai [police]
4. Do not intentionally damage or steal the Department's property
5. Do not smoke in the Department's offices
6. Do not drink alcohol or take illegal drugs while in our offices
7. Do not leave personal property unattended while using our offices
8. If one of our staff has already dealt with you, please do not loiter

Please use our public offices in a responsible and considerate way by observing these rules.

How the state acts as an engine of (mis)recognition can also be illustrated by the treatment accorded to those seeking to obtain asylum. The late Bourdieusian scholar Abdelmalek Sayad memorably observed that the 'secret virtue of immigration' is that it 'provides an introduction, and perhaps the best introduction of all, to the sociology of the state' (Sayad, 2004, p 279). Unlike the promoters of recognition theory within social work, who, as we have seen, do not dwell on the role of the state, Sayad asserts that it is:

> as though it were the very nature of the state to discriminate ... between the 'nationals' it recognizes ... and 'others' with whom it deals only in 'material' and instrumental terms. It deals with them only because they are present within the field of its national sovereignty. (Sayad, 2004, p 279; see also Anderson, 1991)

The 'legal and administrative categories of "asylum seekers", "refugee" and "economic migrant" are important in that they confer different rights and entitlements' (Loyal, 2003, p 83). Such bureaucratic state classification schemes engender systematic patterns of discrimination, which are reinforced beyond the micro-level of face-to-face encounters. Moreover, these 'administrative categories and classifications used by the state play an important role in defining broader discourses of identification and exclusion' (Loyal, 2003, p 83).

Such theoretical insights can contribute to a more rounded understanding of the hardships of asylum seekers in various jurisdictions. For example, in the Republic of Ireland, asylum seekers are rigidly segregated, with 52 direct provision centres established in April 2000 and almost 6,000 asylum seekers still living in them for more than three years. These are privately operated establishments with contracts with the Reception and Integration Agency (RIA): residents are given €19.10 each week to live on and provided with a shared room and meals in 'hotel-style' accommodation. A person waiting for their asylum claim to be decided by the state has no right to work, even though adjudicating on an asylum application can – illuminating the aptness of Bourdieu's comments on power and waiting – take up to 10 years.

Conclusion

This chapter should not be read as a peremptorily dismissive response to the politics of recognition as a corpus of social theory. Recent attempts to import this theory into social work are significant, thought-provoking and important contributions to social work's engagement with core ethical themes and preoccupations. A renewed attentiveness to social suffering is timely for social work practitioners and educators because dwelling on such themes may promote a new interrogation of how routine forms of disparagement and diminishment impact on those having recourse to services. Nevertheless, there is a need to be wary about the promotion of recognition theory in social work and associated fields. Such wariness becomes particularly necessary because recent years have also witnessed this theorisation being harnessed to the workfare agenda. For example, in Norway, there have been attempts to incorporate notions of 'respect' and 'recognition' into schemes intent on 'engaging the young or marginalized to become involved in *positive* social activities like working in the local community, learning general work skills and developing *positive* behaviour' (Marthinsen and Skjefstad, 2011, p 210, emphases added).

The theorisation of Honneth is highly problematic, particularly because of his rather 'naive psychologism' (McNay, 2008, p 135). In contrast, Fraser's approach to recognition – with its focus on 'axes of subordination' and 'perspectival dualism' – gels, in some respects, with some of the more conceptually sophisticated and persuasive accounts of the multifaceted nature of oppression. Like most accounts of recognition theory, however, Fraser's own theorisation tends to under-theorise the state and its role in generating and sustaining patterns of 'othering' and (mis)recognition. Often, in fact, the state is apt to *disappear* and the resolution of issues partly rooted in (mis)recognition is almost entirely displaced onto micro-encounters. In this way, such encounters become conceptually overburdened with expectation because they are exchanges lacking the capacity to eradicate and combat structurally generated (mis)recognition.

If the politics of recognition is, therefore, too deficient a foundation for social work, what new theoretical resources might there be to better equip social work educators and practitioners to operate in neoliberal times? This will be the subject of Chapter Ten.

◀◀Reflection and Talk Box 9▶▶

- What are your views on the ideas of Axel Honneth?

- What are your views on the ideas of Nancy Fraser?

- How successful have some writers been in seeking to take recognition theory into social work? Can recognition theory aid your own social work practice?

- Why is the politics of recognition appearing to gain a higher profile in the social work literature?

- Is the politics of recognition an obstacle to practice that is critically informed and attentive to the demands mapped out by the International Federation of Social Work's definition of the profession?

- Look again at the 'Customer Charter' featured earlier in the chapter: what issues does this document give rise to? How can we theoretically comprehend similar documents or posters that you are aware of in your work with the users of services?

Notes

[1.] This chapter revisits and revises some of the material featured in my 'Recognizing the limitations of the political theory of recognition: Axel Honneth, Nancy Fraser and social work', *British Journal of Social Work*, vol 40, no 5, pp 1517–33. I am grateful to Oxford Journals for giving me permission to make use again of my earlier work.

[2.] Axel Honneth (1949–) is a Professor of Philosophy at the University of Frankfurt, Germany. In 2001, he became director of the Institute for Social Research, originally home to the Frankfurt School. Nancy Fraser (1947–) is an American feminist and critical theorist. She is a Professor within The New School in New York, USA.

[3.] Symbolic violence can be interpreted as a form of ideological violence that is apt to stigmatise or devalue, but which is apt to be viewed as legitimate, by those subjected to it, because of previous patterns of socialisation (see Bourdieu, 2000, ch 5). According to Eagleton (1991, p 158), symbolic violence is 'Bourdieu's way of rethinking and elaborating the Gramscian concept of hegemony' and 'his work as a whole represents an original contribution to what one might call the "microstructures" of ideology'.

CHAPTER TEN

New directions? Boltanski and Chiapello, Negri and Badiou

Introduction

This chapter draws critical attention to a number of additional writers whose work should, perhaps, be wider known within the social work literature. All of these authors inhabit a conceptual space in which neoliberalism is dominant, but unstable, edgy and vulnerable. In contrast with the rather jaded contributions of more canonical social theorists such as Giddens, Beck and Bauman, these thinkers present us with alternative ways of viewing the world and share a distinct 'leftist' orientation. Luc Boltanski (1940–) and Ève Chiapello (1965–) are in dialogue with key Marxist preoccupations; Antonio Negri (1933–) is a Marxist and Alain Badiou (1937–) is a quixotic Marxist. Remaining within the European context within which *Social theory and social work* has largely been concerned, their work presents thematic continuity with other theorists examined in the book. For example, although Boltanski and Chiapello do not operate within a specifically Gramscian perspective, they 'offer a classic analysis of the mechanics by which hegemony is exercised' (Couldry et al, 2010, p 110).

Seeking to identify some of the key unifying concerns shared by post-postmodern theorists, such as the authors analysed here, Therborn (2007, pp 80–3) has identified something of a 'theological turn'. This inclination is detectable, for example, in Badiou's interest in the figure of Saint Paul (Badiou, 2003a [1997] [1997]), which is also shared by Italian political philosopher Giorgio Agamben (2005). Indeed, such is the popularity of the saint that a columnist in a UK national newspaper has light-heartedly avowed that Paul 'remains topical today in a way that no one else in the Bible (with the admitted exception of God) can rival' (Holland, 2010, p 37). A similar interest in biblical texts is present in the recent work of Negri (2009) and in that of the prolific Slavoj Žižek (2000; see also Wright and Wright, 1999). From an older generation of theorists, Habermas has begun to explore the role of religion in a 'post-secular age' (Habermas et al, 2010).

Another unifying theme connecting a number of the theorists examined in this chapter is the project to bring communism in from the cold and create a rupture with the 'squalor of capitalist-parliamentarism' (Badiou, 2003a [1997]). Hardt and Negri (2000, p 413) usefully illustrate the twin interests in communism and early Christianity in the attention that they pay to the figure of Saint Francis:

There is an ancient legend that might serve to illuminate the future of communist militancy: that of Saint Francis of Assisi....To denounce the poverty of the multitude he adopted that common condition and discovered there the ontological power of a new society. The communist militant does the same ... Francis in opposition to the nascent capitalism refused every instrument of discipline ... he posed a joyous life....Once again ... we find ourselves in Francis's situation, posing against the misery of power the joy of being.This is a revolution that no power will control....This is the irrepressible lightness and joy of being a communist. (Hardt and Negri, 2000, p 413)

The revolutionary theme is at the heart of Luc Boltanski's (2002, p 11) query:

[what] has become today of the longing for total revolution? This longing constituted the left's most characteristic and permanent trait, the ideological centre that it cannot completely deny without breaking with an identity established over two centuries of critique and struggle.

Similar claims are present in the work of Badiou (2010) and Negri, along with his frequent co-writer Michael Hardt (1960–). As for the habitually controversial Žižek (2002), revolution is coupled with an even less popular topic, that of Leninism (see also Budgen et al, 2007).

Aside from these broader thematic commonalities, the range of theoretical interests covered by the authors whose work is outlined in this chapter is of great relevance to key concerns in social work (see Table 10.1).

Table 10.1: New social theory resources for social work

Theorists	Themes
Boltanski and Chiapello	Managerialism, contemporary workscapes, the language of 'change' and transformation, hegemony
Negri and the Marxist autonomists	The changing nature of work within capitalism's 'social factory', 'immaterial' labour and 'affective' labour
Badiou	Multiculturalism', 'diversity', 'difference' and, for him, how such ideas are retrogressive in terms of progressive political projects. Opposition to the dominance of 'human rights' discourse

The new spirit of capitalism: Boltanski and Chiapello

The new spirit of capitalism was originally published in France in 1999 with an English edition appearing in 2005. To simplify a complex and lengthy analysis,

Boltanski and Chiapello's key preoccupation is how the social order is legitimised and what motivates people to participate in the 'spirit of capitalism'. The authors maintain that it is possible to identify three spirits linked to different phases in the evolution of capitalism. Stretching to almost 600 pages, their research hones in on management literature from the 1960s and early 1990s, arguing that 'managerial ideology is heavily indebted to the anti-capitalist discourse of the 1960s' (Callinicos, 2006, p 60).

Capitalism has the capacity to co-opt and absorb the arguments of its opposition, becoming ideologically energised and discursively reinvigorated in the process. Boltanski and Chiapello (2005, p xiii) identify two – not always easily separable – critiques: 'the "social critique" (associated with the history of the working-class movement, and stressing exploitation) and the "artistic critique" (derived from intellectual and artistic circles which takes the dehumanization of the capitalist sphere as its particular target)'. Although the perspective developed in *The new spirit of capitalism* is problematic, the book is a serious and enlightening intervention into contemporary European social theory.[1]

Boltanski and Chiapello maintain that 'the spirit of capitalism' is the ideology that justifies engagement in capitalism. At every stage of its evolution, capitalism must have a series of 'moral justifications' *binding* people to it. These justifications must be sufficiently strong to be accepted as self-evident by enough people to check and to overcome, 'the despair or nihilism which the capitalist order … constantly induces' – not only in those whom it oppresses but also … in those who have responsibility for maintaining it and, via education, transmitting its values' (p 10). The 'spirit' works, therefore, to 'sustain the forms of action and predispositions compatible' with the capitalist order. Such justifications 'local or global, expressed in terms of virtue or justice, support the performance of more or less unpleasant tasks, and, more generally, adhesion to a lifestyle conducive' to capitalism (pp 10–11).

Implicitly conjoined with Gramsci's views on hegemony, they maintain that if people are to be genuinely won over to a particular worldview, they need it to make sense and cohere with their own interpretations of the world and their aspirations. One of the 'difficulties capitalism faces in getting itself accepted is that it addresses itself to people who are by no means ready to sacrifice everything to the accumulation process' (p 487). People are not 'wholly identified with this regime, and have experience of different ones – for example, family attachments, civic solidarity, intellectual or religious life and so on – a 'plurality of value orders' (p 487). Nobody can 'be set to work and kept working by force' and so a measure of freedom needs to be 'embedded in capitalism and [this economic system] would negate itself were it to rely exclusively on forcibly enlisting people' (p 485). The role that management discourse fulfils is vital since today it 'constitutes the form *par excellence* in which the spirit of capitalism is incorporated and received' (p 14). This discourse is addressed initially to those whom they term 'cadres', or key groups of managers within private sector corporations, because their support is especially important in terms of running and maintaining companies and creating profits and new markets. If this 'legitimating apparatus' is not responsive and resilient, the entire system could become destabilised (p 15).

The fluid and dynamic character of this apparatus is reflected in how the 'spirits' of capitalism have changed. From the 1930s into the 1960s, the army and military organisation played an important role in helping to constitute capitalism's 'spirit'. Indeed, although the UK does not form part of the analysis, social work reflects this form of organisation with employees of local authorities being referred to as 'officers' even in the final years of the 20th century. Beckett (2003) has also discussed how military metaphors continue to be applied to aspects of social workers' day-to-day engagement with the users of services.

Writing prior to the economic crash of 2007/08, Boltanski and Chiapello identify a 'new spirit', more capable of attracting support and more inclined to encompass the themes of justice and social well-being (p 19). This dimension is apparent in radio, television and cinema advertisements and in how these 'landscapes' of capital seek to foster popular support. As Goldman and Papson (2011, p 14) maintain, capital not 'only produces flows of goods and monies but also flows of signs'. Their analysis of television 'legitimation' advertisements indicates that these 'seem designed to represent corporations as good citizens and ethical actors: environmentally concerned, responsible neighbors supporting local communities' (Goldman and Papson, 2011, p 11). These advertisements 'depict capitalist relations not only as they are, not even as they have been, but as they might be – full of openness, hope, and possibility' (Goldman and Papson, 2011, p 17). This analysis entirely gels with the work of Boltanski and Chiapello, who stress that the aim is to 'galvanize workers' by 'restor[ing] meaning to the accumulation process, and combin[ing] it with the requirements of social justice' (p 19). Unable to discover 'a moral basis in the logic of the insatiable accumulation process (which in itself, on its own, is amoral), capitalism must borrow the legitimating principles it lacks from orders of justification external to it' (p 487).

Over the past quarter-century, multiculturalism and the multicultural imaginary have played a vital role. For Žižek (2002, p 172), the global market 'thrives on the diversification of demand' and multiculturalism 'perfectly fits the logic' of contemporary capitalism. According to Boltanski and Chiapello, capitalism has commodified 'difference', internalising 'the intense demand for differentiation and demassification that marked the end of the 1960s and the beginning of the 1970s' (p 441). Ecological movements and a new green sensibility have also had an impact on the evolution of this 'new spirit' in that nature is now accorded value as 'the locus of the authentic' (p 447). The cutting edge of this 'spin' tends to be the large multinational information and communications technology (ICT) and consultancy corporations. However, given the symbolic capital held by these large corporate players, their logic (embodied in advertisements, 'values' and 'mission' statements) is transmitted beyond the private sector and into the public sector, where capital accumulation is not the main driver. Within social services, the dominance of managerialism was evinced, in the mid-1980s, by the popularity of Masters in Business Administration (MBA) qualifications among directors and middle managers.

Capitalism 'mobilizes "already existing" things' and is responsible for audacious acts of appropriation, colonisation and annexation. It puts to work 'cultural products that are contemporaneous with it and which … have been generated to quite different ends than justifying capitalism' (p 20). In order to maintain its power of attraction, to excite and to soothe, capitalism has to draw 'upon resources external to it, beliefs which at a given moment in time, possess considerable powers of persuasion … even when they are hostile to it' (p 20). Thus, management literature, which forms the main data for the analysis, must 'demonstrate how the prescribed way of making profit might be desirable, interesting, exciting, innovative or commendable. It cannot stop at economic motives and incentives' (p 58). According to this perspective, making money must appear to be a fun, 'chilled', an incessantly 'cool' endeavour (McGuigan, 2009). This is no mere trick or ideological sleight of hand on the part of the ruling class because, to some extent, this 'spirit' can act as a brake on capital accumulation. If the 'justifications proffered are taken seriously, not all profit is legitimate, not all enrichment is just, not all accumulation, even substantial accumulation, is licit' (p 25). This capacity to absorb critique serves, however, to 'help to disarm anti-capitalist forces' (p 27). The paradox for political opponents of capitalism is that the 'price paid by critique for being listened to' is often to 'see some of the values it had mobilized to oppose the form taken by the accumulation process being placed at the service of accumulation' (p 29).

Boltanski and Chiapello use the term 'cities' to try and capture the shifting logics and 'spirits' of justification. Bearing some resemblance to Gramsci's 'hegemony' and Bourdieu's 'doxa', the notion of 'city' suggests a 'composite amalgam of grounds and reasons … variable over time, depending on the expectations of those that must be mobilised and the hopes that they have grown up with, as well as the forms taken by accumulation in different periods' (p 25). They chart the evolution of seven 'cities', which represent the dominant ethos, polity or hegemonic ambiance of particular periods of economic expansion.[2] Crucially, for them, we have made the transition from the 'industrial city' to the one that makes possible the kinds of justification appropriate to the 'network world'. This they term the 'projective city', which represents a break with Taylorist forms of working (see Chapter Six). The main promoters of this 'new flexible world, composed of multiple projects conducted by autonomous persons' are management authors (p 92).

Making work more 'human': examining the literature of management

Examining two corpora of management literature from the periods 1959–69 and 1989–94, respectively, Boltanski and Chiapello found that the shared focal issue was how firms tried to invest work with meaning. In both eras, it was recognised that profit is not 'a very inspiring goal' (p 63). Rather, stress was placed on more 'genuine reasons' for engaged commitment (p 63). While literature from the 1960s lays emphasis on meritocracy, management by objectives and the downplaying of personal judgement, 1990s' texts view 'these large, hierarchized, planned organizations' as anachronistic and conceive the firm as a network in which employers willingly and enthusiastically breach the boundaries formerly separating 'home' and 'work' (p 64). The popular writer on management Tom Peters wrote of the 'liberated firm' and the shift that needed to take place within organisations from 'control to self-control' (pp 80–1). Here, the emphasis is on flexibility, being able to 'ride the wave' of change, obsessive attention to adaptation, lean production and the benefits of outsourcing. To the fore is a stress on 'leadership', on the role of the managers and their 'principal quality', 'mobility' (pp 76, 79). Although Boltanski and Chiapello do not make this connection, facets of dominant social theory – Giddens, Beck and the later Bauman – appear to simply amplify such ideas. Indeed, tropes, such as 'life politics' and 'liquid modernity', can be viewed as largely derived from the corporate management literature of the late 1980s and early 1990s (see Chapters Two and Three).

In neo-management discourse, the emphasis is on interaction and authentic human relations. With new organisations, 'the bureaucratic prison explodes…. Discovery and enrichment can be constant' (p 90). On becoming leader of the Conservative Party, David Cameron was alert to this dominant strain in management and keen to stress that his political plans, later to include his 'Big Society' programme, were devised for a 'post-bureaucratic age' (*The Guardian*, 2008).

While, in the 1960s, reason was the dominant ethos, the later management literature favoured feelings, emotion and creativity. According to Boltanski and Chiapello, one of the main attractions of the proposals formulated in the 1990s is that they 'adumbrate a certain liberation' (p 90). In this 'new world, anything is possible, since creativity, reactivity and flexibility are the new watchwords. Now no one is restricted by belonging to a department or wholly subject to the boss' authority, for all boundaries are transgressed' via the channels of networking and project work (p 90). That is to say, what in Chapter Five was termed 'precariousness', here becomes a way to 'grow' and evolve as a person. A 'seductive aspect of neo-management' is the notion that everyone should 'develop themselves personally' because this management literature maintains that the new work 'organizations are supposed to appeal to all the capacities of human beings, who will be in a position to fully blossom' (p 90). Within the new model of organisation, employees will gain genuine autonomy based 'on self-knowledge and personal fulfilment, not the false autonomy, framed by the career paths, job descriptions' and the systems of the 1960s (p 90). In this sense, job security – associated with status, hierarchy, bureaucracy – is denounced not only as an obstacle to profitability, but also because it impinges on the ability of workers to become fully human, fully liberated. Indeed, these 'trends in neo-management are often … presented as an attempt to inflect the world of work in a "more human" direction' (p 98).

Neo-management literature and its wider discourse aims, therefore, to 'respond to demands for authenticity and freedom' (p 97). This fits with the analysis articulated by Boltanski and Chiapello because it indicates how capitalism reformulates or annexes critique to serve its own purposes and to revitalise the processes of capital accumulation. Thus, it is 'not difficult to find an echo here of the denunciation of hierarchy and aspirations to autonomy that were insistently expressed at the end of the 1960s and 1970s' (p 97). More specifically, they argue that the 'spirit' of capitalism that began to dominate neo-management discourse and other fields in the 1990s was heavily influenced by the political aspirations and desires of 1968 and the period prior to neoliberalisation. The:

> qualities that are guarantees of success in this new spirit – autonomy, spontaneity, rhizomorphous capacity, multitasking (in contrast to the narrow specialization of the old division of labour), conviviality, openness to others and novelty, availability, creativity, visionary intuition, sensitivity to differences, listening to lived experience and receptiveness to a whole range of experiences, being attracted to informality and the search for interpersonal contacts – these are taken directly from the repertoire of May 1968. (p 97)

Thus, many of the 'mechanisms' associated with the new spirit of capitalism – such as 'outsourcing, the proliferation of autonomous profit centres within firms, quality circles and new forms of work organization', have, in part, been developed to address the demands for autonomy that made 'themselves heard at the beginning of the 1970s in an oppositional register' (p 429). What is more, as McRobbie (2010, p 64) suggests, we can also interpret this development as a 'dispensation or permission-to-think'.

The 'little' and the 'great' in 'projective city'

Within Boltanski and Chiapello's developmental model, the 'projective city' now provides the justificatory register in which acts, things and persons are judged. In Gramscian terms, we could say that this is a new hegemony since it comprises the 'main normative fulcrum on which the new spirit of capitalism rests' (p 151). Whereas in the previous 'city' – the 'industrial city' – the key measure was one of efficiency, in this new 'connectionist world', life is 'conceived as a succession of projects' (pp 111, 110). Here, the distinction between private life and professional life tends to diminish, even become erased. In addition, a new importance is 'accorded to the role of mediators, personal relations, friendship or trust in profit creation' (p 443). New technologies, the 'instruments of connection', contribute to this development (p 117). A blurring also occurs 'between the qualities of the person and the properties of their labour power' (p 155). This appears, in fact, to be a world in which the 'brand' is actually 'you' (Peters, 1997; Baréz-Brown, 2011).

Those endowed with the qualities most valued and esteemed within the 'projective city' are the most likely to prosper and succeed. They are 'nodes' at the 'intersection of bundles of relations' (p 148). In Bourdieusian terms, such characters know, understand and even generate the 'rules of the game'. Entirely comprehending their 'field' and its functioning, they monopolise the 'symbolic capital' in the 'projective city' (see Chapter Seven). For Boltanski and Chiapello, this is the 'condition of great men', those towering above 'the little persons' who are too 'rigid' and security-oriented to become autonomous, 'flexible' and self-activating (pp 112, 119). The 'great man' – and here the gendering seems intentional – possesses a range of characteristics and attributes, including being enthusiastic, involved, adaptable, versatile, non-prescriptive, able to engage with others and tolerant. He is a 'connectionist man', able and eager to renounce 'having a single project that lasts a lifetime (a vocation, a profession, a marriage etc.) He is mobile. Nothing must hamper his movements' (p 122): he is a 'streamlined human being' (p 123). The first requirement to become streamlined is:

> renouncing stability, rootedness, attachment to the local, the security of longstanding links…. Great men in the projective city are also *streamlined* in that they are liberated from the burden of their own passions and values…. Nothing must get the upper hand over the imperative of adjustment, or hamper their movements. (p 123)

For Boltanski and Chiapello, the idea of 'liberation' is significant in that it has always been an essential component of the shifting logics of capitalism: under the 'sway of capitalism, the promise of liberation … functions as an ideology' (p 427). Originally, capitalism promised liberation from oppressive 'tradition'. Within this framework, it was, in fact, capitalism that was able to furnish a route map on 'how to be modern' and to achieve individual self-fulfilment (see Chapter Two). However, in its subsequent formulations, the 'spirit of capitalism' has been more subtly capable of integrating 'critiques denouncing capitalist oppression – that is to say, the failure in practice to realize promises of liberation under the capitalist regime' (p 424). Thus, it is possible to identify seemingly paradoxical cycles of 'recuperation … a succession of periods of liberation *by* capitalism and periods of liberation *from* capitalism' (p 425, emphasis in original).

Criticisms

A range of criticisms of varying importance can be directed at the analysis furnished by Boltanski and Chiapello. First, because the book is concerned with France and – more specifically – the private sector, the analysis may not be transferrable to areas beyond France and public sector fields where social workers, for example, are often situated. Nevertheless, this does not entirely dilute the book's theoretical usefulness.

Second, Boltanski and Chiapello mostly rely on management literature as data and do not undertake any ethnography to find out what 'people really *believe* in' (Couldry et al, 2010, p 221, emphasis added). In a later book, Boltanski (2011, p 24) stresses the sociological importance of actors *en situation*, but in *The new spirit of capitalism*, we have no sense as to how workers actually respond to the messages and exhortations contained in management literature. Again, this is a telling criticism given that other research conducted among public sector employees in the UK reveals the 'gaps' that exist between the dominant discourse of managerialist 'reforms' and what actually takes place 'on the ground' in practitioner locations (see, eg, Clarke et al, 2007). Expressed in Bourdieusian terms, workplace 'transformation' programmes have to contend with resistance in embedded 'field' practices and the particular habitus of specific workers.

A third criticism is that the scope of their research fails to grasp the bigger picture, since it covers only what is 'merely epiphenomenal to … re-structuring' (Couldry et al, 2010, p 220). That is to say, the core concern should not be the discursive moves and the narrative – or 'spirit' – of capitalism, but, rather, the evolution of capitalism as a series of *materially* interconnected practices (see, eg, Harvey, 2010). Although this is a valid point, analysing how the neoliberal 'change agenda' is orchestrated and assembled in particular fields of operation is of vital importance in trying to forge effective counter-hegemonic strategies (Garrett, 2009; see also Reflection and Talk Box 10). Indeed, within social work, the inflated tone of the discourse associated with the neoliberal change agenda, one of aspirational libertarianism, owes more to the type of language identified by Boltanski and Chiapello than it does to masculinity, rationality and technicity (Ruch, 2011). Paradoxically, it can seem that liberation, both professional *and* personal, is at hand, albeit at a time when social work services are being divested of resources and subjected to 'austerity' measures.

A fourth criticism is that the book may strike us as rather pessimistic in its portrayal of capitalism's seemingly unfailing resilience and adaptiveness. No possibility of genuine progressive change is articulated: capitalism is voracious and, it would appear, continually able to absorb critique, transforming it into another pillar of the system. In contrast with Marx, the working class are 'curiously lacking in any agency' within Boltanski and Chiapello's perspective (Couldry et al, 2010, p 119). According to the French thinkers, there is 'no ideology, however radical in its principles and formulations, that has not eventually proved open to assimilation' (p xv). Indeed, critical movements even serve the interests of the ruling class by alerting it to the 'dangers threatening it' (p 514). This is a powerful argument that illuminates how hegemony is maintained, but a feature of Boltanski and Chiapello's analysis that is often overlooked by commentators is their aside that the 'mobilizing capacity contained in the new spirit of capitalism as deployed in 1990s management literature seems to us poor' (p 96). So it could be argued that the hegemony of the ruling bloc is always vulnerable, always fragile.

A final criticism is that the book – written during a period when capitalism appeared revived and able, for some, to 'deliver the goods' – may strike us as dated in our post-crash context (see Chapter Five). In the present time of austerity, it is perhaps a grim compulsion that binds people to the system, not the lure of 'liberation' and 'exciting' work. Although such enticements are part of the 'mix', particularly in the zones of limited autonomy available to the creative class (Peck, 2005), the threat of losing one's job and being replaced by the next in the long line of unemployed is, once again, the chief means of disciplining workers.

Another set of theoretical tools that may aid our understanding of the changing nature of contemporary social work is supplied by Antonio Negri, whose contribution is explored in the next section.

Constraint and possibility within the 'social factory': Negri and autonomist Marxists

In Chapter Four, attention was drawn to the idea that we now live in a 'social factory'. This conceptualisation is associated with Antonio Negri and a current within Italian Marxism known, in the 1960s, as *operaismo* and, in the 1970s, as *autonomia* or autonomism.[3] The popular *Empire* (Hardt and Negri, 2000) is also connected to this theoretical and political tradition (see also Boron, 2005).[4] More recently, the same authors' work on 'multitude' is likewise partly rooted in this body of theorisation (Hardt and Negri, 2006).

At odds with dominant interpretations of Gramsci's Marxism in Italy, the autonomists considered a long-drawn struggle for 'hegemony', by means of a 'war of position', to be disastrous for the Left (see Chapter Six). The strategy had proven incapable of achieving revolutionary transformation and even the gains resulting from the Italian Communist Party's participation in social democracy had been rescindable or meagre. The autonomists felt it necessary to embark on a more direct confrontation with the ruling class, what Gramsci had dubbed a 'war of manoeuvre' against capital (see also Landy, 1994). However, they differed in a number of ways from classical Marxism. In place of 'an account of the power of capital', autonomism stresses 'the autonomy and creativity of labour, and labour's power to bring about change' (Gill and Pratt, 2008, p 5).

Rooting their theorisation in a rereading of Marx, a key belief articulated by the autonomists was that organisational and technological innovations within the workplace were driven by workers' insubordination and defiance of capital and its logics. For example, the introduction of the assembly line or, in more recent times, the deployment of ICTs can be interpreted as 'a defensive, *reactive* attempt by capital to escape its dependence on ... labour' (Bowring, 2004, p 104); that is to say, the 'history of the successive attempts of the capitalist class to emancipate itself from the working class' (Tronti, in Bowring, 2004, p 104). This approach clearly amounted to a challenge to the idea that the scientific and technological apparatuses of production were politically neutral.

Negri identified three key stages of capitalist development. The first phase of 'large-scale industry' spanned from 1848 to the First World War. This was a period when an artisan workforce still possessed a degree of autonomy and Negri refers to it as the period of the 'professional worker' (Negri, 2005a). A second phase of large-scale industry extended from 1914 to 1968. This was the era of the 'mass worker', who became deskilled, a mere appendage to the assembly line (see Chapter Six). However, this form of organisation was collectively to the advantage of workers in that it engendered a sense of solidarity and enabled them to develop a better bargaining capacity with employers. The period of the 'mass worker' is one of Fordist regulation and an interventionist state. Through collective bargaining, trade unions were able to secure full employment and rising levels of consumption for a 'labour aristocracy'. In this way, though, these politically passive unions colluded with capital and promoted a form of stability that was, in the long-term, injurious to workers. During the 1960s, Mario Tronti (1931–), among other autonomist writers and activists, called for a 'radical refusal' to participate in this arrangement; hence the call for disruptive interventions in the workplace such as the *autoriduzione* or 'go-slow', absenteeism, the wildcat strike and acts of mass sabotage (Bowring, 2004, pp 108–9). The 'refusal to work' was also perceived as a political and potentially revolutionary act. This position ran counter to much of leftist thinking, opposing some Marxists' 'tendency to romanticize labour' and become victim to 'productivism' (Gill and Pratt, 2008, p 5). More recently, Hardt and Negri (2000, pp 203–4) returned to this theme, reiterating that the:

> refusal to work and authority, or really the refusal of voluntary servitude, is the beginning of liberatory politics.... Beyond this simple refusal, or as part of that refusal, we need also to construct a new mode of life and above all a new community.

Importantly, this statement captures the sense that, for these writers, 'refusal' contains a positive, constructive dimension in that the aspiration is to 'bring into existence new ways of being, living and relating' (Gill and Pratt, 2008, p 6).

This third phase becomes detectable from 1968 and is characterised by the high level of computerisation and automation of productive processes (see Dyer-Witherford, 1999). 'Labour itself is now "completely abstract, immaterial, intellectual". The norms of consumption are highly individualistic and market oriented, while capital itself exists in predominantly multinational forms' (Bowring, 2004, p 110). Normally used to dilute capitalism's reliance on workers and sidestep their opposition, technology can best be perceived as a 'response to the mass rejection of work ... an attempt to capture and exploit the new sources of production and wealth opened up by the counter-culture revolution of the 1960s – the anti-conformism, experiments in lifestyle' (Bowring, 2004, pp 110–11). In this third and still current phase, wage-labour permeates – or as the autonomists prefer 'subsumes' – all spheres of society. Given that metropolitan capitalism is now less able to expand to other territories by means of imperialist expansion, it needs to absorb all those spaces at home that formerly appeared off-limits to commodification. As a result, we witness the privatisation of what were previously public services and resources, for example, in the areas of communications and media, water and energy supplies, education, health, social work, and social care (see Chapter Five). This third period is also one in which sites of production are decentralised at the global level with 'the division of workers into a small, privileged core and a marginalised and insecure majority' (Bowring, 2004, pp 110–11).

The key figure that emerges during this phase is the *operaio sociale* or 'socialised worker', who replaces the 'mass worker' of the preceding period of capitalist development (Negri, 2005a). Work 'permeates the entire society in a multitude of ways' (Landy, 1994, p 221), with 'free time' becoming 'free labour' (Gill and Pratt, 2008, p 17). It is in this context that Negri (2005a) refers to the 'social factory' or 'the factory without walls'. From this perspective, 'labour is deterritorialized, dispersed and decentralized' (Gill and Pratt, 2008, p 7). As a consequence, the whole society is placed at the disposal of profit (see Negri, 2005a, pp 102–15). Capitalism is now, therefore, a social system 'in which life is arranged around, and subordinated to, work' that is increasingly insecure, casualised and 'precarious' (Gill and Pratt, 2008, p 11). However, the autonomists discern in this precarious labour the possibility for new forms of sociality, new forms of antagonism and new forms of resistance. The 'precariat is to post-Fordism what the proletariat was to the industrial age' (Gill and Pratt, 2008, p 11). Critical engagement with such themes, as they relate to the hardships and possibilities associated with precarious working lives, has resulted in new forms of political activism. In Italy, for example, the progressive spread of the term *precario* has gradually eroded the stigma associated with it. In the late 1990s, 'political activists reclaimed it ... [and it was used] with increasing pride.... This change was inspired by the similar successes of reclaiming words like "gay" and "queer"' (Fantone, 2007, p 7).

Negri's periodisation applied to social work

Table 10.2 provides an outline of Negri's periodisation of capitalist development mapped against the evolution of social work in the UK. As is clear, although the periodisation furnishes interesting comparisons, it is not possible to neatly map Negri's three phases onto social work: there is no clear congruence between changes to social workers' working practices and those he identifies taking place in other forms of work. Although not engaging with the autonomist perspective, Carey (2009) surveys the literature on practitioners' changing roles (Parsloe, 1981; Pithouse, 1998 [1987]) and new empirical research with care managers to suggest that social workers retained more control and discretion over their work for much longer than Negri's theorisation would imply. Other conceptual difficulties also apply in relation to the Italian's analysis. He appears, for example, to neglect work undertaken by public sector staff within state welfare bureaucracies. However, this work location is unlike private sector employment and continues to contain residues of a different set of values not entirely driven by the profit motive (Clarke et al, 2007). This gives rise to tensions that may be absent or not as pronounced as in the corporate and private sector.

Table 10.2: Negri's three phases of capitalist development and social work in the UK

Period	Defining characteristics of this industrial phase	Key figure	Main attributes and skills demanded from workers	Social work dimension
1848–1914	Evolution of large-scale industry and hyper-exploitation of labour in the colonies.	The 'professional worker'.	Craft skills and the 'dignity of labour' recognised, but slowly eroded.	Outside the sphere of production, an inchoate social work constructed as largely charitable enterprise demarcating the 'deserving' from the 'undeserving'.
1914–68	Fordist production and the dominance of the assembly line. 'Taylorism' in the workplace. A gendered order in which a 'public' and a 'private' sphere are rigidly maintained. Founded on unpaid domestic labour by women. 'Labour' and 'leisure' fairly clearly demarcated.	The 'mass worker'.	Manual labour reduced to a mere appendage of the machine. The 'mass consumer' beyond the workplace.	Social work beyond the 'factory walls' was a mix of public and voluntary provision. Helps to 'reproduce' the 'mass worker'. Tends to 'problem families', regulates 'deviance'. Social worker retains, to some extent, the character of 'professional worker'.
1968–	The 'factory without walls' and the wage-labour relationship subsumes all areas of society. Life becoming inseparable from work (Lazzarato, 1996). Reframed in official discourses as dilemmas over 'work–life' balance. 'Flexible' work and 'precarious' work begin to dominate workscapes. Also interpreted as period of 'post-Fordism' or emerging neoliberalisation.	The 'socialised worker'.	'Immaterial labour'. Computer proficiency. 'Inflexible flexibility' (Morini, 2007). 'Unemployed' (now 'jobseekers') subject to more coercive interventions to propel them into work. 'Jobseekers' to be 'job-ready' and compliant potential workers.	Arguably, the social worker becoming more akin to the 'mass worker' *from* 1968 with, in England, the setting up of 'Seebohm factories' (Simpkin, 1983). Introduction of LAC system. Social work's 'e-turn' (Garrett, 2005). Strategic attentiveness to affect and on the need for social workers to be able to be 'free' and 'creative' (Le Grand, 2007).

Despite these problems, Negri does provide a useful theoretical framework in which to locate social work's evolving work practices. However, in applying his periodisation to the evolution of social work, there appears to be something of a time-lag. If, according to Negri's formulations, the 'mass worker' period was coming to a close in 1968, an equivalent phase in social work history may have *begun* around that time with the introduction of the 'Seebohm factories' (Simpkin, 1983). Such a shift was to become even more marked in the 1990s in relation to child care social work, with the introduction of the 'looking after children' system (Parker et al, 1991; Ward, 1995), which endeavoured to separate the 'conception' and 'execution' of social work assessments. These materials continue to exert a considerable influence in relation to the design of contemporary assessment schedules and e-templates.

'Immaterial labour' and 'services of proximity'

Specifically in terms of social work, a key feature of the autonomist analysis is its emphasis on 'immaterial labour'. For the autonomists, producing no material or durable goods has assumed a dominant position with respect to other forms of labour in the global, post-Fordist capitalist economy. This does not mean that industrial production will be done away with – the 'shift toward services is most recognizable in the dominant capitalist countries' (Hardt, 1999, p 92). According to Hardt (1999, p 94), this particular form of labour 'produces an immaterial good, such as a service, knowledge, or communication' and 'covers a large range of activities from health care, education, and finance, to transportation, entertainment and advertising. The jobs, for the most part, are highly mobile and involve flexible skills' (Hardt, 1999, p 91). Here, the computer plays a pivotal role. During the period of the 'mass worker':

> workers learned how to act like machines both inside and outside the factory. Today, as general social knowledge becomes ever more a direct force of production, we increasingly think like computers, and the interactive model of communication technologies become more and more central to our laboring activities. (Hardt, 1999, p 95)

Indeed, this description may illuminate aspects of social work following the profession's 'e' or 'electronic turn' (Garrett, 2005). However, Hardt concedes that the growth of such jobs is inseparable from a corresponding growth in low-value and low-skill jobs such as data entry and word processing (Hardt, 1999, p 95).

Although computers are central to a post-Fordist economy, the 'most important aspect, the binding aspect' of immaterial labour, pertains to the *affective* domain of human contact and interaction (Hardt, 1999, p 96). This is most apparent in the area of health services focused on caring, 'in-person' services or 'services of proximity' (Hardt, 1999, p 96). In this sense, social work constitutes a form of 'immaterial labour' containing both the computerised element and the more affective dimension. Increasingly, 'immaterial labour' tends to spread throughout the entire workforce, informing the disposition of a range of, what Bourdieu terms, 'fields' (see Chapter Seven). At a rather banal level, this may relate to the notion of 'customer care' promoted by large service-led corporations. For Hardt (1999, p 96), though, the products of 'immaterial labour' are frequently 'intangible' in that what is furnished is often 'a feeling of ease, well-being, satisfaction, excitement, passion – even a sense of connectedness or community'.

However, the autonomist writers do not tend to 'conceive of immaterial labour as purely functional to capitalism, but see it as providing potential for a kind of spontaneous, elementary communism' (Gill and Pratt, 2008, p 8):

> [As] in so much autonomous Marxist writing the notion has a double face – it speaks on the one hand to the extent to which emotions, feelings, relationships are 'put to work' in post-Fordist capitalism, and on the other to the immanent human cooperative capacities and potentialities that may be set free by such labour. (Gill and Pratt, 2008, p 15)

Affect is, in this way, construed as potentially exceeding power relations, breaking through them, 'offering a glimpse of a better world, with new ways of being and relating' (Gill and Pratt, 2008, p 16). This perspective can, therefore, be seen as a riposte to Foucauldian presumptions on the scope and capacity of power.

'Immaterial labour', specifically the use of ICTs, is often utilised to organise and mobilise opposition to budget cuts and austerity measures. In this sense, younger workers particularly may be more alert to the possibilities afforded by electronic networking to help facilitate, what Gramscians would term, the politics of counter-hegemony (see Chapter Six). In terms of social work, the values of the profession, reflected in day-to-day provision of affective, 'in-person' services, might be perceived as prefigurative of social change and contain the seeds of a new social order in which people are valued before profit.

Criticisms

The attention given to 'immaterial labour', and, more broadly, the autonomist analysis, has prompted a range of meshed criticisms. First, the 'central role given to immaterial labour in Hardt and Negri's analysis may ... be challenged for its Western bias, and its failure to acknowledge the growth of low-tech factory production in the least developed countries of the South' (Bowring, 2004, p 124). Indeed, the 'stubborn materiality of most work' represents a substantial challenge to autonomist claims (Gill and Pratt, 2008, p 9). A second criticism argues that the image of a society dominated 'by knowledge and information work is seen as too redolent of the language used by the prophets of capitalism and management gurus', who are the focus of the research by Boltanski and Chiapello (Gill and Pratt, 2008, p 9).

Third, there is a failure to analyse the profound differences between different groups of workers involved in 'immaterial labour' – between, for example, the fast food worker, the designer of a new advert for a multinational corporation, those involved in other forms of artistic or cultural production, and a child protection social worker (see Graeber, 2008). Since the shifts in work patterns 'have been largely discussed only at the moment when the western, male worker began feeling the negative effects of the new, post-industrial, flexible job market' (Fantone, 2007, p 7), feminist commentators have also been concerned that dominant perceptions within this body of theory are based on a 'politically imaginary subject: the single, male, urban artist or creative worker, idealized as the vanguard of the precariat' (Fantone, 2007, p 9). McRobbie (2010, p 62) has asserted that the work of those such as Hardt and Negri is:

> locked within a class model which permits no space at all for reflecting on the centrality of gender and sexuality in the post-Fordist era, with the result that there is a failure to consider the meaning of what is often referred to as the feminisation of work.

Reaffirming the 'communist hypothesis' and 'one world' politics: Badiou

Arguably, Badiou's theorisation can be connected to Maoism, a form of Marxism owing allegiance to the Chinese Revolution (1949), the politics of Mao Zedong (1893–1976) and to some of the ideas sparking and sustaining the 'Great Proletarian Cultural Revolution' in China (1966–76). This was always a minority current within French and, more generally, European Marxism but it did have some influence on student activists associated with the 'events' of May 1968 in France. Whether or not Badiou remains a Maoist, or even post-Maoist, is a question that preoccupies a number of his commentators. Bosteels (2005, p 578) maintains that Badiou's 'concept of politics as a procedure of truth remains to a large extent inseparable, despite apparent self-criticisms, from the theory and practice of Maoism' (Bosteels, 2005, p 578). Moreover, Badiou continues to refer to Mao to amplify his arguments (see, eg, Badiou, 2008a).

Badiou's major books are *Being and event* (Badiou, 2005; see also Norris, 2009) and, what is sometimes referred to as 'Being and event 2', *The Logic of worlds* (Badiou, 2009; see also Hallward, 2008). These represent his 'defiant riposte to the post-modern condition, a condition which claims that philosophy has exhausted its universal history' (Barker, 2002, p 4). Badiou's perspective is entirely antithetical to postmodernist theorising, which, as mentioned in Chapter Two, had an impact within the academic literature of social work in the 1990s. His own philosophy hinges on the concept of 'the "event" as a form of momentous change ... in the realms of science, art, love, and emancipatory politics'. For him, 'humans become "subjects" only when acting in a way that is "faithful" to such events' (Bassett, 2008, p 897): only when they are loyal to, and active within, 'a revolutionary break'

(Hewlett, 2006, p 375). Critical of the 'liberal model where the philosopher with a social conscience is impartial intellectual during the day and activist intellectual at night', Badiou reclaims the tradition of Sartre and Althusser, maintaining that 'in order to understand, one simply must intervene, both as activist and intellectual' (Hewlett, 2006, p 376). This perspective leads him to criticise 'left-leaning social scientists', such as Bourdieu, who despite their analysis are:

> politically very weak, for the simple reason that they do not break with parliamentarism, with 'democratic' consensus. They can only contribute to an 'oppositional' stance, i.e. a position of protest from *within* the state-sanctioned structures and rules (parties, elections, trade unions, constitutional amendments …). But unfortunately, the category of 'opposition' is precisely a central category of parliamentarism, of 'democracy'. No genuine break can be made from within this category. (Badiou, in Hallward, 2002, emphasis in original)

In contrast, 'events' are breaks or 'ruptures with the established order of things, which happen in certain times and places in unpredictable ways' (Bassett, 2008, p 898). Such 'events' also transform the objects of sociologists' discussions into 'militant subjects in their own right' (Hallward, 2002), prising open the social world and inaugurating new ways of being.

Although not against universal suffrage, he views elections as 'incorporated into a form of state, the capitalist parliamentary state, appropriate for the maintenance of the established order, and that they have a conservative function, which in case of troubles becomes a repressive one' (Badiou, 2008b, p 34). Thus, Badiou (2010) believes in the need for a radical rupture with the current global order through a reactivation of the communist project. This is not a nostalgic yearning for the USSR, but part of his endeavour to rethink and reinvent communism for the contemporary world. All those who abandon the 'communist hypothesis' immediately 'resign themselves to the market economy, to parliamentary democracy … and to the inevitable and "natural" character of the most monstrous inequalities' (Badiou, 2008a, p 98). Badiou is especially scathing of those on 'the Left' who joined the administration of Nicolas Sarkozy (2007–2012). More fundamentally, he is disdainful of the parliamentary Left which, lacking sufficient political commitment and vibrancy, merely seek a 'bit of social politeness' to blunt processes of neoliberalisation (Badiou, 2008a, p 102).

Despite his attacks on parliamentarism, Badiou's actual political practice can be interpreted as rather 'reformist'. His activism is reflected in the group *Organisation Politique* (OP) and its publication *La Distance Politique* (LDP). Formed in 1984, the OP, spearheaded by Badiou, Sylvain Lazarus and Natacha Michel, has tended to explain its political practice as making 'prescriptions against the state' (Badiou, in Badiou and Hallward, 1998, p 114). While seeking to abstain from parliament, OP activists therefore press political demands on the state, campaigning and mobilising around the plight of the *sans-papiers* and other migrant workers. The statement *'tous les gens qui sont ici sont d'ici'* ('everyone who is here is from here') is the 'most frequently printed slogan' of LDP (Hallward, 2002). This facet of his politics, which directly relates to the sameness–difference dialectic, will be returned to later.

Saint Paul

In the light of Badiou's radical politics, his interest in Saint Paul the apostle may, at first, appear somewhat incongruous. Yet, Badiou argues that the experience of Paul, when he comes to believe in 'the resurrection of Christ and its universal significance, is an excellent example of an individual becoming a subject through a life-changing faithfulness to and belief in an event' (Hewlett, 2004, pp 343–4). While acknowledging that the saint is frequently associated with 'Christianity's least appealing aspects: the institutional Church, moral discipline, social conservatism' and even 'suspiciousness toward the Jews', Badiou confesses that he never 'really connected Paul with religion' (Badiou, 2003a [1997], pp 4, 1). Along with his admiration for the epistles, 'whose poetry astonishes' (Badiou, 2003a [1997], p 1), Badiou extols the political significance of Saint Paul, who represents for him 'the ultimate model of the modern, post-Bolshevik activist' (Hewlett, 2006, p 396). He concentrates on a corpus of just six rather brief epistles regarded by some biblical scholars as the most authentic, most likely to have been written by Paul: Romans, Corinthians 1 and 2, Galatians, Phillippians, and Thessalonians 1. The recipients of these letters were likely to be a 'few "brothers" – which is an archaic form of our "comrades" – lost in the city' (Badiou, 2003a [1997], p 20). No matter how far away, Paul 'never loses sight of these enclaves of the faithful whose existence he played midwife to' (Badiou, 2003a [1997], p 20).

According to Badiou, Paul is a man of the city rather than the country and his style owes nothing to the 'rural images and metaphors' which characterise the 'parables of Christ' (Badiou, 2003a [1997], p 21). He was not a desert mystic; on the contrary, he spent time in Antioch, 'the third city of the empire after Rome and Alexandria', and was shaped by his 'urban cosmopolitanism and lengthy voyages' (Badiou, 2003a [1997], p 21). As well as being profoundly revolutionary, the figure of Saint Paul 'fits' in relation to other aspects of Badiou's theoretical architecture. In this sense, at least two aspects of his life are vital. First, he was transformed by an 'event', during which he suddenly became a subject, on the road to Damascus. Nobody converted Saint Paul, his conversion was spontaneous and liquidated all that had gone before; after it, the world was made anew. He then became a turbulent presence within the emerging Christian orthodoxy and its institutional framework. Paul turned 'away from all authority other than the Voice that personally summoned him to his becoming-subject' (Badiou, 2003a [1997], p 18). Despite being pragmatically prepared to compromise with the historical leaders of the Church in the Jerusalemite 'centre', he conceived of himself as a 'leader of a party or faction' (Badiou, 2003a [1997], p 21). On his many voyages he rarely felt the need to consult the 'centre'. For Badiou, the *'ex-centered* dimension of Paul's action' serves to highlight that 'all true universality is devoid of a center' (Badiou, 2003a [1997], p 19, emphasis in original); that is to say, it gives rise to actions in the world that are not the result of hierarchical command.

Second, in Badiou's reading, Paul was committed to a profoundly levelling, singular universality. Although a Roman citizen, Paul rejected 'any legal category [seeking] to identify the Christian subject. Slaves, women, people of every profession and nationality [were] therefore admitted without restriction or privilege' (Badiou, 2003a [1997], pp 13–14). Badiou is able to draw on a number of passages from the epistles to illuminate Paul's perspective. Paradigmatic of the apostle's simple message are the following extracts:

> There is neither Jew nor Greek, there is neither slave nor free, there is neither male nor female. (Galatians 3.28, in Badiou, 2003a [1997], p 9)

> Glory, honor, and peace for every one that does good, to the Jew first and also to the Greek. For God shows not partiality. (Romans 2.10, in Badiou, 2003a [1997], p 9)

On account of this understanding, Paul did not consent to the 'distinction between two circles among those he rallied, the doctrinal sympathizers and the "true" converts' (Badiou, 2003a [1997], p 21). He saw all converts as:

> fully practicing followers, whatever their background, and regardless of whether they [were] circumcised. Judeo-Christians of strict observance [maintained] the practice of distinguishing between degrees of belonging, and [found] it genuinely scandalous that individuals possessing neither the markings nor the ritual practices of the community [could] be considered as equals. (Badiou, 2003a [1997], p 22)

These ideas on Saint Paul and his promotion of a singular universalism are clearly connected to Webb's move to inject similar thinking into social work.

Taking Badiou into social work

Webb (2009) uses Badiou to criticise what he perceives as social work's problematic contemporary ethical base. He maintains that these 'Western liberal ethics' are entirely compatible with neoliberal capitalism. More emphatically, social work 'should be "indifferent to differences" by transcending the politics of difference' (Webb, 2009, p 309). Here, a focal concern is that this alleged centrality of 'difference', within the social work literature is a result of the 'displacement of class as *the* universal signifier of oppression' (Webb, 2009, p 309, emphasis in original). Indeed, Badiou (2003a [1997], p 6) refers to the pervasive 'attempt to promote the cultural virtue of oppressed subjects ... in order to extol communitarian particularisms'. Mindful of what he perceives to be a core Badiousian perspective, Webb avows that:

> identity politics of difference rest on *anti-essentialist* claims that there are multiple starting-points of equal status rather than one single one from which to assess the ethics of social work.... The net effect of the critique of difference and diversity discourse is to demonstrate why ideas and institutions embraced by many progressives, in fields such as social work, can in fact be conservative. (Webb, 2009, p 309, emphasis in original)

The risk associated with identity politics is that it gives rise to divisiveness since a 'predilection towards highlighting difference can lead to a latent form of xenophobia in peoples, a partitioning rather than an understanding' (Webb, 2009, p 310).

What is more, there is a 'contradiction', even duplicity, intrinsic to the 'respect for differences' talk because it shields 'an "idealtype", a unitary identity that is tucked away for the proselytisers of difference': the affluent, white, Westerner against whom all 'differences' are defined (Webb, 2009, p 311). When the liberal rhetoric is viewed more closely, the message being conveyed to immigrants is merely: 'Become like me and I will respect your difference' (Badiou, in Webb, 2009, p 311). Badiou, in fact, argues that 'the fundamental democratic axiom of principled democracy, that is, the right to be defended today is not "the right to difference", but, on the contrary, and more than ever, the right to sameness' (Hallward, in Webb, 2009, p 311). Along with the scorn for 'difference', according to Webb, Badiou disparages the contemporary fixation with 'human rights', holding that 'the rhetoric of human rights serves as a distraction from and support for a radically unjust world order dominated by global capitalism and the great power neo-liberalism' (Webb, 2009, p 313). Webb continues:

> Human rights always have ... something terroristic in them. Simply put, human rights are effective only when there is a power to define and enforce them; they require an agent outside that is above their beneficiaries. For liberalism since the 17th century, this has been the state; for today's human rights ideology, it is ideally a cosmopolitan US humanitocracy. (Webb, 2009, p 312)

Webb's illumination of what he regards as the resonance of Badiou's work for social work has generated critical responses, with Imre (2009, p 256) charging that being 'indifferent to difference' is 'tantamount to a shrug of the shoulders rather than progressive politics' (see also Jose, 2009). How, therefore, can Webb's analysis and this subsequent assertion be assessed?

The profession's 'excitement' about 'difference' is certainly not as prominent as Webb (2009, p 310) maintains; neither does it possess the hegemonic weight or doxic command that is suggested. In Britain, Surinder Guru (2010, p 272) has remarked that in the context of the so-called 'war on terror', social work has 'remained ominously silent' on how the 'discourse and policies … may affect their clients and their own professional practice'. Guru maintains that many communities have become the targets of hysteria and suspicion (see also Nickels et al, 2011).

Beyond the terrain of social work, Western Muslims have been viewed, in recent years, 'exclusively through the prism of counter-terrorism. Sensitive issues of integration and community cohesion have become entangled in the securitised discourse of the war on terror' (Hasan, 2011, p 34). Within the wider polity in which social work is located, multiculturalism has been assailed by Prime Minister David Cameron (2011) in a speech – significantly – held at an international *security* conference. In the keynote intervention, in which his toxic rhetoric can be linked to Badiou's notion of 'authoritarian integration' (Badiou, 2008a, p 65), Cameron called for a 'much more active, muscular liberalism'. He went on:

> we have allowed the weakening of *our* collective identity. Under the doctrine of state multiculturalism, we have encouraged different cultures to live separate lives, apart from each other and apart from the mainstream.…We've even tolerated these segregated communities behaving in ways that run completely counter to *our* values. (Cameron, 2011, emphases added)

Furthermore, this downplaying of 'multiculturalism' is currently detectable within much of mainstream Left thinking in Britain. For example, a brief survey of the 'four evolving strands of progressive thought' neither contained reference to the place of minority groups nor referred to questions pivoting on 'difference' (White, 2009). Within other European jurisdictions, it is likewise debatable whether social workers give the same attention to these themes as perhaps their counterparts do in North America and Australasia (where Webb is based). For example, in the Republic of Ireland, there is 'little evidence' of 'practices or policies in social work' seeking to address this issue (Walsh et al, 2010, p 1984). Walsh and her colleagues maintain:

> the development of specific texts on working with refugees and asylum seekers and the inclusion of equality and human rights on social work courses have not translated into visible anti-racist or anti-oppressive policies or practices in social work.…The lack of attention to cultural differences in child protection guidelines and child welfare legislation is one tangible example of a continuing inertia. (Walsh et al, 2010, p 1984)

Meanwhile, Irish people in Britain have themselves tended to be ignored within the dominant discourse on 'race', ethnicity, 'diversity' and 'difference' (see, eg, Hickman et al, 2005; Jeyasingham, 2011).

More broadly, notions of 'diversity' and 'difference' pivot on complex and highly charged theoretical (and political) questions. This is apparent, as we saw in Chapter Nine, if one looks at some of the debates generated on recognition theory that have begun to find a place within social work's academic literature. Although not theoretically framed and articulated within a Badiousian problematic, these exchanges are deliberating and contesting similar issues. Likewise, McLennan's (2001) 'critical universalism' idea can be perceived as trying to grapple with the same questions (see also Modood and Dobbernack, 2011). In what follows, the aim will be to clarify some of these key theoretical questions and specifically as they relate to Badiou. In this context, it is important to recognise that his interventions are, perhaps, a little more nuanced than has been acknowledged by either Webb or those prompted to respond to his article.

'There is only one world'

Within and beyond social work, a progressive politics must identify areas of commonality and solidarity, if not 'sameness', if it is to counter neoliberalisation. However, as evidenced in his theorisation and political practice, Badiou is aware that the promotion of a confining, stultifying 'sameness' is socially retrogressive. In a note sketching the new imperative for leftist activists following the victory of Sarkozy in May 2007, Badiou asserted that the foundational statement the Left should coalesce around should to be the assumption that 'all workers labouring here belong here, and must be treated on a basis of equality, and respected accordingly – especially workers of foreign origin' (Badiou, 2008a, p 44). His position is particularly significant given that foreign workers in contemporary France are subjected to heightened immigration control policies, the imposition of mandatory competence in the French language, the putting in place of obstacles to family reunions, the abolition of the right to asylum, police raids and – what Badiou terms – 'repression in dress' (Badiou, 2008a, p 44; see also Chrisafis, 2012). He also objects to 'the wretched "civilizing" campaigns against the customs of people who arrive in our country' and to the development of Sarkozy's 'authoritarian integration' (Badiou, 2008a, pp 44, 65).

To a cursory commentator, Badiou's interventions on these points may seem at odds with his apparent promotion of 'universalism' and with what Webb identifies as an antipathy for ideas pivoting on 'difference'. However, Badiou's perspective is integral to the 'one world' politics at the root of his 'communist hypothesis'. His commitment to 'one world' politics has little in common with the shallow rhetoric of 'globalisation' dominating the discourse of so-called 'world leaders' which percolates, on occasions, into the social work literature. He clearly articulates this fundamental distinction declaring that the:

> thesis of a democratic unity of the world realized by the market and the 'international community' is a complete sham. If it were true, we would have to welcome ... 'foreigners' as people coming from the same

world as ourselves. We would have to treat them as we would treat someone from another region who stops over in our town, then finds work and settles there. But this is not at all what happens. The most widespread conviction, that which government policies constantly seek to reinforce, is that *these people come from a different world*. (Badiou, 2008a, p 57, emphasis in original)

He elaborates:

The unity of the world is one of living and acting beings, here and now. And I must absolutely insist on this test of unity: these people who are here, different from me in terms of language, clothes, religion, food, education, exist in the same world, exist just as I myself do. Since they exist like me, I can converse with them, and then, as with anyone else, we can agree and disagree about things. But on the absolute precondition that they exist as I do – in other words, in the same world. (Badiou, 2008a, p 61)

For Badiou, holding fast to the idea that we all inhabit the same world does not negate a person's right to 'maintain and develop' what they may conceive as their sense of 'identity' and to 'preserve and organize those invariant properties' such as 'religion, mother tongue, forms of recreation and domesticity, and so on' (Badiou, 2008a, p 65). This would be particularly important, in fact, for migrant workers, who feel compelled to refuse 'the imposition of integration' (Badiou, 2008a, p 65). He, therefore, argues:

The single world of living women and men may well have laws. What it cannot have is subjective 'cultural' preconditions for existence within it. It cannot demand that, in order to live in it, you have to be like everyone else – still less, like a minority of these others, for example like the 'civilized' white petty bourgeois. If there is a single world, all of those who live in it exist as much as I do, even though they are not like me, they are different. The single world is precisely the place where an unlimited set of differences exists.… If, on the contrary, those who live in the world are asked to be the same, this means that the world is closed in on itself and becomes, as a world, different from another world. Which inevitably sets the scene for separations, walls, controls, contempt, death, and finally war. (Badiou, 2008a, p 63)

Following this line of reasoning, if 'preconditions' are placed on migrants – if the state is able to label them as 'asylum seekers' and confine them to 'reception centres' – the 'same world' principle has been abandoned (Badiou, 2008a, p 63; see also Chapter Nine). Badiou's engagement with the theme of difference is therefore more complex than what may be inferred from Webb's commentary. Rather than denying 'differences', Badiou alerts his reader to the 'immense differentiating unity of the world of human beings' (Badiou, 2008a, p 64):

> [To] say 'there is only one world' is to say that this world is precisely, in its very unity, a series of identities and differences. These differences, far from raising an objection to the unity of the world, are in fact its principle of existence. (Badiou, 2008a, p 62)

Criticisms

For those sharing the political aspiration to rekindle the communist hypothesis, there remain, at least, three problems with Badiou's conceptual scheme.[5] First, despite being a philosopher associated with Marxism, there is a startling lack of an economic dimension attached to his theorisation. As Hewlett (2004, p 342) argues, there 'seems to be no residual influence of Marx's political economy on the philosophical infrastructure, however much he might condemn and combat the social effects of today's all-pervasive, virtually unfettered drive for profits'. This may be because in seeking to avoid economic determinism, Badiou pays insufficient attention to the shifting modes and relations of production. It is as though the 'event' is the engine of history. Although it is clear that his political sympathies are with the working class and the dispossessed, class plays no central role and he is sceptical about the importance of trade unions, preferring the self-organisation of smaller, close-knit groups or clusters (*Noyaux*) of workers located within factories (Hallward, 2002).

Second, Badiou (2003b, p 132) has articulated a theory encompassing four types of change: modifications (consistent with the existing regime); weak singularities (novelties with no existential consequences); strong singularities (implying an important existential change but whose consequences remain measurable); and events (strong singularities whose consequences are virtually infinite). Nevertheless, it is not always be clear what constitutes an 'event'. How significant and momentous does an occurrence need to be in order to be defined as such? What are its boundaries and perimeters? In Badiou's articulation, social change is unpredictable, a rupture in time and space, seemingly from 'nowhere'. Typically, he insists, for example, that the French Revolution 'event and all others must be seen as a development which owed a large part to chance and contingency' (Hewlett, 2004, p 345). This perspective has made him 'vulnerable to the charge that the event becomes a "miracle" whose cause cannot be explained' (Bassett, 2008, p 902). When light is shone on specific 'events', there is usually a more gradual unfolding as opposed to a sudden irruption. Indeed, what Badiou portrays as 'events' cannot really be 'understood without recourse to a thorough examination of what goes before them – the context of their genesis – just as much as what follows them' (Hewlett, 2006, p 380). Such an approach would lead to a more Gramscian reading, which asks more searching questions about the molecular composition of an 'event', its 'causal structures, and its contradictions'

(Bassett, 2008, p 903). A Gramscian perspective, as mentioned in Chapter Six, also aids an examination of how hegemony functions, or becomes anachronistic and vulnerable, at specific historical conjunctures. In this context, Bourdieu's formulations of habitus, field and capital might also help to articulate why events happen or never even appear as possibilities.

The difficulties with this aspect of Badiou's theorisation are also apparent in his approach to the Paris Commune: a two-month period in the spring of 1871, during which the working poor and unemployed took control over certain areas of Paris, intent on establishing a new communistic order. For Badiou, the Commune is another illustration of an unpredictable and momentous 'event' providing the opportunity for transformed subjectivities and new fidelities to new truths. However, as Bassett (2008, p 903) observes, in his exploration of the social and economic dynamics that provided the shifting context for the Commune, it is 'difficult to imagine new subjects emerging who had not been radicalised in the network of debating clubs, mass meetings, and revolutionary organisations active in every neighbourhood' (Bassett, 2008, p 903). The Commune insurgents were not 'unknowns', but communist, socialist, syndicalist and anarchist activists. The Paris insurrection was hardly, despite spontaneous and unpredictable components, an entirely spontaneous event. Rather, many had spent years organising and trying to convince their fellows of the need for such action. Such evidence suggests, therefore, that a fuller explanation requires:

> knowledge of longer term changes in social and economic structures, as well as the development of political culture and organisation into which 'unknowns' were mobilised and radicalised. New subjectivities certainly emerged, but in ways more entwined with the past, more imbricated in political cultures, memories, and traditions. (Bassett, 2008, pp 903–4)

A third criticism is that, implicitly and sometimes more overtly, Badiou's theorisation can seem dominated by a fascination with the heroic, male figure. Paul is one example of this tendency, Robespierre another. Related to this, there is a hint of a certain lofty, aristocratic disdain for the everyday, and people's strategic, often faltering and failing, struggles *inside* the fabric of capitalism. Such criticisms gel, in part, with Lenin's (1981) castigation of the 'infantile disorder' of ultra-leftism. Badiou's theorisation often fails to allow any room or possibility for those, many social workers included, actively struggling within – to use Gramsci again – the 'trenches' and 'earthworks' of civil society (Forgacs, 1988). More damagingly, with Badiou, and this probably reflects his intentional positioning, politics is only authentically political when it takes the form of 'a sudden rupture with the status quo; slow, ongoing efforts to convince others in the ideological realm or small gains apparently do not count as politics' (Hewlett, 2006, p 381). In this sense, Badiou's position does not appear to allow sufficient space for the evolution of a more progressive or 'radical' social work (Lavalette, 2011a). However, the compelling iconoclastic energy and enlightening insights that characterise Badiou's work fully warrant his inclusion within the profession's academic literature and are likely to expand and deepen social work's engagement with social theory.

Conclusion

Having outlined the diverse body of theorisation of Boltanski and Chiapello, Negri and the autonomist Marxists, and Badiou, we cannot ignore the considerable problems posed both in terms of conceptualisation and of its linkages with social work. Nevertheless, the contributions of these prominent European intellectuals remain insightful and furnish innovative perspectives on change and transformation. When brought into conversation with Gramsci and Bourdieu, explored earlier in the book, these new directions potentially help us to break away from the stale theoretical frameworks that have delimited theorisation within social work in recent years.

◀◀Reflection and Talk Box 10▶▶

- Ferguson (2004, p 135) has maintained that creativity and 'more soulful forms of work are being suppressed'. The Munro review has also asserted that there is a pressing 'need to strip away much of the top down bureaucracy that previous reforms have put in the way of frontline services. Giving professionals greater opportunity for responsible innovation and space for professional judgment' (Department of Education, 2011, p 22). These perspectives hint at what real or authentic social work should look and feel like. Can we link such comments to the ideas of Boltanski and Chiapello? Can you identify any other 'change agenda' within your area of work that might lend itself to their theorisation?

- How persuasive are the ideas of Negri and his colleagues on 'the social factory' and 'immaterial labour'? Do they help us to understand contemporary social work?

- How do you respond to the ideas of Badiou as these relate to issues of 'diversity' and 'difference' within social work?

Notes

[1.] In the following section, for ease of reference, only the relevant page numbers from the book will be provided.

[2.] Boltanski and Chiapello's seven 'cities' are: the 'inspired city'; the 'domestic city'; the 'city of opinion or renown'; the 'civic city'; the 'market city'; the 'industrial city'; and the 'projective city'.

[3.] Negri spent many years in prison because he was alleged to be the 'mastermind' behind the terrorist actions of the Red Brigades (*Brigate Rosse* in Italian). There was no real basis for this charge, but fragments of Negri's writings from the late 1970s remain at best problematic, see, for example, the pamphlet 'Domination and sabotage' featured in Negri (2005b [1997]).

[4.] Boron (2005, pp 23–4) has maintained that:

> almost all the citations are taken from books or articles published within the limits of the French–American academic establishment.... In short *Empire* offers a vision that wants to be a critical examination going to the root of the problem, but given the fact that it cannot emancipate itself from the privileged place from where it observes the social scene of its time ... it is trapped in the ideological nets of the dominant classes.

[5.] His views on children, children's rights and child abuse are also deeply problematic, although there is insufficient space available here to be able to examine this dimension to his work.

CHAPTER ELEVEN

Conclusion

> I mean it's almost like you need less and less bright people doing social work because actually what you don't want them to do is to kind of really think too much about the wider issues, the wider aspects of what they're doing, what you want them to do really is to do what they're told. (Joe, a social work team manager who works with disabled children and their families, in Thomas and Davies, 2005, p 724)

Perhaps Joe's comments apply specifically to a UK context, where, as Jones argued over two decades ago:

> social-work education is ... unique in its anti-intellectualism and its hostile stance to the social sciences.... There is no comparable system of social-work education in the world which is so nationally uniform, uninspired and tailored so closely to the requirements of major state employers. (Jones, 1996, pp 190–1; see also Jones, 2011)

Since the foundation of social work in England, the aspiration to 'produce' social workers with an appropriate ideological disposition is evidenced by the efforts made by the leadership of the Charity Organization Society (COS) to contain and regulate the curriculum for professional education (Jones, 1983, ch 6).

In order to win and maintain hegemony within a field, there is a need to instil specific ways of thinking and acting that impact on and transform the 'habitus' of people, their very sense of themselves and their place in the world. This process is not 'set out or imposed in an explicit way'; rather, with each new entrant to a field, this accommodation takes 'place insensibly, in other words gradually, progressively and imperceptibly': this is how 'a sense of the game' is inculcated and internalised (Bourdieu, 2000, p 11). Thus, the rise of a pervasive neoliberal mentality in the late 1970s coincided with new attempts to regulate and control social work education. This was most apparent in the aftermath of the social workers' strike in 1978–79, when a 'growing body of opinion ... asserted that social work education [had] been partly responsible for the increasing politicization and radicalism of social workers who then went on to become "difficult" employees' (Jones, 1983, p 103). During this period, the discipline of sociology was especially targeted for criticism and at least one local authority considered compiling a so-called 'blacklist of social work courses' whose graduates it 'was not prepared to employ' irrespective of their professional calibre (Jones, 1983, p 103). These rather naive measures were founded on the assumption that small cadres of 'Marxist' social work lecturers were intent on – and, even more mistakenly, *able to* – entirely transform the students' worldview, reorienting them in a leftist direction. Although there may have been a number of Marxist social work educators, universities remained even then largely conservative and elitist locations: the truth was, perhaps, that it 'was not so much that social work courses had radicalised students, but more critical students were coming into social work' (Jones, 1983, p 106).

More recently, some writers have become more optimistic about the possibilities provided by the social work degree introduced in the UK in 2003, trusting that this programme has given new impetus to the teaching of knowledge based on sociological understandings (Cree, 2010). The determination of some social work academics to 'consistently [resist] the obliteration of sociology' from the curriculum (Cunningham and Cunningham, 2008, p 178) was, in some instances, backed by the former New Labour government's own literature on social work education. In her interviews with focus groups on the future of social work training, Barnes (2002, p 13) insisted on 'a need for courses to develop curricula which will ensure that students acquire knowledge about the origins and development of those social problems which they are routinely likely to encounter and strategies to deal with them'.

Nevertheless, 'there is still a latent concern to keep social workers "safe"' (Cunningham and Cunningham, 2008, p 179). As if to soften the theoretical edge of the curriculum, official statements on the new degree stressed that the aim of the programme was to 'prepare students for the reality of becoming a social worker' and would focus on 'practical training' (Department of Health, 2002). The then Health Minister in the New Labour administration elaborated: 'Social work is a very practical job. It is about protecting people and changing their lives, not about being able to give fluent and theoretical explanations about why they got into difficulties in the first place' (Department of Health, 2002). Somewhat similarly, in her review into the status of social care services, published in April 2007, Dame Denise Platt drew attention to a criticism of the *British Journal of Social Work* with its 'small readership' and articles that are 'tortuously theoretical and get nowhere' (Platt, 2007, p 17). Coming from a primary definer of the purpose and intent of social work and social care, such an acerbic comment is no mere expression of subjective disgruntlement but deliberately seeks to discredit the journal's willingness to engage with theoretical and frequently *political* questions.

A number of writers have commented on how their personal attempts to develop more sociologically informed and radical ways of thinking and working have resulted in pressures within the workplace. Recently, a practitioner and writer, has exposed the less than positive response of his local office to his attendance at a conference on the future direction of social work (Rogowski, 2010, pp 1–2). In a less overtly political manner, another respected author of textbooks for students remarked that when he began his career in social work, he was 'discouraged from asking questions or developing' his knowledge base:

I was simply urged to 'get on with the job', without any real clarity about what the job actually was or how to go about it. It was largely a case of copying what other staff did and doing the best I could without any real depth of understanding. (Thompson, 2010, p xi)

These accounts are troubling in that they reveal how an anti-theorising culture is prevalent in many social work workplaces.

Stressing to challenge such a culture, *Social work and social theory* has also been addressed to students, such as Angela, whose comments were referred to in Chapter One. This book has been founded on the understanding that in a neoliberal world, it is vital for social workers (and social work and social policy academics) to try and theoretically comprehend the nature of their work and their role in society. This perspective stems from a belief that social workers, social work academics and those operating in related fields should be *critical* thinkers willing, when necessary, to be constructively disruptive of dominant ways of thinking, seeing and acting within, and beyond, the professional field. Expressed rather more elaborately by Calhoun (2003, p 63), this would entail seeking to wed practice to *critical* theory, understood as 'the project of social theory that undertakes simultaneously critique of received categories, critique of theoretical practice, and critical substantive analysis of social life in terms of the possible, not just the actual'.

The conviction underpinning this book has been that critical theory, mainly but not exclusively emerging from Europe, is a vital resource for a progressive social work whose aim is to put people before profit. In seeking to create this counter-hegemonic project and new bonds of solidarity in hard times, we have much to lose, but everything to gain.

References

Adam, B. (2004) *Time*, Cambridge: Polity.

Adkins, L. (2004a) 'Reflexivity: freedom or habit of gender?', *Sociological Review*, vol 52, no 3, pp 191–211.

Adkins, L. (2004b) 'Introduction: feminism, Bourdieu and after', *Sociological Review*, vol 53, no 2, pp 3–19.

Adorno, T. (2000) *Minima moralia*, London: Verso.

Adorno, T.W. (2003) *Can one live after Auschwitz: a philosophical reader*, Stanford, CA: Stanford University Press.

Agamben, G. (2005) *A time that remains*, Stanford, CA: Stanford University Press.

Alexander, J.C. and Lara, M.P. (1996) 'Honneth's new critical theory of recognition', *New Left Review*, vol 220, pp 126–36.

Allen, A. (2008) *The politics of ourselves: power, autonomy, and gender in contemporary critical theory*, New York, NY: Columbia University.

Alzheimer's Research Trust (2009) 'Government promises to cut the use of antipsychotic drugs by two thirds', press release, 12 November.

Anderson, B. (1991) *Imagined communities*, London: Verso.

Anderson, J. (1995) 'Translator's introduction', in A. Honneth, *The struggle for recognition*, Cambridge: Polity.

Anderson, K. (2010) 'Irish secularization and religious identities: evidence of an emerging new Catholic habitus', *Social Compass*, vol 57, no 1, pp 15–39.

Anderson, P. (1976) 'The antinomies of Antonio Gramsci', *New Left Review*, vol 100, pp 5–79.

Anderson, P. (1998) *The origins of postmodernity*, London: Verso.

Anderson, P. (2005) 'Arms and rights: Rawls, Habermas and Bobbio in an age of war', *New Left Review*, vol 31, pp 5–43.

Arnold, B. (2009) *The Irish gulag*, Dublin: Gill & Macmillan.

Asen, R. (2000) 'Seeking the "counter" in counterpublics', *Communication Theory*, vol 10, no 4, pp 424–46.

Askeland, G.A. and Payne, M. (2006) 'Social work education's cultural hegemony', *International Social Work*, vol 49, no 6, pp 731–43.

Back, L. (2009) 'Portrayal and betrayal: Bourdieu, photography and sociological life', *Sociological Review*, vol 57, no 3, pp 471–91.

Badiou, A. (2003a [1997]) *Saint Paul*, Stanford, CA: University of California.

Badiou, A. (2003b) 'Beyond formalisation', *Angelaki*, vol 8, no 2, pp 111–37.

Badiou, A. (2005) *Being and event*, New York, NY: Continuum.

Badiou, A. (2007) *The century*, Cambridge: Polity.

Badiou, A. (2008a) *The meaning of Sarkozy*, London: Verso.

Badiou, A. (2008b) 'Communist hypothesis', *New Left Review*, vol 49, pp 29–47.

Badiou, A. (2009) *Logic of worlds*, London: Continuum.

Badiou, A. (2010) *The communist hypothesis*, London: Verso.

Badiou, A. and Hallward, P. (1998) 'Politics and philosophy', *Angelaki*, vol 3, no 3, pp 113–34.

Baert, P. (2001) 'Jürgen Habermas', in A. Elliott and B. Turner (eds) *Profiles in contemporary social theory*, London: Sage.

Bailey, R. (2011) 'Foreword', in M. Lavalette (ed) *Radical social work today: social work at the crossroads*, Bristol: The Policy Press.

Bailey, R. and Brake, M. (eds) (1975) *Radical social work*, London: Edward Arnold.

Baines, D. (2004a) 'Caring for nothing: work organization and unwaged labour in social services', *Work, Employment and Society*, vol 18, no 2, pp 267–95.

Baines, D. (2004b) 'Pro-market, non-market: the dual nature of organizational change in social services delivery', *Critical Social Policy*, vol 24, no 1, pp 5–29.

Baines, D. (2006) 'Staying with people who slap us around: gender, juggling responsibilities and violence in paid (and unpaid) care work', *Gender, Work and Organization*, vol 13, no 2, pp 129–52.

Baines, D. (2010) '"If we don't get back to where we were before": working in the restructured non-profit social services', *British Journal of Social Work*, vol 40, no 3, pp 928–45.

Baker, J. (2009) 'Young mothers in late modernity: sacrifice, respectability and the transformation of the neoliberal subject', *Journal of Youth Studies*, vol 12, no 3, pp 275–88.

Balibar, E. (2007) 'Uprisings in the *Banlieues*', *Constellations*, vol 14, no 1, pp 47–72.

Bambery, C. (2006) *A rebel's guide to Gramsci*, London: Bookmarks.

Baréz-Brown, C. (2011) 'How to build brand "you"', *The Guardian*, Money Section, 9 July, p 1.

Barker, J. (2002) *Alain Badiou: a critical introduction*, London: Pluto.

Barnes, J. (2002) 'Reform of social work education and training'. Available at: http://www.doh.gov.uk/swqualification/focusgroup.pdf

Bar-On, A. (1999) 'Social work and the "missionary zeal to whip the heathen along the path of righteousness"', *British Journal of Social Work*, vol 29, pp 5–26.

Barrett, M. (1992) 'Words and things: materialism and method in contemporary feminist analysis', in M. Barrett and A. Phillips (eds) *Destabilizing theory: contemporary feminist debates*, Cambridge: Polity.

Barrett, M. and McIntosh, M. (1982) *The antisocial family*, London: Verso.

Bassett, K. (2008) 'Thinking the event: Badiou's philosophy of the event and the example of the Paris Commune', *Environment and Planning D: Society and Space*, vol 26, pp 895–910.

Bauman, Z. (1989) *Modernity and the Holocaust*, Cambridge: Polity.

Bauman, Z. (1993) *Postmodern ethics*, Oxford: Blackwell.

Bauman, Z. (1995) *Life in fragments: essays in postmodern morality*, London: Blackwell.

Bauman, Z. (1997) *Postmodernity and its discontents*, Cambridge: Polity.

Bauman, Z. (1998a) *Globalization*, Cambridge: Polity.

Bauman, Z. (1998b) *Work, consumerism and the new poor*, Buckingham: Open University.

Bauman, Z. (2000a) 'Am I my brother's keeper?', *European Journal of Social Work*, vol 3, no 1, pp 5–11.

Bauman, Z. (2000b) *Liquid modernity*, Cambridge: Polity.

Bauman, Z. (2000c) 'Social issues of law and order', *British Journal of Criminology*, vol 40, no 2, pp 205–21.

Bauman, Z. (2002a) *Society under siege*, Cambridge: Polity.

Bauman, Z. (2002b) 'Reconnaissance wars of the planetary frontierland', *Theory, Culture & Society*, vol 19, no 4, pp 81–90.

Bauman, Z. (2003) *Liquid love*, Cambridge: Polity.

Bauman, Z. (2004) *Wasted lives: modernity and it outcasts*, Cambridge: Polity.

Bauman, Z. (2005) *Liquid life*, Cambridge: Polity.

Bauman, Z. (2006) *Liquid fear*, Cambridge: Polity.

Bauman, Z. (2008) *The art of life*, Cambridge: Polity.

Bauman, Z. (2009) 'Getting to the roots of radical politics today', in J. Pugh (ed) *What is radical politics today?*, Houndmills: Palgrave Macmillan.

Bauman, Z. (2010) *Letters from the liquid modern world*, Cambridge: Polity.

Bauman, Z. (2011a) *Culture in a liquid modern world*, Cambridge: Polity.

Bauman, Z. (2011b) *Collateral damage: social inequalities in a global age*, Cambridge: Polity.

Bauman, Z. and Haugaard, M. (2008) 'Liquid modernity and power: a dialogue with Zygmunt Bauman', *Journal of Power*, vol 1, no 2, pp 111–30.

Beck, U. (1994) 'The reinvention of politics: towards a theory of reflexive modernization', in U. Beck, A. Giddens and S. Lash (eds) *Reflexive modernization*, Cambridge: Polity.

Beck, U. (1998) *Risk society* (5th reprint), London: SAGE.

Beck, U. (2000a) 'Zombie categories', in J. Rutherford (ed) *The art of life*, London: Lawrence & Wishart.

Beck, U. (2000b) 'Living your own life in a runaway world: individualisation, globalisation and politics', in W. Hutton and A. Giddens (eds) *On the edge: living with global capitalism*, London: Jonathan Cope.

Beck, U. and Beck-Gernsheim, E. (1999) *The normal chaos of love* (1st reprint), Cambridge: Polity.

Beckett, C. (2003) 'The language of siege: military metaphors in the spoken language of social work', *British Journal of Social Work*, vol 33, no 5, pp 625–39.

Beilharz, P. (ed) (2001) *The Bauman reader*, Oxford: Blackwell.

Bellamy, R. (ed) (1994) *Gramsci: pre-prison writings*, Cambridge: University of Cambridge.

Bensaid, D. (2002) *Marx for our times, adventures and misadventures of a critique*, London: Verso.

Bergdolt, K. (2008) *Wellbeing: a cultural history*, Cambridge: Polity.

Bhambra, G.K. (2007) *Rethinking modernity*, Houndmills: Palgrave Macmillan.

Blair, T. (2006) 'Interview with BBC on social exclusion', 31 August. Available at: http://www.pm.gov.uk/output/Page10023.asp

Bohman, J. (1999) 'Practical reason and cultural constraint: agency in Bourdieu's theory of practice', in R. Shusterman (ed) *Bourdieu: a critical reader*, Oxford: Blackwell.

Boltanski, L. (2002) 'The Left after May 1968 and the longing for total revolution', *Thesis Eleven*, vol 69, pp 1–20.

Boltanski, L. (2011) *On critique: a sociology of emancipation*, Cambridge: Polity.

Boltanski, L. and Chiapello, E. (2005) *The new spirit of capitalism*, London: Verso.

Boron, A.A. (2005) *Empire & imperialism*, London: Zed Books.

Bosteels, B. (2005) 'Post-Maoism: Badiou and politics', *positions*, vol 13, no 3, pp 575–635.

Bourdieu, P. (1991) *Language and symbolic power*, Cambridge: Polity.

Bourdieu, P. (1994) *In other words*, Cambridge: Polity.

Bourdieu, P. (1996) *Photography: a middlebrow art*, Cambridge: Polity.

Bourdieu, P. (1998a) 'The essence of neoliberalism', *Le Monde Diplomatique*, December. Available at: http://mondediplo.com/1998/12/08bourdieu

Bourdieu, P. (1998b) *On television and journalism*, London: Pluto.

Bourdieu, P. (2000) *Pascalian meditations*, Cambridge: Polity.

Bourdieu, P. (2001a) *Homo Academicus*, Cambridge: Polity.

Bourdieu, P. (2001b) *Acts of resistance: against the new myths of our time*, Cambridge: Polity.

Bourdieu, P. (2002a) 'Social space and symbolic power', in M. Haugaard (ed) *Power: a reader*, Manchester: Manchester University Press.

Bourdieu, P. (2002b) 'Habitus', in J. Hillier and E. Rooksby (eds) *Habitus: a sense of place*, Aldershot: Ashgate.

Bourdieu, P. (2003a) *Firing back: against the tyranny of the market 2*, London: Verso.

Bourdieu, P. (2003b) *Outline of a theory of practice* (17th printing), Cambridge: Cambridge University.

Bourdieu, P. (2004 [1984]) *Distinction* (10th reprint), London: Routledge.

Bourdieu, P. (2007) *Sketch for self-analysis*, Cambridge: Polity.

Bourdieu, P. (2008) *Political interventions: social science and political action*, London: Verso.

Bourdieu, P. and Eagleton, T. (1994) 'Doxa and the common life: an interview', in S. Zizek (ed) *Mapping ideology*, London: Verso.

Bourdieu, P. and Wacquant, L. (1999) 'On the cunning of imperialist reason', *Theory, Culture & Society*, vol 16, no 1, pp 41–59.

Bourdieu, P. and Wacquant, L. (2001) 'NewLiberalSpeak: notes on the new planetary vulgate', *Radical Philosophy*, Jan/Feb, 105, pp 2–6.

Bourdieu, P. and Wacquant, L. (2004) *An invitation to reflexive sociology*, Cambridge: Polity.

Bourdieu, P., Accardo, A., Balazas, G., Beaud, S., Bonvin, F., Bourdieu, E., Bourgois, P., Broccolichi, S., Champagne, P., Christin, R., Faguer, J.P., Garcia, S., Lenoir, R., Euvrard, F., Pialoux, M., Pinto, L., Podalydes, D., Sayad, A., Soulie, C. and Wacquant, J.D. (2002) *The weight of the world: social suffering in contemporary society*, Cambridge: Polity.

Bowlby, J. (1990) *Child care and the growth of love* (3rd edn), Harmondsworth: Penguin.

Bowring, F. (2004) 'From the mass worker to the multitude', *Capital & Class*, vol 83, pp 101–33.

Boym, S. (2001) *The future of nostalgia*, New York, NY: Basic Books.

Brandist, C. (1996) 'Gramsci, Bakhtin and the semiotics of hegemony', *New Left Review*, vol 216, pp 94–110.

Brandist, C., Shepherd, D. and Tihanov, G. (eds) (2004) *The Bakhtin circle*, Manchester: Manchester University.

Braverman, H. (1974) 'Labour and monopoly capital', *Monthly Review*, vol 26, no 3, pp 1–134.

Braverman, H. (1998) *Labour and monopoly capitalism: the degradation of work in the twentieth century – 25th anniversary edition*, New York, NY: Monthly Review Press.

Bren, P. (2010) *The greengrocer and his TV: the culture of communism after the 1968 Prague Spring*, London: Cornell University.

Brenner, N. and Theodore, N. (eds) (2002) *Spaces of neoliberalism*, Oxford: Blackwell.

Brewer, C. and Lait, J. (1980) *Can social work survive?* London: Temple Smith.

Bridge, G. (2004) 'Pierre Bourdieu', in P. Hubbard, R. Kitchin and G. Valentine (eds) *Key thinkers on space and place*, London: Sage.

Broadhurst, K., Wastell, D., White, S., Hall, C., Peckover, S., Thompson, K., Pithouse, A. and Davey, D. (2010) 'Performing "initial assessment" identifying the latent conditions for error at the front-door of local children's services', *British Journal of Social Work*, vol 40, no 2, pp 352–70.

Broberg, G. and Roll-Hansen, N. (eds) (1996) *Eugenics and the welfare state*, East Lansing, MI: Michigan State University.

Brown, M. (2003) 'Survival at work: flexibility and adaptability in American corporate culture', *Cultural Studies*, vol 17, no 5, pp 713–33.

Browne, V. (2011) 'Let's own up to our part in the burst bubble', *The Irish Times*, 4 April, p 14.

Brunt, R. (1989) 'The politics of identity', in S. Hall and M. Jacques (eds) *New times: the changing face of politics in the 1990s*, London: Lawrence & Wishart.

Budgen, S., Kouvelakis, S. and Žižeck, S. (eds) (2007) *Lenin reloaded*, London: Duke University.

Bunting, M. (2009) 'Workfare has arrived in Britain, smuggled in with slippery rhetoric', *The Guardian*, 23 February, p 29.

Bunting, M. (2011) 'Hectored, humiliated, bullied: women are bearing the brunt of flexible labour', *The Guardian*, 2 May, p 23.

Burdett, C. (2007) 'Eugenics old and new', *Soundings*, vol 60, pp 7–13.

Butler, I. and Drakeford, M. (2003) *Scandal, social policy and social welfare*, Bristol: The Policy Press.

Butler, J. (1999) 'Performativity's social magic', in R. Shusterman (ed) *Bourdieu: a critical reader*, Oxford: Blackwell.

Butler, J. (2004) *Precarious life*, London: Verso.

Buttigieg, J.A. (1986) 'The legacy of Antonio Gramsci', *Boundary 2*, vol 14, no 3, pp 1–17.

Cabinet Office (2010) 'Prime Minister launches the Big Society Bank and announces the first four big society communities', Press Notice, 19 July. Available at: http://www.cabinetoffice.gov.uk/newsroom/news_releases/2010/100719-bigsociety.aspx

Calhoun, C. (2003) 'Habitus, field and capital: the question of historical specificity', in C. Calhoun, E. LiPuma and M. Postone (eds) *Bourdieu: critical perspectives* (3rd reprint), Cambridge: Polity.

Callinicos, A. (1999a) *Social theory*, Cambridge: Polity.

Callinicos, A. (1999b) 'Social theory put to the test of politics: Pierre Bourdieu and Anthony Giddens', *New Left Review*, July/August, pp 77–102.

Callinicos, A. (2000) 'Impossible anti-capitalism?', *New Left Review*, March/April, pp 117–125.

Callinicos, A. (2006) *The resources of critique*, Cambridge: Polity.

Callinicos, A. (2010) *Bonfire of illusions*, Cambridge: Polity.

Cameron, D. (2010) 'Together in the national interest', Speech to the Conservative Party Conference, 6 October. Available at: http://www.conservatives.com/News/Speeches/2010/10/David_ig_Together_in_the_National_Interest.aspx

Cameron. D. (2011) 'PM's speech at Munich Security Conference', 5 February. Available at: http://www.number10.gov.uk/news/pms-speech-at-munich-security-conference/

Camilleri, P. (1999) 'Social work and its search for meaning: theories, narratives and practices', in B. Pease and J. Fook (eds) *Transforming social work: postmodern critical perspectives*, London: Routledge.

Cardy, S. (2010) '"Care matters" and the privatization of looked after children's services in England and Wales: developing a critique of independent "social work practices"', *Critical Social Policy*, vol 30, no 3, pp 430–442.

Carel, H. (2008) *Illness*, Durham: Acumen.

Carey, M. (2003) 'Anatomy of a care manager', *Work, employment and society*, vol 17, no 1, pp 121–35.

Carey, M. (2007) 'White-collar proletariat? Braverman, the deskilling/upskilling of social work and the paradoxical life of the agency care manager', *Journal of Social Work*, vol 7, no 1, pp 93–114.

Carey, M. (2008) 'Everything must go? The privatization of state social work', *British Journal of Social Work*, vol 38, no 5, pp 918–35.

Carey, M. (2009) 'It's a bit like being a robot or working in a factory', *Organization*, vol 16, no 4, pp 505–27.

Carver, T. (1998) *The postmodern Marx*, Manchester: Manchester University.

Chambon, A.S., Irving, A. and Epstein, L. (ed) (1999) *Reading Foucault for social work*, New York, NY: Columbia University.

Charlesworth, S.J. (2000a) *A phenomenology of working class experience*, Cambridge: Cambridge University.

Charlesworth, S. (2000b) 'Bourdieu, social suffering and the working class', in B. Fowler (ed) *Reading Bourdieu on society and culture*, Oxford: Blackwell.

Children's Right's Alliance for England (2010) 'CRAE statement on physical control in care manual', Press Notice, 13 July. Available at: http://www.crae.org.uk/news-and-events/news/physical-control-in-care-manual-released-to-crae.html

ChildStats.gov (2011) 'America's children: key national indicators of well-being'. Available at: http://www.childstats.gov/americaschildren/index3.asp

Chopra, R. (2003) 'Neoliberalism as *doxa*: Bourdieu's theory of the state and the contemporary Indian discourse on globalization and liberalization', *Cultural Studies*, vol 17, nos 3/4, pp 419–44.

Chrisafis, A. (2012) 'French anti-terror raids: security, protection or electioneering?', *The Guardian*, 4 April. Available at: http://www.guardian.co.uk/world/2012/apr/04/french-terror-raids-security-electioneering

Circourel, A.V. (2003) 'Aspects of structural and processual theories of knowledge', in C. Calhoun, E. LiPuma and M. Postone (eds) *Bourdieu: critical perspectives* (3rd reprint), Cambridge: Polity, pp 89–116.

Clarke, J. (2004) *Changing welfare, changing states: new directions in social policy*, London: Sage.

Clarke, J. (2005) 'New Labour's citizens: activated, empowered, responsibilized, abandoned', *Critical Social Policy*, vol 25, no 4, pp 447–63.

Clarke, J., Newman, J., Smith, N., Vidler, E. and Westmarland, L. (2007) *Creating citizen-consumers: changing publics and changing public services*, London: Sage.

Coates, K. and Silburn, R. (1970) *The forgotten Englishman*, Harmondsworth: Penguin.

Cohen, S. (2001) *States of denial: knowing about atrocities and suffering*, Cambridge: Polity.

Coleman, N. and Harris, J. (2008) 'Calling social work', *British Journal of Social Work*, vol 38, no 3, pp 580–99.

Coleman, R. and Sim, J. (2005) 'Contemporary statecraft and the "punitive obsession": a critique of the new penology', in J. Pratt, D. Brown, M. Brown, S. Hallsworth and W. Morrison (ed) *The new punitiveness: trends, theories and perspectives*, Devon: Willan.

Commission of Investigation (2009) *Report into the Catholic Archdiocese of Dublin*, Dublin: Department of Justice, Equality and Law Reform.

Commission of Investigation (2010) *Report into the Catholic Diocese of Cloyne*, Dublin: Department of Justice, Equality and Law Reform.

Commission to Inquire into Child Abuse (2009) *Commission to Inquire into Child Abuse report*, Dublin: Stationery Office.

Conservative Party (2007) 'No more blame game – the future for children's social workers'. Available at: http://www.fassit.co.uk/leaflets/No%20More%20Blame%20Game%20-%20The%20Future%20for%20Children's%20Social%20Workers.pdf

Cook, D. (2001) 'The talking cure in Habermas's republic', *New Left Review*, vol 12, pp 135–52.

Cooper, J. (2011) 'Cuts causing child abuse to be downgraded, say social workers', *Community Care*, 14 April. Available at: http://www.communitycare.co.uk/Articles/2011/04/14/116661/cuts-causing-child-abuse-to-be-downgraded-say-social-workers.htm

Cooper, M. (2008) *Life as surplus: biotechnology and capitalism in the neoliberal era*, Seattle, WA: University of Washington.

Corrigan, P. (1982) 'The Marx factor', *Social Work Today*, 26 January, pp 8–11.

Corrigan, P. and Leonard, P. (1978) *Social work practice under capitalism*, London: Macmillan.

Couldry, N., Gilbert, J., Hesmondhalgh, D. and Nash, K. (2010) 'The new spirit of capitalism', *Soundings*, vol 45, pp 109–24.

Coulshed, V. (1988) *Social work practice: an introduction*, London: MacMillan.

Coward, R. (2011) 'Southern Cross wakes us up to the business of caring', *The Guardian*, 12 July, p 28.

Cree, V.E. (2010) *Sociology for social workers and probation officers* (2nd edn), Abingdon: Routledge.

Crehan, K. (2002) *Gramsci, culture and anthropology*, London: Pluto.

Cresswell, T. (2001) 'The production of mobilities', *Soundings*, vol 43, pp 11–26.

Crew, D.F. (1998) *Germans on welfare: from Weimar to Hitler*, Oxford: Oxford University.

Cronin, C. (1996) 'Bourdieu and Foucault on power and modernity', *Philosophy & Social Criticism*, vol 22, no 6, pp 55–85.

Cruddas, J. (2011) 'Robert Tressell – the ragged trousered philanthropist', The Roscoe Lecture, Liverpool John Moore's University, 3 March.

Cunningham, J. and Cunningham, S. (2008) *Sociology and social work*, Exeter: Learning Matters.

Danaher, G., Schirato, T. and Webb, J. (2000) *Understanding Foucault*, London: Sage.

Dant, T. (2004) 'The driver-car', *Theory, Culture & Society*, vol 21, nos 4/5, pp 61–79.

Davies, M. (1981) *The essential social worker*, London: Heinemann.

Davis, M. (2006) *Planet of slums*, London: Verso.

Deacon, A. and Mann, K. (1999) 'Agency, modernity and social policy', *Journal of Social Policy*, vol 28, pp 413–35.

Department for Education and Skills (2007) *Care matters: time for change*, London: Department for Education and Skills.

Department of Education (2010) 'Review of child protection: better frontline services to protect children', Press Notice, 10 June. Available at: http://www.education.gov.uk/news/press-notices-new/reviewofchildprotection

Department of Education (2011) *The Munro review of child protection: final report*, London: TSO.

Department of Health (1988) *Protecting children: a guide for social workers undertaking a comprehensive assessment*, London: HMSO.

Department of Health (2002) 'New social work degree will focus on practical training', Press Release, 22 May.

Department of Health, Department for Education and Employment, and Home Office (2000) *Framework for the assessment of children in need and their families*, London: Stationery Office.

Derbyshire, P. (2004) 'Spotless', *Radical Philosophy*, vol 126, pp 48–50.

Derrida, J. (1994) *Specters of Marx: the state of debt, the work of mourning and the new international*, London: Routledge.

Devine, F. and Savage, M. (2005) 'The cultural turn, sociology and class analysis', in F. Devine, M. Savage, J. Scott and R. Crompton (eds) *Rethinking class: culture, identities and lifestyle*, London: Palgrave.

Dikec, M. (2006) 'Guest editorial', *Environment and Planning D: Society and Space*, vol 24, pp 159–63.

Dolowitz, D.P., with Hulme, R., Nellis, M. and O'Neill, F. (eds) (2000) *Policy transfer and British social policy*, Maidenhead: Open University.

Dominelli, L. (1997) *Sociology for social work*, London: MacMillan.

Dominelli, L. (2002) *Feminist social work theory and practice*, London: Palgrave.

Duncombe, J. and Marsden, D. (1993) 'Love and intimacy: the gender division of emotion and "emotion work"', *Sociology*, vol 27, no 2, pp 221–43.

Dunning, J. (2011) 'Councils line up to transfer care staff to trading companies', *Community Care*, 21 March. Available at: http://www.communitycare.co.uk/Articles/2011/03/21/116506/councils-line-up-to-transfer-care-staff-to-trading-companies.htm

Dustin, D. (2007) *The McDonaldization of social work*, Aldershot: Aldgate.

Dyer-Witheford, N. (1999) *Cyber-Marx: cycles and circuits of struggle in high-technology capitalism*, Urbana and Chicago, IL: University of Illinois.

Eagleton, T. (1991) *Ideology: an introduction*, London: Verso.

Eagleton, T. (2003) *After theory*, New York, NY: Basic Books.

Ebert, T.L. (1996) *Ludic feminism and after*, Ann Arbor, MI: University of Michigan.

Edemariam, A. (2007) 'Professor with a past', *The Guardian*, 28 April, p 31.

Elliott, L. (2010) 'A brand of austerity about as progressive as Thatcher's', *The Guardian*, 26 August, p 30.

Elliott, L. (2011) 'Three years on, it's as if the crisis never happened', *The Guardian*, 30 May, p 22.

Ellison, N. (2011) 'The Conservative Party and the "Big Society"', in C. Holden, M. Kilkey and G. Ramia (eds) *Social Policy Review 23*, Bristol: The Policy Press.

Emirbayer, M. and Williams, E.M. (2005) 'Bourdieu and social work', *Social Service Review*, vol 79, no 4, pp 689–724.

Emond, R. (2003) 'Putting the care into residential: the role of young people', *Journal of Social Work*, vol 3, no 3, pp 321–37.

Fabian Society (2008) 'Flint: we must break link between council housing and worklessness', Press Release, 5 February. Available at: http://fabians.org.uk/events/socialhousing-conference-08/speech

Fabricant, M. (1985) 'The industrialization of social work practice', *Social Work*, vol 30, no 5, pp 389–96.

Fantone, L. (2007) 'Precarious changes: gender and generational politics in contemporary Italy', *Feminist Review*, vol 87, pp 5–21.

Federici, S. (2004) *Caliban and the witch: women, the body and primitive accumulation*, Brooklyn, NY: Autonomedia.

Federici, S. (2011) 'Feminism and the politics of the commons', *The Commoner*. Available at: http://www.commoner.org.uk/wp-content/uploads/2011/01/federici-feminism-and-the-politics-of-commons.pdf

Feldman, L.C. (2002) 'Redistribution, recognition, and the state: the irreducibly political dimension of injustice', *Political Theory*, vol 30, no 3, pp 410–40.

Ferguson, H. (2001) 'Social work, individualization and life politics', *British Journal of Social Work*, vol 31, no 1, pp 41–55.

Ferguson, H. (2003) 'In defence (and celebration) of individualization and life politics for social work', *British Journal of Social Work*, vol 33, no 5, pp 699–707.

Ferguson, H. (2004) *Protecting children in time: child abuse, child protection and the consequences of modernity*, Houndmills: Palgrave Macmillan.

Ferguson, H. (2005) 'Working with violence, the emotions and the psycho-social dynamics of child protection: reflections on the Victoria Climbié case', *Social Work Education*, vol 24, no 7, pp 781–95.

Ferguson, H. (2008) 'Liquid social work: welfare interventions as mobile practices', *British Journal of Social Work*, vol 38, no 3, pp 561–79.

Ferguson, H. (2010a) 'Walks, home visits and atmospheres: risk and the everyday practices and mobilities of social work and child protection', *British Journal of Social Work*, vol 40, no 4, pp 1100–17.

Ferguson, H. (2010b) 'Therapeutic journeys: the car as a vehicle for working with children and families and theorizing practice', *Journal of Social Work Practice*, vol 24, no 2, pp 121–38.

Ferguson, H, (2011) *Child protection practice*, Houndmills: Palgrave Macmillan.

Ferguson, I. (2007) 'Neoliberalism, happiness and well-being', *International Socialism*, vol 117, pp 123–43.

Ferguson, I. and Lavalette, M. (2004) 'Beyond power discourse: alienation and social work', *British Journal of Social Work*, vol 34, pp 297–312.

Ferguson, I. and Lavalette, M. (2006) 'Globalization and global justice: towards a social work of resistance', *International Social Work*, vol 49, no 3, pp 309–18.

Fine, R. (2007) *Cosmopolitanism*, Abingdon: Routledge.

Finlayson, A. (2007) 'Making sense of David Cameron', *Public Policy Research*, March–May, pp 3–11.

Finlayson, A. (2010) 'The broken society versus the social recession', *Soundings*, vol 44, pp 22–35.

Finlayson, J.G. (2005) *Habermas: a very short introduction*, Oxford: Oxford University.

Fiori, G. (1990) *Antonio Gramsci: life of a revolutionary*, London: Verso.

Fischman, G.E. and McLaren, P. (2005) 'Rethinking critical pedagogy and the Gramscian and Freirean legacies: from organic to committed intellectuals or critical pedagogy, commitment, and praxis', *Cultural Studies/Critical Methodologies*, vol 5, no 4, pp 425–47.

Forgacs, D. (1988) *A Gramsci reader*, London: Lawrence and Wishart.

Foucault, M. (1977) *Discipline and punish*, Harmondsworth: Penguin.

Foucault, M. (1980) 'The eye of power', in C. Gordon (ed) *Michel Foucault: power/knowledge*, Brighton: Harvester Press.

Foucault, M. (1988a) 'The ethic of care for the self as a practice of freedom', in J. Bernauer and D. Rasmussen (eds) *The final Foucault*, London: MIT Press.

Foucault, M. (1988b) 'The minimalist self' and 'Power and sex', in L.D. Kritzman (ed) *Michel Foucault: politics, philosophy and culture*, New York, NY: Routledge.

Foucault, M. (1988c) 'Technologies of the self', in L.H. Martin, H. Gutman and P.H. Hutton (eds) *Technologies of the self: a seminar with Michel Foucault*, Amherst, MA: University of Massachusetts.

Foucault, M. (1988d) 'Critical theory/intellectual history', in L.D. Kritzman (ed) *Michel Foucault: politics, philosophy and culture*, New York, NY: Routledge.

Fowler, B. (1997) *Pierre Bourdieu and cultural theory: critical investigations*, London: Sage.

Fowler, B. (2001) 'Pierre Bourdieu', in A. Elliot and B.S. Turner (eds) *Profiles in contemporary social theory*, London: Sage.

Fowler, B. (2003) 'Reading Pierre Bourdieu's *Masculine domination*: notes towards an intersectional analysis of gender, culture and class', *Cultural Studies*, vol 17, nos 3/4, pp 468–94.

Fram, M.S. (2004) 'Research for progressive change: Bourdieu and social work', *Social Service Review*, vol 78, no 4, pp 553–76.

Fraser, N. (1989) *Unruly practices: power, discourse and gender in contemporary social theory*, Cambridge: Polity.

Fraser, N. (1997) *Justice interruptus: critical reflections on the post-socialist condition*, London: Routledge.

Fraser, N. (1999) 'Rethinking the public sphere', in C. Calhoun (ed) *Habermas and the public sphere*, London: MIT.

Fraser, N. (2000) 'Rethinking recognition', *New Left Review*, vol 3, pp 107–20.

Fraser, N. (2003) 'Social justice in an age of identity politics: redistribution, recognition and participation', in N. Fraser and A. Honneth (eds) *Redistribution or recognition?*, London: Verso.

Fraser, N. and Gordon, L. (1997) 'A genealogy of dependency', in N. Fraser (ed) *Justice interruptus: critical reflections on the post-socialist condition*, London: Routledge.

Fraser, N. and Honneth, A. (2003) 'Introduction: redistribution or recognition?', in N. Fraser, and A. Honneth (eds) *Redistribution or recognition?*, London: Verso.

Freire, P. (1972) *Pedagogy of the oppressed*, Harmondsworth: Penguin.

Friedman, J. (2000) 'Americans again, or the new age of imperial reason', *Theory, Culture & Society*, vol 17, no 1, pp 139–46.

Friedman, P.K. (2009) 'Ethical hegemony', *Rethinking Marxism*, vol 21, no 3, pp 355–66.

Friedmann, J. (2002) 'Placemaking as project? Habitus and migration in transnational cities', in J. Hillier and E. Rooksby (eds) *Habitus: a sense of place*, Aldershot: Ashgate.

Frisby, D. (2002) *Georg Simmel*, London: Routledge.

Froggett, L. (2004) 'Holistic practice, art, creativity and the politics of recognition', *Social Work & Social Science Review*, vol 11, no 3, pp 29–51.

Furedi, F. (2004) *Therapy culture*, London: Routledge.

Gardiner, M.E. (2004) 'Wild publics and grotesque symposiums: Habermas and Bakhtin on dialogue, everyday life and the public space', *Sociological Review*, vol 52 (Supplement 1), pp 28–48.

Garrett, P.M. (1999) 'The pretence of normality: intra-family violence and the response of state agencies in Northern Ireland', *Critical Social Policy*, vol 19, no 1, pp 31–56.

Garrett, P.M. (2002) 'Social work and the "just society": diversity, difference and the sequestration of poverty', *The Journal of Social Work*, vol 2, no 2, pp 187–210.

Garrett, P.M. (2003) *Remaking social work with children and families: a critical discussion on the 'modernisation' of social care*, London: Routledge.

Garrett, P.M. (2004) *Social work and Irish People in Britain*, Policy Press: Bristol.

Garrett, P.M. (2005) 'Social work's "electronic turn": notes on the deployment of information and communication technologies in social work with children and families', *Critical Social Policy*, vol 25, no 4, pp 529–54.

Garrett, P.M. (2007a) '"Sinbin" solutions: the "pioneer" projects for "problem families" and the forgetfulness of social policy research', *Critical Social Policy*, vol 27, no 2, pp 203–30.

Garrett, P.M. (2007b) 'Learning from the "Trojan Horse"? The arrival of "Anti-Social Behaviour Orders" in Ireland', *European Journal of Social Work*, vol 10, no 4, pp 497–511.

Garrett, P.M. (2009) *'Transforming' children's services? Social work, neoliberalism and the 'modern' world*, Maidenhead: McGraw Hill/Open University.

Garrett, P.M. (2012) 'Adjusting "our notions of the nature of the state": a political reading of Ireland's child welfare crisis', *Capital and Class*, vol 36, no 2, pp 263–81.

Garrett, P.M. (forthcoming) 'A "catastrophic, inept, self-serving" Church? Re-examining three reports on child abuse in the Republic of Ireland', *Journal of Progressive Human Services*.

Garrity, Z. (2010) 'Discourse analysis, Foucault and social work research', *Journal of Social Work*, vol 10, no 2, pp 193–210.

Garvey, T.G. (2000) 'The value of opacity: a Bakhtian analysis of Habermas's discourse ethics', *Philosophy and Rhetoric*, vol 33, no 4, pp 370–90.

Gaughan, L. and Garrett, P.M. (2011) 'The "most twisted and unaccountable force in the state"? Newspaper accounts of social work in the Republic of Ireland in troubled times', *Journal of Social Work*, vol 12, no 3, pp 267-86.

Geoghegan, L. and Lever, J., with McGimpsey, I. (2004) *ICT for social welfare*, Bristol: The Policy Press.

Geoghegan, R. and Boyd, E. (2011) *Inside job: creating a market for real work in prison*, London: Policy Exchange.

Germino, D. (1986) 'Antonio Gramsci: from the margins to the center, the journey of a hunchback', *Boundary 2*, vol 14, no 3, pp 19–30.

Giddens, A. (1991) *Modernity and self-identity*, Cambridge: Polity.

Giddens, A. (1994a) 'Living in a post-traditional society', in U. Beck, A. Giddens and S. Lash (ed) *Reflexive modernization*, Cambridge: Polity.

Giddens, A. (1994b) *Beyond left and right*, Cambridge: Polity.

Giddens, A. (1998) *The Third Way: the renewal of social democracy*, Cambridge: Polity.

Giddens, A. (ed) (2001) *The global Third Way debate*, Cambridge: Polity.

Giddens, A. (2003) 'Introduction – neoprogressivism: a new agenda for social democracy', in A. Giddens (ed) *The progressive manifesto*, Cambridge: Polity.

Giddens, A. (2007) *Over to you, Mr Brown: how Labour can win again*, Cambridge: Polity.

Gill, R. and Pratt, A. (2008) 'Precarity and cultural work: in the social factory?', *Theory, Culture & Society*, vol 25, nos 7–8, pp 1–30.

Gill, S. (2000) 'Toward a postmodern prince? The Battle in Seattle as a moment in the new politics of globalisation', *Millennium: Journal of International Studies*, vol 29, no 1, pp 131–40.

Gilroy, P. (2000) *Between camps: nations, cultures and the allure of race*, Harmondsworth: Penguin.

Goffman, I. (1971 [1959]) *The presentation of self in everyday life*, Harmondsworth: Pelican.

Goldman, E. (1969) *Anarchism and other essays*, New York, NY: Dover.

Goldman, R. and Papson, S. (2011) *Landscapes of capital*, Cambridge: Polity.

Goldson, B. (2009) '"Child incarceration": institutional abuse, the violent state and the politics of impunity', in P. Scraton (ed) *The violence of incarceration*, London: Routledge.

Goode, L. (2005) *Jürgen Habermas: democracy and the public sphere*, London: Pluto.

Good Goodrich, L. (2010) 'Single mothers, work(fare), and managed precariousness', *Journal of Progressive Human Services*, vol 21, no 2, pp 107–35.

Graeber, D. (2008) 'The sadness of post-workerism', *Tate Britain*, 19 January. Available at: http://www.commoner.org.uk/wp-content/uploads/2008/04/graeber_sadness.pdf

Gramsci, A. (1979) *Letters from prison*, London: Quartet.

Grandin, G. (2010) *Fordlandia*, London: Icon.

Grass, G. and Bourdieu, P. (2002) 'The "progressive" restoration', *New Left Review*, March/April, 14, pp 63–79.

Gray, M. and Webb, S. (eds) (2009) *Social work theories and methods*, London: Sage.

Gregg, M. (2011) *Work's intimacy*, Cambridge: Polity.

Gregg, P. (2008) *Realising potential: a vision for personalised conditionality and support*, London: Department for Work and Pensions.

Griffiths, T. (2007) *Three plays 1*, Nottingham: Russell House.

Guillari, S. and Shaw, M. (2005) 'Supporting or controlling? New Labour's housing strategy for teenage parents', *Critical Social Policy*, vol 25, no 3 pp 402–17.

Gunn, S. (2005) 'Translating Bourdieu: cultural capital and the English middle class in historical perspective', *British Journal of Sociology*, vol 56, no 1, pp 50–65.

Guru, S. (2010) 'Social work and the "war on terror"', *British Journal of Social Work*, vol 40, no 1, pp 272–89.

Habermas, J. (1984) *The theory of communicative action, vol 1*, Cambridge: Polity.

Habermas, J. (1987) *The theory of communicative action, vol 2*, Cambridge: Polity.

Habermas, J. (1990) *Moral consciousness and communicative action*, Cambridge: Polity.

Habermas, J. (1996) *Between facts and norms*, Cambridge: Polity.

Habermas, J. (1997) *A Berlin republic: writings on Germany*, Lincoln, NE: University of Nebraska.

Habermas, J. (2001a) *On the pragmatics of social interaction*, Cambridge, MA: MIT.

Habermas, J. (2001b) *The postnational constellation: political essays*, Cambridge: Polity.

Habermas, J. (2003) 'Interpreting the fall of a monument', *Constellations*, vol 10, no 3, pp 364–71.

Habermas, J. (2006) *The structural transformation of the public space*, Cambridge: Polity (first published in German in 1962 and in English in 1989).

Habermas, J. et al. (2010) *An awareness of what is missing*, Cambridge: Polity.

Haddour, A. (2009) 'Bread and wine: Bourdieu's photography of colonial Africa', *Sociological Review*, vol 57, no 3, pp 385–06.

Hall, S. (1993) 'Thatcherism today', *New Statesmen and Society*, 26 November, pp 14–17.

Hall, S. (1996) 'Gramsci's relevance for the study of race and ethnicity', in D. Morley and K.-H. Chen (eds) *Stuart Hall: critical dialogues in cultural studies*, London: Routledge.

Hall, S. (1998) 'The great moving nowhere show', *Marxism Today*, Nov/Dec, pp 9–15.

Hall, S. (2002) 'Gramsci and us', in J. Martin (ed) *Antonio Gramsci: critical assessments of leading political philosophers*, London: Routledge.

Hall, S. (2003) 'New Labour's double-shuffle', *Soundings*, vol 24, pp 10–25.

Hall, S. and Jacques, M. (1989) *New times: the changing face of politics in the 1990s*, London: Lawrence & Wishart.

Hall, S., Critcher, C., Jefferson, T., Clarke, J. and Roberts, B. (1978) *Policing the crisis: mugging, the state and law and order*, Houndmills: MacMillan Education.

Hallsworth, S. (2005) 'Modernity and the punitiveness', in J. Pratt, D. Brown, M. Brown, S. Hallsworth and W. Morrison (eds) *The new punitiveness: trends, theories and perspectives*, Devon: Willan.

Hallward, P. (2002) 'Badiou's politics: equality and justice', *Culture Machine*, 2. Available at: http://www.culturemachine.net/index.php/cm/article/view/271/256

Hallward, P. (2008) 'Order and event', *New Left Review*, vol 53, pp 125–35.

Hanna, S. (2010) 'Call centres as sites of professional practice: "where old social workers go to die"?', *Australian Social Work*, vol 63, no 3, pp 266–80.

Hardt, M. (1999) 'Affective labor', *Boundary 2*, vol 26, no 2, pp 89–101.

Hardt, M. and Negri, A. (2000) *Empire*, Cambridge, MA: Harvard University.

Hardt, M. and Negri, A. (2006) *Multitude*, London: Penguin.

Hardt, M. and Weeks, K. (eds) (2000) *The Jameson reader*, Oxford: Blackwell.

Hare, I. (2004) 'Defining social work for the 21st century: the International Federation of Social Workers' revised definition of social work', *International Social Work*, vol 47, no 3 pp 407–27.

Harlow, E. (2004) 'Why don't women want to be social workers anymore? New managerialism, postfeminism and the shortage of social workers in Social Services Departments in England and Wales', *European Journal of Social Work*, vol 7, no 2, pp 167–79.

Harlow, E. and Webb, S.A. (eds) (2003) *Information and communication technologies in the welfare services*, London: Jessica Kingsley.

Harman, C. (2008) 'Theorising neoliberalism', *International Socialism*, vol 117, pp 25–49.

Harris, J. (1998) 'Scientific management, bureau-professionalism, new managerialism: the Labour process of state social work', *British Journal of Social Work*, vol 28, pp 839–62.

Harris, J. (2003) *The social work business*, London: Routledge.

Harvey, D. (2005) *A brief history of neoliberalism*, Oxford: Oxford University.

Harvey, D. (2006a) *Limits to capital*, London: Verso.

Harvey, D. (2006b) *Spaces of global capitalism*, London: Verso.

Harvey, D. (2010) *The enigma of capital*, London: Verso.

Hasan, M. (2011) 'How fear of criminalization forces Muslims into silence', *The Guardian*, 9 September, p 34.

Haugaard, M. (ed) (2002) *Power: a reader*, Manchester: Manchester University Press.

Hayes, D. and Houston, S. (2007) '"Lifeworld", "system" and family group conferences: Habermas's contribution to discourse in child protection', *British Journal of Social Work*, vol 37, no 6, pp 987–1006.

Haylett, C. (2001) 'Modernisation, welfare and "third way" politics: limits in "thirds"?', *Transactions of the Institute of British Geographers*, vol 26, no 1, pp 43–56.

Hayward, C.R. (2003) 'The difference states make: democracy, identity, and the American city', *American Political Science Review*, vol 97, no 4, pp 501–15.

Haywood, K. and Yar, M. (2006) 'The "chav" phenomenon: Consumption, media and the construction of a new underclass', *Crime, Media, Culture*, vol 2, no 1, pp 9–28.

Heller, A. (1982) 'Habermas and Marxism', in J.B. Thompson and D. Held (eds) *Habermas: critical debates*, London: Macmillan.

Hennessy, M. (2011) 'Englishman's council house may not always be his home', *The Irish Times*, 17 November, p 12.

Hewlett, N. (2004) 'Engagement and transcendence: the militant philosophy of Alain Badiou', *Modern & Contemporary France*, vol 12, no 3, pp 335–52.

Hewlett, N. (2006) 'Politics as thought? The paradoxes of Alain Badiou's theory of politics', *Contemporary Political Theory*, vol 5, pp 371–404.

Hickman, M.J., Morgan, S., Walter, B. and Bradley, J. (2005) 'The limitations of whiteness and the boundaries of Englishness', *Ethnicities*, vol 5, no 2, pp 160–82.

Hietala, M. (1996) 'From race hygiene to sterilisation: the eugenics movement in Finland', in G. Broberg and N. Roll-Hansen (eds) *Eugenics and the welfare state*, East Lansing, MI: Michigan State University.

Hirschkop, K. (1999) *Mikhail Bakhtin*, Oxford: Oxford University.

Hirschkop, K. (2000) 'Its too good to talk: myths of dialogue in Bakhtin and Habermas', *New Formations*, vol 41, pp 83–94.

Hirschkop, K. (2004) 'Justice and drama: on Bakhtin as a complement to Habermas', *Sociological Review*, vol 52 (Supplement), pp 49–66.

Hirschkop, K. and Shephard, D. (eds) (2001) *Bakhtin and cultural theory*, Manchester: Manchester University.

Hoare, Q. (ed) (1988) *Antonio Gramsci: selections from political writings (1910–1920)*, London: Lawrence and Wishart.

Hoare, Q. and Nowell Smith (eds) (2005) *Antonio Gramsci: selections from prison notebooks* (10th reprint), London: Lawrence and Wishart.

Hobsbawm, E. (2007) 'Critical sociology and social history', *Sociological Research Online*, vol 12, no 4. Available at: http://www.socresonline.org.uk/12/4/2.html

Hobsbawm, E. (2008) 'The £500bn question', *The Guardian*, 9 October, p 28.

Hobsbawm, E. (2011) *How to change the world: tales of Marx and Marxism*, London: Little, Brown.

Hoggett, P. (2001) 'Agency, rationality and social policy', *Journal of Social Policy*, vol 30, no 1, pp 37–56.

Holland, T. (2010) 'Face to faith', *The Guardian*, 27 February, p 37.

Holt, S. (2003) 'Child protection social work and men's abuse of women: an Irish study', *Child and Family Social Work*, vol 8, pp 53–65.

Honneth, A. (1995) *The struggle for recognition*, Cambridge: Polity.

Hourigan, N. (ed) (2011) *Understanding Limerick: social exclusion and change*, Cork: Cork University.

Houston, S. (2002) 'Reflecting on habitus, field and capital: towards a culturally sensitive social work', *Journal of Social Work*, vol 2, no 2, pp 149–67.

Houston, S. (2003) 'Moral consciousness and decision-making in child and family social work', *Adoption & Fostering*, vol 27, no 3, pp 61–71.

Houston, S. (2008) 'Transcending ethnoreligious identities in Northern Ireland: social work's role in the struggle for recognition', *Australian Social Work*, vol 61, no 1, pp 25–41.

Houston, S. (2009) 'Jürgen Habermas', in M. Gray and S.A. Webb (eds) *Social work: theories and methods*, London: Sage.

Houston, S. (2010a) 'Further reflections on Habermas's contribution to discourse in child protection: an examination of power in social life', *British Journal of Social Work*, vol 40, no 6, pp 1736–53.

Houston, S. (2010b) 'Beyond Homo Economicus: recognition, self-realization and social work', *British Journal of Social Work*, vol 40, no 3, pp 841–57.

Houston, S. and Dolan, P. (2008) 'Conceptualising child and family support: the contribution of Honneth's critical theory of recognition', *Children & Society*, vol 22, no 6, pp 458–69.

Houston, S., Skehill, C., Pinkerton, J. and Campbell, J. (2005) 'Prying open the space for social work in the new millenium: four theoretical perspectives on transformative practice', *Social Work & Social Sciences Review*, vol 12, pp 35–52.

Howe, D. (1994) 'Modernity, postmodernity and social work', *British Journal of Social Work*, vol 24, no 5, pp 513–32.

Hudis, P. and Anderson, K.B. (eds) (2004) *The Rosa Luxemburg reader*, New York, NY: Monthly Review Press.

Hussein, A.A. (2004) *Edward Said: criticism and society*, London: Verso.

Hutton, W. (2011) 'In focus', *The Observer*, 7 August, pp 24–5.

Hutton, W. and Giddens, A. (eds) (2000) *On the edge: living with global capitalism*, London: Jonathan Cope.

Iarskaia-Smirnova, E. and Romanoz, P. (2002) 'A salary is not important here: the professionalization of social work in contemporary Russia', *Social Policy & Administration*, vol 36, no 2, pp 123–41.

ICO (Information Commissioner's Office) (2006) 'A report on the surveillance society: for the Information Commissioner by the surveillance studies network'. Available at: http://www.ico.gov.uk/upload/documents/library/data_protection/practical_application/surveillance_society_full_report_2006.pdf

ICO (2010) 'Information Commissioner's report to Parliament on the state of surveillance'. Available at: http://www.ico.gov.uk/~/media/documents/library/Corporate/Research_and_reports/ surveillance_report_for_home_select_committee.ashx

IFSW (International Federation of Social Workers) (2000) 'Definition of social work'. Available at: http://www.ifsw.org/f38000138.html

Imre, R. (2009) 'Badiou and the philosophy of social work', *International Journal of Social Work*, vol 19, pp 253–8.

Irish Prison Chaplains (2010) 'The Irish Chaplains' annual report'. Available at: http://www.catholicbishops.ie/2010/11/29/irish-prison-chaplains-annual-report-2010/

Irving, A. and Young, T. (2002) 'Paradigm for pluralism: Mikhail Bakhtin and social work practice', *Social Work*, vol 47, no 1, pp 19–29.

Ives, P. (2004a) *Language and hegemony in Gramsci*, London: Pluto.

Ives, P. (2004b) *Gramsci's politics of language: engaging the Bakhtin Circle and the Frankfurt School*, Toronto: University of Toronto.

Jackson, N. and Carter, P. (1998) 'Labour as dressage', in A. McKinley and K. Starkey (eds) *Foucault, management and organization theory*, London: Sage.

Jacques, M. (2008) 'Northern Rock's rescue is part of a geopolitical sea change', *The Guardian*, 18 January, p 23.

James, A.L. (2004) 'The McDonaldization of social work – or "come back Florence Hollis, all is (or should be) forgiven', in R. Lovelock, K. Lyons and J. Powell (eds) *Reflecting on social work – discipline and profession*, Aldershot: Ashgate.

Jameson, F. (1991) *Postmodernism, or the cultural logic of late capitalism*, London: Verso.

Jameson, F. (2000) 'Postmodernism, or the cultural logic of late capitalism', in M. Hardt and K. Weeks (eds) *The Jameson reader*, Oxford: Blackwell.

Jayaram, N. (2011) 'Caste, corporate disabilities and compensatory disabilities in India: colonial legacy and post-colonial paradox', in J. Midgley and D. Piachaud (eds) *Colonialism and welfare: social policy and British imperialism*, Cheltenham: Edward Elgar.

Jeffery, L. (2011) *Understanding agency: social welfare and social change*, Bristol: The Policy Press.

Jenkins, R. (2002) *Pierre Bourdieu*, London: Routledge.

Jeyasingham, D. (2011) 'White noise: a critical evaluation of social work education's engagement with whiteness studies', *British Journal of Social Work*, advanced electronic access from 7 August.

Jones, C. (1983) *State social work and the working class*, London: MacMillan.

Jones, C. (1996) 'Anti-intellectualism and the peculiarities of British social work education', in N. Parton (ed) *Social theory, social change and social work*, London: Routledge.

Jones, C. (2001) 'Voices from the front line: state social workers and New Labour', *British Journal of Social Work*, vol 31, no 4, pp 547–62.

Jones, C. (2011) 'The best and worst of times: reflections on the impact of radicalism on British social work education in the 1970s', in M. Lavalette (ed) *Radical social work today: social work at the crossroads*, Bristol: Policy Press.

Jones, O. (2011) *Chavs: the demonization of the working class*, London: Verso.

Jones, R. (2012) *Border Walls*, London: Zed Books.

Jones, S. (2006) *Antonio Gramsci*, London: Routledge.

Jordan, B., with Jordan, C. (2000) *Social work and the Third Way*, London: Sage.

Jordan, B. (2001) 'Tough love: social work, social exclusion and the Third Way', *British Journal of Social Work*, vol 31, pp 527–46.

Jordan, B. (2007) *Social work and well-being*, Lyme Regis: Russell House.

Jose, J. (2009) 'Rethinking social work ethics: what is the real question?', *International Journal of Social Welfare*, vol 19, pp 246–52.

Joseph, J. (2006) *Marxism and social theory*, Houndmills: Palgrave Macmillan.

Joyce, P., Corrigan, P. and Hayes, M. (1988) *Striking out: trade unionism and social work*, London: Macmillan Education.

Kagarlitsky, B. (2009) *Back in the USSR*, London: Seagull.

Karakayli, N. (2004) 'Reading Bourdieu with Adorno: the limits of critical theory and reflexive sociology', *Sociology*, vol 38, no 2, pp 351–68.

Kendall, L. and Harker, L. (2002) *From welfare to wellbeing: the future of social care*, London: IPPR.

Kentikelenis, A., Karanikolos, M., Papanicolas, I., Basu, S., McKee, M. and Stuckler, D. (2011) 'Health effects of financial crisis: omens of a Greek tragedy', *The Lancet*, published online 10 October. Available at: http://www.thelancet.com/journals/lancet/article/PIIS0140-6736(11)61556-0/fulltext

Kitson, F. (1991 [1971]) *Low intensity operations: subversion, insurgency and peacekeeping*, London: Faber and Faber.

Klein, N. (2001) *No logo*, London: Flamingo.

Klein, N. (2007) *The shock doctrine: the rise of disaster capitalism*, London: Allen Lane.

Klein, N. (2011) 'If you rob people of the little they have, expect resistance', *The Guardian*, 18 August, p 35.

Krane, J. and Davies, L. (2000) 'Mothering and child protection practice: rethinking risk assessment', *Child and Family Social Work*, vol 5, pp 35–45.

Kunstreich, T. (2003) 'Social welfare in Nazi Germany', *Journal of Progressive Human Services*, vol 14, no 2, pp 23–53.

Laclau, E. and Mouffe, C. (1985) *Hegemony and socialist strategy*, London: Verso.

Landy, M. (1986) 'Culture and politics in the work of Antonio Gramsci', *Boundary 2*, vol 14, no 3, pp 49–70.

Landy, M. (1994) *Film, politics and Gramsci*, Minneapolis, MN: University of Minnesota.

Lane, J. (2000) *Pierre Bourdieu: a critical introduction*, London: Pluto.

Lane, T. (1987) *Liverpool: gateway of empire*, London: Lawrence and Wishart.

Langan, M. (2011) 'Rediscovering radicalism and humanity in social work', in M. Lavalette (ed) *Radical social work today: social work at the crossroads*, Bristol: The Policy Press.

Langman, L. and Ryan, M. (2009) 'Capitalism and the carnival character', *Critical Sociology*, vol 35, no 4, pp 471–92.

Lasdun, J. (2007) *Seven lies*, London: Vintage.

Lash, S. (1990) *Sociology of postmodernism*, London: Routledge.

Lau, R.W.K. (2004) 'Habitus and the practical logic of practice', *Sociology*, vol 38, no 2, pp 369–87.

Laurier, E. (2004) 'Doing office work on the motorway', *Theory, Culture & Society*, vol 21, nos 4/5, pp 261–77.

Lavalette, M. (ed) (2011a) *Radical social work today: social work at the crossroads*, Bristol: The Policy Press.

Lavalette, M. (2011b) 'Introduction', in M. Lavalette (ed) *Radical social work today: social work at the crossroads*, Bristol: The Policy Press.

Lazzarato, M. (1996) 'Immaterial labor', in P. Virno and M. Hardt (eds) *Radical thought in Italy*, Minneapolis, MN: University of Minneapolis.

Leggett, W. (2009) 'Prince of modernisers: Gramsci, New Labour and the meaning of modernity', in M. McNally and J. Schwarzmantel (eds) *Gramsci and global politics*, London: Routledge.

Le Grand, J. (2007) *Consistent care matters: exploring the potential of social work practices*, London: Department for Education and Skills.

Lemert, C. (2000) 'The clothes have no emperor: Bourdieu on American imperialism', *Theory, Culture & Society*, vol 17, no 1, pp 97–106.

Lenin, V.I. (1981) *Left-wing communism, an infantile disorder* (8th printing), Moscow, USSR: Progress Publishers.

Levy, A. and Kahan, B. (1991) *The pindown experience and the protection of children*, Stafford: Staffordshire County Council.

Lewis, G. (2005) 'Welcome to the margins: diversity, tolerance, and the politics of exclusion', *Ethnic and Racial Studies*, vol 28, no 3, pp 536–58.

Lewis, G. and Neal, S. (2005) 'Introduction: contemporary political contexts, changing terrains and revisited discourses', *Ethnic and Racial Studies*, vol 28, no 3, pp 423–44.

Lindner, K. (2010) 'Marx's Eurocentrism: postcolonial studies and Marx scholarship', *Radical Philosophy*, vol 161, pp 27–42.

Liogier, R. (2010) 'The attack on the veil is a huge blunder', *The Guardian*, 27 January, p 30.

Llewellyn, A., Agu, L. and Mercer, D. (2008) *Sociology for social workers*, Cambridge: Polity.

Lombard, D. (2010) 'More councils likely to follow Suffolk in outsourcing services', *Community Care*, 24 September. Available at: http://www.communitycare.co.uk/Articles/2010/09/24/115418/more-councils-likely-to-follow-suffolk-in-outsourcing-services.htm

Lopez, J. and Potter, G. (2001) *After postmodernism*, London: Athlone.

Lorenz, W. (1993) *Social work in a changing Europe*, London: Routledge.

Lorenz, W. (2005) 'Social work and a new social order – challenging neo-liberalism's erosion of solidarity', *Social Work & Society*, vol 3, no 1. Available at: http://socwork.net/Lorenz2005.pdf

Lovell, T. (2000) 'Thinking feminism with and against Bourdieu', in B. Fowler (ed) *Reading Bourdieu on society and culture*, Oxford: Blackwell.

Lovell, T. (2004) 'Bourdieu, class and gender: "the return of the living dead"', *Sociological Review*, vol 53, no 2, pp 37–57.

Lovell, T. (ed) (2007) *(Mis)recognition, social inequality and social justice: Nancy Fraser and Pierre Bourdieu*, London: Routledge.

Loyal, S. (2003) 'Welcome to the Celtic Tiger: racism, immigration and the state', in C. Coulter and S. Coleman (eds) *The end of Irish history?*, Manchester: Manchester University.

Loyal, S. (2009) 'The French in Algeria, Algerians in France: Bourdieu, colonialism and migration', *Sociological Review*, vol 57, no 3, pp 406–28.

Lyon, D. (1994) *Postmodernity*, Buckingham: Open University Press.

Lyon, D. (2001a) *Surveillance society: monitoring everyday life*, Buckingham: Open University.

Lyon, D. (2001b) 'Surveillance after September 11', *Sociological Research Online*, vol 6, no 3. Available at: http://www.socresonline.org.uk/6/3/lyon.html.

Lyon, D. (2003) *Surveillance after September 11*, Cambridge: Polity Press.

Lyon, D. (ed) (2006) *Theorizing surveillance*, Devon: Willan.

Lyotard, J.-F. (1984) *The postmodern condition: a report on knowledge*, Manchester: Manchester University.

MacCormaic, R. (2009) 'Four years after the riots, and little has changed in the French suburbs', *The Irish Times Weekend Review*, p 3.

MacGregor, D. (1996) *Hegel, Marx, and the English state*, London: University of Toronto.

MacKinnon, S.T. (2009) 'Social work intellectuals in the twenty-first century: critical social theory, critical social work and public engagement', *Social Work Education*, vol 28, no 5, pp 512–27.

Mancini Billson, J. and Fluehr-Lobban, C. (eds) (2005) *Female well-being: towards a theory of social change*, London: Zed Books.

Marcuse, H. (1991) *One-dimensional man*, Oxford: Routledge.

Marcuse, H. (2001) *Legacies of Dachau: the uses and abuses of a concentration camp, 1933–2001*, Cambridge: Cambridge University.

Markell, P. (2003) *Bound by recognition*, Princeton, NJ, and Oxford: Princeton University.

Marthinsen, E. and Skjefstad, N. (2011) 'Recognition as a virtue in social work practice', *European Journal of Social Work*, vol 14, no 2, pp 195–213.

Martin, J. (1998) *Gramsci's political analysis*, Houndmills: Macmillan.

Martin, J. (2002) 'The political logic of discourse: a neo-Gramscian view', *History of European Ideas*, vol 28, pp 21–31.

Martin, J. (2006) 'Piero Gobetti's agonistic liberalism', *History of European Ideas*, vol 32, pp 205–22.

Marx, K. (1990) *Capital, volume 1*, London: Penguin.

Marx, K. and Engels, F. (1978) *The communist manifesto*, Harmondsworth: Penguin.

Massey, D. (2010) 'The political struggle ahead', *Soundings*, vol 45, pp 9–19.

Mathiason, N. (2007) 'Children's homes hit by buyout fears', *The Observer*, 14 October. Available at: http://society.guardian.co.uk/children/story/0,,2191473,00.html

Matthewman, S. and Hoey, D. (2006) 'What happened to postmodernism?' *Sociology*, vol 40, no 3, pp 529–47.

May, T. (2005) 'Transformations in academic production', *European Journal of Social Theory*, vol 8, no 2, pp 193–209.

McClintock, A. (1995) *Imperial Leather: race, gender and sexuality in the colonial conquest*, London: Routledge.

McGregor, K. (2011a) 'Tenth of social care workers paid less than minimum', *Community Care*, 11 April. Available at: http://www.communitycare.co.uk/Articles/2011/04/11/116645/tenth-of-social-care-workers-paid-less-than-minimum-wage.htm

McGregor, K. (2011b) 'Social work assistants asked to take complex cases', *Community Care*, 13 April. Available at: http://www.communitycare.co.uk/Articles/2011/04/13/116673/social-work-assistants-asked-to-take-complex-cases.htm

McGuigan, J. (2009) *Cool capitalism*, London: Pluto.

McKay, S. (1998) *Sophie's story*, Dublin: Gill & Macmillan.

McKinley, A. and Starkey, K. (eds) (1998) *Foucault, management and organization theory*, London: Sage.

McLaughlin, K. (2007) 'Regulation and risk in social work: the general social care council and the social care register in context', *British Journal of Social Work*, vol 37, no 2, pp 1263–77.

McLaughlin, K. (2008) *Social work, politics and society*, Bristol: Policy Press.

McLaughlin, K. (2010) 'The social worker versus the general social care council: an analysis of care standards tribunal hearings and decisions', *British Journal of Social Work*, vol 40, no 1, pp 311–27.

McLellan, D. (ed) (2000) *Karl Marx: selected writings* (2nd edn), Oxford: Oxford University Press.

McLennan, G. (2001) 'Can there be a "critical" multiculturalism?', *Ethnicities*, vol 1, no 3, pp 389–422.

McLennan, G. and Squires, J. (2004) 'Intellectuals and tendencies', *Soundings*, vol 27, pp 86–95.

McNay, L. (1999) 'Gender, habitus and field: Pierre Bourdieu and the limits of reflexivity', *Theory, Culture & Society*, vol 16, no 1, pp 95–117.

McNay, L. (2008) *Against recognition*, Cambridge: Polity.

McRobbie, A. (2010) 'Reflections on feminism, immaterial labour and the post-Fordist regime', *New Formations*, vol 70, pp 60–77.

Mental Health Commission (2011a) 'The use of seclusion, mechanical means of bodily restraint and physical restraint in approved centres: activities report 2009'. Available at: http://www.mhcirl.ie/Publications/Seclusion+Restraint_Report%20_2009.pdf

Mental Health Commission (2011b) 'The human cost: an overview of the evidence on economic adversity and mental health and recommendations for action'. Available at: http://www.mhcirl.ie/News_Events/HCPaper.pdf

Merrill Lynch and Capgemini (2011) 'Merrill Lynch global wealth management and Capgemini release 15th annual world wealth report', Press Release, 22 June. Available at: http://www.capgemini.com/news-and-events/news/merrill-lynch-global-wealth-management-and-capgemini-release-15th-annual-world-wealth-report/

Mickel, A. (2011) 'Pain at the pumps for social workers as the value of their driving allowances fall', *Community Care*, 22 March. Available at: http://www.communitycare.co.uk/Articles/2011/03/22/116509/rising-petrol-prices-put-the-squeeze-on-social-work-practitioners.htm

Midgley, J. and Piachaud, D. (eds) (2011) *Colonialism and welfare: social policy and British imperialism*, Cheltenham: Edward Elgar.

Miliband, E. (2011) 'Responsibility in 21st century Britain', Coin Street Neighbourhood Centre, 13 June.

Miller, J. (1993) *The passion of Michel Foucault*, London: Harper Collins.

Miller, P. and Rose, N. (2008) *Governing the present*, Cambridge: Polity.

Milne, S. (2011) 'The fallout from the crash of 2008 has only just begun', *The Guardian*, 10 March, p 33.

Milner, J. (1993) 'A disappearing act: the differing career paths of fathers and mothers in child protection investigations', *Critical Social Policy*, vol 13, no 2, pp 48–64.

Mirsepassi, A. (2000) *Intellectual discourse and the politics of modernization*, Cambridge: Cambridge University.

Modood, T. and Dobbernack, J. (2011) 'A left communitarianism? What about multiculturalism?', *Soundings*, vol 48, pp 54–66.

Moi, T. (1991) 'Appropriating Bourdieu: feminist theory and Pierre Bourdieu's sociology of culture', *New Literary History*, vol 22, pp 1017–49.

Mooney, T. (2003) 'Celebrity chairs', *Education Guardian*, 20 August.

Morini, C. (2007) 'The feminization of labour in cognitive capitalism', *Feminist Review*, vol 87, pp 40–60.

Morton, A.D. (2003) 'Historicising Gramsci: situating ideas in and beyond their context', *Review of International Political Economy*, vol 10, no 1, pp 118–46.

Moss, J. (ed) (1988) *The later Foucault*, London: Sage.

Mottier, V. and Gerodetti, N. (2007) 'Eugenics and social democracy: or, how the European left tried to eliminate "weeds" from its national gardens', *Soundings*, vol 60, pp 35–50.

Mullaly, B. (1997) *Structural social work*, Toronto: Oxford University.

Munck, R. (2005) 'Neoliberalism and politics, and the politics of neoliberalism', in A. Saad-Filho and D. Johnston (eds) *Neoliberalism: a critical reader*, London: Pluto.

Munro, E. (2011) 'The Munro review of child protection: interim report – the child's journey'. Available at: http://www.education.gov.uk/munroreview/downloads/Munrointerimreport.pdf

Murphy, F.D., Buckley, H. and Joyce, L. (2005) *The Ferns report*, Dublin: Stationery Office.

Murray, G. (2006) 'France: the riots and the Republic', *Race & Class*, vol 47, no 4, pp 26–45.

Nairn, T. (1964) 'The British political elite', *New Left Review*, vol 23, pp 19–26.

Negri, A. (2005a) *The politics of subversion: a manifesto for the twenty-first century*, Cambridge: Polity.

Negri, A. (2005b [1997]) *Books for burning: between civil war and democracy in 1970s Italy*, London: Verso.

Negri, A. (2009) *The labor of job*, Durham, NC: Duke University.

Neilson, G. (1995) 'Bakhtin and Habermas: towards a transcultural ethics', *Theory and Society*, vol 24, pp 803–34.

Neilson, G. (2002) *The norms of answersability: social theory between Bakhtin and Habermas*, Albany, NY: State University of New York.

Nickels, H.C., Thomas, L., Hickman, M.J. and Silvestri, S. (2011) 'De/constructing "suspect' communities", *Journalism Studies*, IFirst Article.

Noble, G. and Watkins, M. (2003) 'So, how did Bourdieu learn to play tennis? Habitus, consciousness and habitation', *Cultural Studies*, vol 17, nos 3/4, pp 520–38.

Norris, C. (2009) *Badiou's being and event*, London: Continuum.

NSWQB (National Social Work Qualification Board) (2006) *Social work posts in Ireland*, Dublin: NSWQB.

Ofsted, Healthcare Commission and HMIC (Her Majesty's Inspectorate of Constabulary) (2008) *Joint area review: Haringey children's services authority area.* Available at: http://www.ofsted.gov.uk/oxcare_providers/la_download/ (id)/4657/(as)/JAR/jar_2008_309_fr.pdf

Oliver, K. (2004) 'Witnessing and testimony', *Parallax*, vol 10, no 1, pp 79–88.

Orzeck, R. (2007) 'What does not kill you: historical materialism and the body', *Environment and Planning D: Society and Space*, vol 25, no 3, pp 496–514.

Osborne, D. and Gaebler, T.A. (1992) *Reinventing government: how the entrepreneurial spirit is transforming the public sector*, Reading, MA: Addison Wesley.

Outhwaite, W. (1996) *The Habermas reader*, Cambridge: Polity.

Ovenden, K. (2000) 'The politics of protest', *Socialist Review*, vol 242. Available at: http://pubs.socialistreviewindex.org.uk/sr242/ovenden.htm

Parker, D. (2000) 'The Chinese takeaway and the diasporic habitus: space, time and power geometrics', in B. Hesse (ed) *Unsettled multiculturalisms*, London: Zed Books.

Parker, R., Ward, H., Jackson, S., Aldgate, J. and Wedge, P. (1991) *Looking after children: assessing outcomes in child care*, London: HMSO.

Parsloe, P. (1981) *Social services area teams*, London: George Allen and Unwin.

Parton, N. (1994) 'Problematics of government, (post)modernity and social work', *British Journal of Social Work*, vol 24, no 1, pp 9–32.

Parton, N. and Marshall, W. (1998) 'Postmodernism and discourse approaches to social work', in R. Adams, L. Dominelli and M. Payne (eds) *Social work, themes, issues and critical debates*, London: Macmillan.

Parton, N. and O'Byrne, P. (2000) *Constructive social work*, London: MacMillan.

Pease, B. and Fook, J. (eds) (1999) *Transforming social work practice: postmodern critical perspectives*, London: Routledge.

Peck, J. (2005) 'Struggling with the creative class', *International Journal of Urban and Regional Research*, vol 29, no 4, pp 740–70.

Peck, J. (2010) *Constructions of neoliberal reason*, Oxford: Oxford University.

Peillon, M. (1998) 'Bourdieu's field and the sociology of welfare', *Journal of Social Policy*, vol 27, no 2, pp 213–29.

Pemberton, C. (2010) 'Sterilise parents who abuse children', *Community Care*, 24 August. Available at: http://www.communitycare.co.uk/ Articles/2010/08/24/115157/sterilise-parents-who-abuse-children-top-professor-says.htm

Pemberton, C. (2011) 'Council seeks to close down its children homes', *Community Care*, 25 May. Available at: http://www.communitycare.co.uk/ Articles/2011/05/25/116879/council-seeks-to-close-down-its-children-homes.htm

Perelman, M. (2000) *The invention of capitalism*, Durham, NC, and London: Duke University.

Peters, T. (1997) 'The brand called you', *Fast Company*, 31 August. Available at: http://www.fastcompany.com/magazine/10/brandyou.html

Pileggi, M.S. and Patton, C. (2003) 'Bourdieu and cultural studies', *Cultural Studies*, vol 17, nos 3/4, pp 313–25.

Pine, L. (1995) 'Hasude: the imprisonment of "asocial" families in the Third Reich', *The Germany History Society*, vol 13, no 2, pp 182–98.

Pine, L. (1997) *Nazi family policy 1933–1945*, Oxford: Berg.

Pithouse, A. (1998 [1987]) *Social work: the social organisation of an invisible trade*, Aldershot: Avebury.

Platt, D. (2007) 'The status of social care – a review'. Available at: http://www.dh.gov. uk/en/Publicationsandstatistics/Publications/PublicationsPolicyAndGuidance/ DH_074217

Polansky, N.A., Ammons, P.W. and Weathersby, B.L. (1983) 'Is there an American standard of child care?', *Social Work*, vol 23, no 5, pp 341–7.

Pollard, R. (2008) *Dialogue and desire: Mikhail Bahktin and the linguistic turn in psychotherapy*, London: Karnac.

Pope John Paul II (1981) *Laborem exercens: encyclical letter of the Supreme Pontiff on human work*, London: Catholic Truth Society.

Poupeau, F. and Discepolo, T. (2005) 'Scholarship with commitment: on the political engagements of Pierre Bourdieu', in L. Wacquant (ed) *Pierre Bourdieu and democratic politics*, Cambridge: Polity.

Powell, F. (1998) 'The professional challenges of reflexive modernization: social work in Ireland', *British Journal of Social Work*, vol 28, pp 311–28.

Pratt, J., Brown, D., Brown, M., Hallsworth, S. and Morrison, W. (ed) (2005) 'Introduction', in J. Pratt, D. Brown, M. Brown, S. Hallsworth and W. Morrison (eds) *The new punitiveness: trends, theories and perspectives*, Devon: Willan.

Price, V. and Simpson, G. (2007) *Transforming society? Social work and sociology*, Bristol: Policy Press.

Prideaux, S. (2005) *Not so New Labour: a sociological critique of New Labour's policy and practice*, Bristol: The Policy Press.

Prout, A. (2000) 'Children's participation: control and self-realisation in British late modernity', *Children & Society*, vol 14, pp 304–15.

Puwar, N. (2009) 'Sensing a post-colonial Bourdieu', *Sociological Review*, vol 57, no 3, pp 371–85.

Ramesh, R. (2010) 'The reluctant seer', *Society Guardian*, 3 November, pp 1–2.

Ransome, P. (2010) *Social theory for beginners*, Bristol: The Policy Press.

Reay, D. (2000) 'A useful extension of Bourdieu's conceptual framework? Emotional capital as a way of understanding mothers' involvement in their children's education', *Sociological Review*, vol 48, no 4, pp 568–86.

Reay, D. (2004) 'Gendering Bourdieu's concepts of capitals? Emotional capital, women and social class', *Sociological Review*, vol 53, no 2, pp 57–75.

Reisch, M. and Andrews, J. (2002) *The road not taken: a history of radical social work in the United States*, New York, NY: Brunner-Routledge.

Robbins, D. (2002) 'Pierre Bourdieu, 1930–2002', *Theory, Culture & Society*, vol 19, no 3, pp 113–16.

Roberts, A. (2000) *Fredric Jameson*, London: Routledge.

Roberts, J.M. (2004) 'The stylistic of competence: a Bakhtinian exploration of some Habermasian themes', *Theory, Culture & Society*, vol 21, no 6, pp 91–114.

Robinson, A. (2006) 'Towards an intellectual reformation: the critique of common sense and the forgotten revolutionary project of Gramscian theory', in A. Bieler and A. Morton (eds) *Images of Gramsci*, London: Routledge.

Robinson, G. (2003) 'Technicality and indeterminacy in probation practice: a case study', *British Journal of Social Work*, vol 33, no 5, pp 593–610.

Roets, G., Roose, R., Claes, L., Vandekinderen, C., Van Hove, G. and Vadnerplasschen, W. (2011) 'Reinventing the employable citizen: a perspective for social work', *British Journal of Social Work*, advance access published 7 April.

Rogers, C. (1980) *A way of being*, Boston, MA: Houghton Mifflin Company.

Rogowski, S. (2010) *Social work: the rise and fall of a profession*, Bristol: Policy Press.

Rose, N. (2000) 'Government and control', *British Journal of Criminology*, vol 40, no 2, pp 321–39.

Rosenau, P.M. (1991) *Postmodernism and the social sciences*, Chichester: Princeton University.

Ruch, G. (2011) 'Where have all the feelings gone?', *British Journal of Social Work*, advanced electronic access from 5 October.

Rupert, M. (2006) 'Reading Gramsci in an era of globalizing capitalism', in A. Bieler and A. Morton (eds) *Images of Gramsci*, London: Routledge.

Rustin, M. (2007) 'What's wrong with happiness?', *Soundings*, vol 36, pp 67–85.

Rutherford, J. (2007) 'New Labour, the market state, and the end of welfare', *Soundings*, vol 36, pp 40–56.

Said, E.W. (2002) 'Conversation with Neeladri Bhattacharya, Suvir Kaul, and Ania Loomba', in D.T. Goldberg and A. Quayson (eds) *Relocating postcolonialism*, Oxford: Blackwell, pp 1–15.

Said, E.W. (2003 [1978]) *Orientalism*, London: Penguin.

Sapey, B. (1997) 'Social work tomorrow: towards a critical understanding of technology in social work', *British Journal of Social Work*, vol 27, no 6, pp 803–14.

Saville, J. (1957) 'The welfare state: an historical approach', *The New Reasoner*, vol 3, pp 5–25.

Sayad, A. (2004) *The suffering of the immigrant*, Cambridge: Polity.

Sayyid, S. (2003) *A fundamental fear: Eurocentrism and the emergence of Islamism*, London: Zed Books.

Scambler, G. (ed) (2001) *Habermas, critical theory and health*, London: Routledge.

Schinkel, W. (2003) 'Pierre Bourdieu's political turn?', *Theory, Culture and Society*, vol 20, no 6, pp 69–93.

Schon, D.A. (1992) 'The crisis of professional knowledge and the pursuit of an epistemology of practice', *Journal of Interprofessional Care*, vol 6, no 1, pp 49–64.

Schultheis, F., Holder, P. and Wagner, C. (2009) 'In Algeria: Pierre Bourdieu's photographic fieldwork', *Sociological Review*, vol 57, no 3, pp 448–71.

Scott, J. (2006) *Social theory: central issues in sociology*, London: Sage.

Scourfield, P. (2007) 'Are there reasons to be worried about the "caretelisation" of residential care', *Critical Social Policy*, vol 27, no 2, pp 155–81.

Scourfield, P. (2012) 'Caretelization revisited and the lesson of Southern Cross', *Critical Social Policy*, vol 32, no 1, pp 137–49.

Secretary of State for Education and Skills (2006*) Care matters: transforming the lives of children and young people in care*, London: HMSO.

Secretary of State for Health and Secretary of State for the Home Department (2003) *The Victoria Climbié inquiry – report of an inquiry by Lord Laming*, Cm 5730, London: HMSO.

Seebohm, F. (1968) *Report of the Committee on Local Authority and Allied Personal Social Services*, Cmnd 3703, London: HMSO.

Showstack Sassoon, A. (1986) 'The people, intellectuals and specialized knowledge', *Boundary 2*, vol 14, no 3, pp 137–68.

Shusterman, R. (1999) 'Introduction', in R. Shusterman (ed) *Bourdieu: a critical reader*, Oxford: Blackwell.

Simpkin, M. (1983) *Trapped within welfare: surviving social work*, London: MacMillan.

Singh, G. and Cowden, S. (2009) 'The social worker as intellectual', *European Journal of Social Work*, vol 12, no 4, pp 1369–457.

Skeggs, B. (1997) *Formations of class and gender*, London: Sage.

Skeggs, B. (2004a) 'Exchange, value and affect: Bourdieu and "the self"', *Sociological Review*, vol 52, no S2, pp 75–95.

Skeggs, B. (2004b) *Class, self, culture*, London: Routledge.

Skeggs, B. (2004c) 'Context and background: Pierre Bourdieu's analysis of class, gender and sexuality', *Sociological Review*, vol 52, no S2, pp 19–33.

Skehill, C. (1999) *The nature of social work in Ireland: a historical perspective*, Lewiston: Edwin Mellen.

Skehill, C. (2004) *History of the present of child protection and welfare social work in Ireland*, Lewiston: Edwin Mellen.

Small, J. (1982) 'New black families', *Adoption & Fostering*, vol 6, no 3, pp 35–40.

Smith, A.L. (2004) 'Heteroglossia, "common sense", and social memory', *American Ethnologist*, vol 1, no 2, pp 251–69.

Smith, A.M. (1998) *Laclau and Mouffe: the radical democratic imaginary*, London: Routledge.

Smith, C. and White, S. (1997) 'Parton, Howe and postmodernity: a critical comment on mistaken identity', *British Journal of Social Work*, vol 27, no 2, pp 275–95.

Smith, H. (2012) 'A good man: tributes to Athens pensioner who killed himself in protest at austerity', *The Guardian*, 6 April, p 22.

Smith, M. (2003) 'Gorgons, cars and the frightful fiend: representations of fear in social work and counselling', *Journal of Social Work Practice*, vol 17, no 2, pp 153–63.

Smith, R. (2008) *Social work and power*, Houndmills: Palgrave Macmillan.

Society Guardian (2006) 'Forced entry', 6 September.

Sointu, E. (2005) 'The rise of an ideal: tracing changing discourses of wellbeing', *Sociological Review*, vol 53, no 2, pp 255–75.

Sointu, E. (2006) 'Recognition and the creation of wellbeing', *Sociology*, vol 40, no 3, pp 493–510.

Soper, K. (2007) 'The other pleasures of post-consumerism', *Soundings*, vol 35, pp 31–41.

Spensky, M. (1992) 'Producers of legitimacy: homes for unmarried mothers in the 1950s', in C. Smart (ed) *Regulating womanhood: essays on marriage, motherhood and sexuality*, London: Routledge.

Spinley, B.M. (1953) *The deprived and the privileged*, London: Routledge & Kegan Paul.

Stabile, C.A. and Morooka, J. (2003) 'Between two evils, I refuse to choose the lesser evil', *Cultural Studies*, vol 17, nos 3/4, pp 326–48.

Standing, G. (2011) 'Workfare and the precariat', *Soundings*, no 47, Spring, pp 35–44.

Steele, J. (2009) 'History is too important to be left to politicians', *The Guardian*, 20 August, p 33.

Steyaert, J. and Gould, N. (2009) 'Social work and the changing face of digital divide', *British Journal of Social Work*, vol 39, no 4, pp 740–53.

Swansen, G. (2007) 'Serenity, self-regard and the genetic sequence: social psychiatry and preventive eugenics in Britain, 1930s–1950s', *Soundings*, vol 60, pp 50–66.

Swanson, J. (2000) 'Self help: Clinton, Blair and the politics of personal responsibility', *Radical Philosophy*, vol 101, pp 29–39.

Sweetman, P. (2009) 'Revealing habitus, illuminating practice: Bourdieu, photography and visual methods', *Sociological Review*, vol 57, no 3, pp 491–512.

Taylor, C. (1992) *Multiculturalism and 'the politics of recognition'*, Princeton, NJ: Princeton University.

Taylor, K. (2009) *Cruelty: human evil and the human brain*, Oxford: Oxford University.

Tester, K. (2004) *The social thought of Zygmunt Bauman*, Houndmills: Palgrave.

Tester, K. and Jacobsen, M.H. (2005) *Bauman before postmodernity*, Aalborg, Denmark: Aalborg University.

The Guardian (2008) 'Cameron wants charities paid market rate for public services', 4 June, p 11.

The Guardian (2010a) 'Minister calls for more child protection volunteers', 30 October, p 21.

The Guardian (2010b) 'Pressure to sack peer who thinks cuts will encourage the poor to "breed"', 26 November, pp 1–2.

The Guardian (2011a) 'Minister blames feminism over lack of jobs for working men', 2 April, p 6.

The Guardian (2011b) 'A nation unified in tolerant scepticism', 25 April.

The Guardian (2011c) 'Editorial: state of emergency', 5 August.

The Independent (1993) 'The Pope decries "savage" effects of all-out capitalism', 3 November.

Therborn, G. (2007) 'After dialectics: radical social theory in a post-communist world', *New Left Review*, vol 43, pp 63–117.

Therborn, G. (2011) *The world: a beginner's guide*, Cambridge: Polity.

Thomas, R. and Davies, A. (2005) 'What have the feminists done for us? Feminist theory and organizational resistance', *Organization*, vol 12, no 5, pp 711–40.

Thompson, G. (2008) 'Are we all neoliberals now? "Responsibility" and corporations', *Soundings*, vol 39, pp 67–75.

Thompson, N. (1997) *Anti-discriminatory practice*, London: Macmillan.

Thompson, N. (2010) *Theorizing social work practice*, Houndmills: Basingstoke.

Thompson, S. (2006) *The political theory of recognition*, Cambridge: Polity.

Tomanovic, S. (2004) 'Family habitus as the cultural context for childhood', *Childhood*, vol 11, no 3, pp 339–60.

Tormey, S. and Townshend, J. (2006) *Key thinkers from critical theory to post-Marxism*, London: Sage.

Toynbee, P. (2010a) 'The "big society" is a big fat lie – just follow the money', *The Guardian*, 7 August, p 27.

Toynbee, P. (2010b) 'Loyal, public service merits more than this cold trashing', *The Guardian*, 24 August, p 27.

Toynbee, P. (2011a) 'This benefit bonanza is more big Serco than big society', *The Guardian*, 5 April, p 29.

Toynbee, P. (2011b) 'Chav: the vile word at the heart of fractured Britain', *The Guardian*, 31 May, p 29.

Tregeagle, S. and Darcy, M. (2008) 'Child welfare and information and communications technology: today's challenge', *British Journal of Social Work*, vol 38, no 8, pp 1481–98.

Trotsky, L. (1971) *Revolution betrayed*, New York, NY: Pathfinder.

Trotsky, L. (1972) *The struggle against fascism in Germany*, Harmondsworth: Pelican.

Trotsky, L. (1979) *Problems of everyday life and other writings on culture and science* (3rd edn), New York, NY: Pathfinder.

Tucker, R.C. (1972) *The Marx–Engels reader* (2nd edn), London: Norton.

Turney, D. (2000) 'The feminizing of neglect', *Child and Family Social Work*, vol 5, pp 47–56.

Tyler, I. (2008) 'Chav mum chav scum: class disgust in contemporary Britain', *Feminist Media Studies*, vol 8, no 1, pp 17–35.

United Nations Development Programme (2005) *Human development report: international cooperation at a crossroads*, New York, NY: Oxford University.

Vice, S. (1997) *Introducing Bakhtin*, Manchester: Manchester University.

Wacquant, L. (1998) 'Pierre Bourdieu', in R. Stones (ed) *Key sociological thinkers*, Houndmills: Palgrave.

Wacquant, L. (2001a) 'The penalisation of poverty and the rise of neo-liberalism', *European Journal on Criminal Policy and Research*, vol 9, pp 401–12.

Wacquant, L. (2001b) 'Further notes on Bourdieu's "Marxism"', *International Journal of Contemporary Sociology*, vol 38, no 1, pp 103–10.

Wacquant, L. (2002) 'Slavery to mass incarceration', *New Left Review*, vol 13, pp 41–61.

Wacquant, L. (2005a) 'The penal leap backward: incarceration in America from Nixon to Clinton', in J. Pratt, D. Brown, M. Brown, S. Hallsworth and W. Morrison (eds) *The new punitiveness: trends, theories and perspectives*, Devon: Willan.

Wacquant, L. (2005b) 'Pointers on Pierre Bourdieu and democratic politics', in L. Wacquant (ed) *Pierre Bourdieu and democratic politics*, Cambridge: Polity.

Wacquant, L. (2009) *Punishing the poor: the neoliberal government of social insecurity*, Durham, NC, and London: Duke University.

Wade, R. (2008) 'Financial regime change', *New Left Review*, vol 53, pp 5–23.

Wagner, P. (2008) *Modernity as experience and interpretation*, Cambridge: Polity.

Walker, R. and Buck, D. (2007) 'The Chinese road', *New Left Review*, vol 46, pp 39–69.

Walsh, T., Wilson, G. and O'Connor, E. (2010) 'Local, European and global: an exploration of migration patterns of social workers into Ireland', *British Journal of Social Work*, vol 40, no 6, pp 1978–95.

Walters, J. (2003) 'Fame academies', *Guardian Education*, 12 August. Available at: http://www.guardian.co.uk/education/2004/sep/14/highereducation. accesstouniversity1

Ward, H. (ed) (1995) *Looking after children: research into practice*, London: HMSO.

Wardhaugh, J. and Wilding, P. (1993) 'Towards an explanation of the corruption of care', *Critical Social Policy*, vol 13, no 1, pp 4–32.

Waterhouse, R. (2000) *Lost in care: report of the Tribunal of Inquiry into the abuse of children in care in the former county council areas of Gwynedd and Clwyd since 1974*, London: The Stationery Office.

Watkins, S. (2010) 'Blue Labour', *New Left Review*, vol 63, pp 5–17.

Webb, S. (2006) *Social work in a risk society*, Houndmills: Palgrave.

Webb, S. (2009) 'Against difference and diversity in social work: the case of human rights', *International Journal of Social Welfare*, vol 18, pp 307–16.

Webb, S. (2010) '(Re)assembling the left: the politics of redistribution and recognition in social work', *British Journal of Social Work*, vol 40, no 8, pp 2364–79.

Weinstein, J. (2011) '*Case Con* and radical social work in the 1970s: the impact of the revolutionaries', in M. Lavalette (ed) *Radical social work today: social work at the crossroads*, Bristol: The Policy Press.

Werbner, P. (2000) 'Who sets the terms of the debate? Heterotopic intellectuals and the clash of discourses', *Theory, Culture & Society*, vol 17, no 1, pp 147–56.

White, S. (2009) 'An ideological map', *New Statesman*. Available at: http://www.newstatesman.com/uk-politics/2009/09/society-guiding-progressive

White, S., Fook, J. and Gardner, F. (eds) (2006) *Critical reflection in health care and social care*, Maidenhead: Open University.

White, S., Hall, C. and Peckover, S. (2009) 'The descriptive tyranny of the common assessment framework: technologies of categorization and professional practice in child welfare', *British Journal of Social Work*, vol 39, no 7, pp 1197–217.

White, V. (2006) *The state of feminist social work*, London: Routledge.

Williams, F. (2001) 'In and beyond New Labour: towards a new political ethics of care', *Critical Social Policy*, vol 21, no 4, pp 467–94.

Williams, F. (2005) 'A good-enough life: developing the grounds for a political ethic of care', *Soundings*, vol 30, pp 17–33.

Williams, R. (1973) 'Base and superstructure in Marxist cultural theory', *New Left Review*, Nov–Dec, pp 3–17.

Williams, R. (1983 [1976]) *Keywords: a vocabulary of culture and society* (2nd edn), New York: Norton.

Winnicott, D.W. (1965) *The family and individual development*, London: Tavistock.

Wolfreys, J. (2000) 'In perspective: Pierre Bourdieu', *International Socialism Journal*, vol 87.

Wolfreys, J. (2002) 'Pierre Bourdieu: voice of resistance', *International Socialism Journal*, vol 94, pp 97–102.

Woodwiss, A. (1997) 'Against "modernity": a dissident rant', *Economy & Society*, vol 26, no 1, pp 1–22.

Worsley, P. (2002) *Marx and Marxism*, London: Routledge.

Wright, E. and Wright, E. (eds) (1999) *The Žižek reader*, Oxford: Blackwell.

Wright Mills, C. (2000) *The sociological imagination: 40th anniversary issue*, Oxford: Oxford University.

Young, I.M. (2007) *Global challenges: war, self-determination and responsibilities for justice*, Cambridge: Polity.

Young, R.J.C. (2001) *Postcolonialism: an historical introduction*, Oxford: Blackwell.

Yuval-Davis, N., Anthias, F. and Kofman, E. (2005) 'Secure borders and safe haven and the gendered politics of belonging: beyond social cohesion', *Ethnic and Racial Studies*, vol 28, no 3, pp 513–35.

Žižek, S. (2000) *The fragile absolute – or, why is the Christian legacy worth fighting for?*, London: Verso.

Žižek, S. (2002) *Revolution at the gates: selected writings of Lenin from 1917*, London: Verso.

Žižek, S. (2004) *Iraq: the borrowed kettle*, London: Verso.

Žižek, S. (2008) 'Use your illusions', *The London Review of Books*, 14 November. Available at: http://www.lrb.co.uk/2008/11/14/slavoj-zizek/use-your-illusions

Index

V

W

Y

Z